MICHAEL D

Out of the Shadows

MICHAEL DOUGLAS

Out of the Shadows
The Unauthorised Biography

ANDY DOUGAN

ROBSON BOOKS

First published in Great Britain in 2001.
This updated edition published in 2003 by Robson Books,
The Chrysalis Building, Bramley Road, London W10 6SP

An imprint of Chrysalis Books Group plc

British Library Cataloguing in Publication Data
A catalogue record for this title is available from the British Library

ISBN 1 86105 694 X

Typeset by SX Composing DTP, Rayleigh, Essex
Printed in Great Britain by
Creative Print & Design (Wales), Ebbw Vale

To Christine, Iain, and Stuart and to the memory of my parents

CONTENTS

GOLDEN
BOXES AND
SILVER
SPOONS

When he cried from the cold or from hunger Bryna Demsky used to console her son Issur with a story of how he had been born in a golden box. The box appeared to her one day in her yard in the dead of winter. When she went to investigate, she found nothing inside this beautiful, shimmering treasure except a baby boy. She took the baby and left the box. Issur, always a practical child and ever aware of their straitened circumstances, would ask why she didn't keep the box. Then his mother would hug him and explain that she had no need of the box when she had already taken the treasure it contained.

Issur grew up and had four sons. He had no stories like this to tell them, but what he was able to give them was a life that he could only have imagined when he was their age. His first son was born, not to a golden box, but to a magnificent mansion. Michael Douglas first saw the light of day at 10.30 in the morning of 25 September

1944, at St Peter's Hospital in New Brunswick. Considering it was her first child it was an exhausting but relatively uncomplicated birth for his mother Diana. His father, as was common at the time, was not present at the birth. Kirk Douglas, the former Issur Danielovich Demsky, was carving a name for himself as a bright young actor on the New York stage. He was playing the part of an army lieutenant in *Kiss and Tell*, a light romantic comedy which had been running on Broadway for well over a year. Indeed, Kirk had taken Diana to see the play on their first date, when he was on leave from the Navy. When they saw it, the part of the lieutenant was being played by Richard Widmark. Now, Widmark having gone to do another show, Douglas took over from him. The war in Europe was drawing to a close but America was still heavily involved in the war in the Pacific and would remain so for almost another year. As a consequence it seemed that Douglas, who had been given an early discharge from the Navy after a severe bout of amoebic dysentery, was one of the few juvenile leads available to Broadway producers. It would not be the first time he would step into the shoes of Widmark, then the much bigger star, and indeed he went on to eventually replace him in *Trio*, the show for which Widmark had left *Kiss and Tell*.

When Michael was born his father had been recording a radio show in a Manhattan studio. Who knows what sort of form he was in, since he had been up all night after taking Diana to the hospital when she had gone into labour the night before. He called St Peter's at lunchtime to be told that he was a father, it was a boy. That afternoon he went on stage for the matinee performance of *Kiss and Tell* before dashing by train to New Brunswick, so he could see his son and be back in time for the evening curtain. His first words as he charged, unshaven and bleary-eyed, into the recovery room were not calculated to endear him to his wife, or indeed his son and heir.

'Christ,' he announced, 'what a day I've had'.

Kirk Douglas was lucky to make it back to Broadway unbloodied that night, but he and Diana were delighted with their first child.

They had already decided on a name. When he was born, Diana had told the nurses that he was to be called Michael. This had been arrived at only after some discussion. Diana had apparently been in favour of naming him after his father and calling him Kirk Douglas Jnr. Douglas balked at that. He seemed to know even then that he himself was destined for great things and he had no desire to burden a son with living in the shadow of not only a famous father but also trying to live up to his name. Besides, Douglas felt calling anyone 'Junior' automatically diminished them, and left them something of a mountain to climb in later life. In addition Douglas, an Orthodox Jew, had religious objections to a child being named after a living family member. In the end a compromise was reached, although neither parent seems entirely certain of their son's given name. His mother insists that their first born is known as Michael Kirk Douglas while his father insists that the boy has no formal middle name, simply the initial 'K'.

Another compromise was reached on the subject of religion. Michael was circumcised, not by a rabbi, but by a doctor at the hospital. His grandmother Bryna was told it had been a religious service to spare her feelings. Despite the wishes of Diana Douglas's family, there was no christening. This was a decision which did nothing to further endear Kirk Douglas to his new in-laws, who already had a low opinion of him for stealing their daughter away from them. Thomas Dill felt that actors were parasites and was occasionally wont to express himself at length on the subject, much to his daughter's annoyance.

After the usual week of recovery and gathering her strength at St Peter's, Diana Douglas left hospital with her new son and went straight into a level of luxury to which he would become accustomed for most of his life. When they were first married Diana had told her new husband that her sister had a house in the country. This was something of an understatement, as Kirk Douglas was soon to discover. Ruth Dill had been married to Seward Johnson of the Johnson & Johnson pharmaceuticals conglomerate. When they were married they set up home in what Diana referred to as the house in the country. It was called Merriewold and was built in 1926. Modelled on a French château, it was an award-winning design which featured both towers and a courtyard. Seward Johnson spared no expense on a home for his new bride. As well as extensive, professionally-designed rose gardens Merriewold also had its own clay tennis court. As a final touch, the roof had been imported from the Cotswolds in England and the stone for the walls had come from Pennsylvania. The house outlasted the marriage. After they had divorced and she had remarried Ruth Dill kept Merriewold. She and her new husband Phil Crocket were living in the gardener's cottage on the estate, but Diana and Kirk Douglas were generously offered the use of the main house. The huge house with its oak beams, high heavy wooden doors, and many turrets was far too big for a couple with a new baby so it was decided by Diana that they would live only in the West Wing, appropriately enough the former nursery wing.

Michael Douglas was a contented but serious baby. Despite strenuous efforts by his parents, his grandparents, and assorted cooing relatives only rarely would anyone's attentions be favoured with a smile from the fine-featured, blond-haired boy. Michael Douglas was, even then, an observer. He was happy to watch the world go by and keep his counsel and his smiles to himself.

This early taste of opulence was destined to be brief. Even before they had moved into their fine but temporary home in New Brunswick, Kirk Douglas had already found a place they could call their own to start their family life. Ruth Crockett had offered them the chance to stay while her sister was pregnant. It made sense. Diana would be close to her parents during the final few weeks of her confinement while Kirk commuted every night via Penn Station to Broadway. It also gave the still relatively newly-weds the chance to save some money and find their feet. After less than three weeks Kirk Douglas decided he could not impose any longer, although in truth the high society lifestyle probably chafed considerably, and moved his wife and new son to Greenwich Village.

The Douglases properly began their family life in a first floor walk-up apartment on West Eleventh Street in Greenwich Village, an area Kirk knew well from his student days. There was no comparison between this and Merriewold, but it was a better place to start their life together than most American families had in the immediate post-war years. It had a balcony in the bedroom which overlooked an interior garden, there was a room next door for baby Michael, and there was a living room, complete with a fireplace, and a small dining room for entertaining. For ninety dollars a month and furnished with antiques which Ruth had encouraged them to take from New Brunswick, it provided the ideal start for what should have been an idyllic family life.

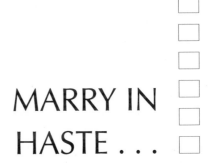

MARRY IN HASTE . . .

When he was in kindergarten Izzy Demsky read a nursery poem about a red robin. It was rapturously received and from that moment on he knew he wanted to be an actor. His next major dramatic role came when he was just in second grade, and he played the pivotal role of the shoemaker in *The Shoemaker and The Elves*. Again it was a rousing success and he was confirmed in his ambition. Acting, or at least the escape into a world of fantasy, must have been an intoxicating release for a small boy who was growing up in abject poverty. He was the son of a ragman who drank, he was the only son and the middle child of seven, and his father never showed him affection or approval when he was growing up.

One of the abiding memories of his childhood is his father turning up unexpectedly at that performance of *The Shoemaker and the Elves* and buying him an ice cream afterwards. A simple act of parental bonding but it stayed with him for more than eighty years, as vivid now as on the day it happened. Another enduring recollection comes from his early teens. By working hours at a time at a succession of menial and thankless jobs, and hoarding the cash he had been given at his Bar Mitzvah, he had amassed $313. This was as close to a king's ransom as a thirteen-year-old in Amsterdam, New York, would ever come. It was to be his ticket out of the slums, it would send him to college. But at the height of the Depression his father 'borrowed' the money for a lunatic get rich quick scheme, speculating on the price of scrap metal. He misjudged the whole calamitous affair. The market collapsed, the metal he had bought for 24 cents a pound he could sell only for two cents a pound and his son's fortune disappeared overnight.

This only strengthened the young man's resolve. Eventually he did run away to Canton in New York with $163 and enrolled in St Laurence University. With his quick mind and vibrant physicality Kirk Douglas – although it would still be several years before he went by that name – quickly established himself on campus. He had nurtured his love of acting and theatre at Wilbur H. Lynch High School, where he had won a prize for public speaking. He continued his acting into university and it was while he was at St Laurence that, Douglas insists, he learned most of his dramatic training, not in the classroom but in the wrestling ring. Douglas was one of the school's star wrestlers. In the summer he would make extra cash as a 'ringer', who stepped out of the crowd in front of the wrestling booth to go into the ring with the Masked Marauder – in reality another member of the university wrestling team. The crowds would flock to the ticket tent to watch this hapless loser get beaten up. Of course the match was fixed and Douglas won. As the crowds were filing out a re-match was announced, which took them straight back to the barker to buy tickets for a bout in which the Masked Marauder would surely triumph. He didn't. In any event the crowds poured in, Douglas learned how to sell a wrestling move and play to an audience, and got $10 a day for his trouble.

Douglas also learned more legitimate theatrical skills at the Tamarack Playhouse in the Adirondacks in upper New York state.

Douglas was hired as a stagehand but as he built sets, placed props, or swept up he watched everything which was going on around him like a hawk. He soaked it up like a sponge and eventually ended up playing a number of small parts in various repertory productions. By the time he went back to St Laurence, where his loyalties had been divided between acting and sport, his mind was made up. As he had several times told his friend Pete Riccio, the boy he had accompanied to St Laurence, he was going to be a Broadway star.

To achieve his ambition the next logical step was to move to New York. Broadway was unlikely to come to Canton in search of Kirk Douglas, so he had to go to Broadway. One thing he left behind in Canton, or more specifically at the Tamarack Playhouse where he spent another summer after graduating, was his name. He was no longer Issur Danielovich Demsky, now he was Kirk Douglas. This started as a stage name, but within weeks of arriving in New York he found a lawyer and had it changed legally. Kirk Douglas's journey to the Great White Way took him first to Greenwich Village, where he had found a job at the Greenwich House putting on theatrical shows for immigrant children. In return for his efforts the Greenwich House agreed to provide him with room and board. The tiny apartment they found for him in Jones Street was not far from the rather more splendid accommodation where he and his wife and son would set up their first family home some five years later.

Kirk Douglas had one more stroke of luck. He had wanted to enrol in the American Academy of Dramatic Arts but could not afford the $500 annual tuition fee. It was hard enough to survive even with the free room and board at the Greenwich House, the Academy fees might as well have been $5 million. But after he had found another school which offered to give him a scholarship, the Academy contacted him to say that they too would be able to subsidise his studies. Douglas was much older than the other students but he was not in the least self-conscious and threw himself into a two year course of speech, drama, dance and movement. Every day he would take the subway from Columbus Circle back to the Village and climb the stairs to his garret in Jones Street, exhausted but with his mind buzzing with new ideas and techniques. After completing that first year he went back to Tamarack for a third summer and then returned to New York for his senior year at the American Academy of Dramatic Art.

By this stage things were becoming serious. The class which had begun the previous year had been reduced to half its size by a rigorous process of attrition. The 80 students who began the second year, including Kirk Douglas, would find things even more difficult and their resolve to act would be tested on a daily basis. Their chief tormentor was Charles Jehlinger, at 80 still one of the grand old men of American theatre. He was the man who was responsible for shaping the careers of such disparate talents as Spencer Tracy and Grace Kelly, who had already graduated from the Academy. Legend had it that the great Edward G. Robinson, when a student there, had become so incensed by Jehlinger's criticism that he picked up a table from the stage and threw it at his tutor. Jehlinger, who was standing in the front stalls, was knocked to the ground, but continued his critique of Robinson's performance without missing a beat. Robinson later confirmed the story, saying his only regret was that he hadn't killed him.

Robinson's response was atypical but Jehlinger's treatment of his students was not. Day after day he would order them to repeat the most trivial pieces of stage craft until they had achieved it to his satisfaction. There were tears and rages and tantrums and many of the class simply could not take the pace and left. Kirk Douglas was on the point of leaving himself. They were doing a play called *Bachelor Born*, in which Douglas was playing the lead role of a 'Mr Chips' style schoolteacher. He had been asked by Jehlinger to repeat a relatively simple entrance so often that he had begun to doubt his sanity. Shaken and dazed, he wandered backstage trying to make sense of what had just happened. But as he did he noticed a young woman sitting sobbing on a trunk. It was Diana Dill, the ingenue in *Bachelor Born*, and she was breaking her heart.

Like Kirk Douglas, acting provided Diana Dill with an escape. In her case it was not a retreat from grinding poverty, but quite the opposite. Diana Dill was born to a wealthy and distinguished family in Bermuda in 1923. Her father, Thomas Dill, was the attorney-general on the island and his family had been there since the early seventeenth century. Her mother, Ruth Neilson, was a New Yorker who was able to trace her family back to Peter Stuyvesant. Diana was the youngest of six children and grew up in a large house with a substantial domestic staff and all the trappings of wealth and status. The family moved to England in 1929, where Diana and her sister Fan were sent to boarding school at Upper Chine School for Girls. There was an eight-year gap between Diana and Fan and as a consequence they were separated at school; Fan went into the seniors and Diana into the juniors. Although she was thoroughly miserable Diana found salvation at the age of eight when she discovered the joy of Shakespeare. She threw herself into school productions of *A Midsummer Night's Dream* and *The Tempest* and discovered, as she later described it, the difference between how things are and how things should be. Acting and Shakespeare enabled Diana to get through a difficult period in her life before the family returned to Bermuda in 1933, when her father was appointed Attorney-General of Bermuda. The fondness for drama which had been stirred in her early days at Upper Chine was further fanned when she returned to the school when she was thirteen. This time an English teacher, Miss Dobbs, encouraged her to stretch herself and her imagination. Slowly but surely Diana, who had been a rebellious girl, was beginning to find a purpose in her life.

Like most well brought up young women of her age and class, Diana was expected to marry well, raise children, and be a good wife and mother. She had other plans. She wanted to go to the Royal Academy of Dramatic Art in London, move into a trendy flat, and live the decadent life of a successful West End star. The war in Europe put paid to those plans and in 1939 the Dills headed for America. The wisdom of their plans was emphatically brought home to them by an incident on their outward journey. They had been due to sail to the United States on the *Athenia*, but because of an administrative mix-up the ship was over-booked. The Dills were transferred to another ship, the *Aquitania*. This meant a frustrating delay, but while they waited to sail they heard that the *Athenia* had been torpedoed by a German submarine and lost.

It was an anxious crossing for the Dill family but Thomas and Ruth and their daughters eventually arrived in the United States and moved into Merriewold, the house which Ruth and Seward Johnson had built in New Brunswick. Like Diana's later sojourn there, when Michael was born, it was intended only as a temporary stay. Her parents were making plans to move on to Bermuda where they would be safe from the conflict but Diana, once again, had ideas of her own. If she could not go to RADA in London then she would try for a place at the American Academy of Dramatic Art in New York. Surprisingly, her parents did not voice any strong opposition. She later said she believed that they felt she needed to get the non-sensical notion of acting out of her system so she could settle down to a normal life. The plan was that she would go to the Academy and live at Merriewold, commuting daily by train and subway. The tuition fees which had been such a problem for Kirk Douglas would not be a problem for Diana Dill, but first there was the audition. Diana, accompanied by her mother, went to see Emil Diestel who ran the school with Charles Jehlinger. The mother and daughter combination was a formidable one and the over-matched Diestel was browbeaten into giving Diana an audition there and then. Undaunted, she played all three lead roles – Celia, Rosalind, and Orlando – in a bravura selection from *As You Like It* and was accepted on the spot.

Diana Dill survived the first year at Carnegie Hall and was, along with Kirk Douglas, one of the 80 who were receiving Charles Jehlinger's special attentions in their senior year. She knew Douglas only slightly, she had her own friends in class, but they were cast opposite each other in *Bachelor Born*. Diana had been having a hard time in the show but nowhere near as difficult as Kirk Douglas. When he walked off the stage white-faced and trembling to find her crying backstage, he had no idea why she was crying. When he stopped to try to help he did not know that the tears were not for her, they were for him. She had been so embarrassed by Jehlinger's humiliation of her fellow student that it was more than she could bear, and weeping was the only response.

He asked her to go and have a cup of coffee with him and she agreed. Over coffee and pie the young man who had wanted nothing more than to be a Broadway star discussed his future with this woman he scarcely knew. Jehlinger had told him he would never be an actor, he was wasting everyone's time. What would he do? He poured out his soul and told her everything about the sacrifices he had made and the sacrifices his sisters had made to help him through college. What was he to do now? Was there nothing for it except to go back to Amsterdam and sell shoes? As they walked together in Central Park they realised that there was only one thing that he could do: he must go back. Diana managed to convince him that Jehlinger had been testing him, attempting to break his resolve, trying to find out just how badly he wanted to be an actor. Douglas agreed. He would go back. They walked a little further, they kissed, and then they said goodnight. The following day Kirk Douglas went back to the Academy, made his peace with Jehlinger and, according to Diana Dill, turned in a devastating performance in *Bachelor Born*.

Solving Kirk Douglas's crisis of confidence had forged a bond between the two aspiring actors. They began to date but not, Diana insists, seriously. She was aware of Douglas's reputation as a ladies' man and was determined to keep him at arm's length. Instead they talked about books and plays and music. He told her about his straitened upbringing and filled her with his enthusiasm for socialism and the rights of trade unions. This was a new world to Diana Dill, who had been raised as someone who would take her place in the next generation of the ruling classes. They had nicknames for each other. She called him 'Doug' while he called her 'Miss Everything-is-Lovely Dill'. Despite her determination not to be won over by his physical charms, Diana was finding her resistance lowering and decided that the easiest thing to do was to take herself out of harm's way. She began to date other men, he continued to see other women, but they remained good friends.

At the end of their senior year Diana Dill was the only member of the graduating class to have an acting job to go to. She had been offered a standard contract by a Warner Brothers scout and was preparing to leave for Hollywood. Everyone was thrilled for her, except Kirk Douglas. Going to Hollywood would be betraying her art, he argued. She should be true to her craft and stay in New York with the rest of them, fighting for the integrity of legitimate theatre. He wrote her a long and impassioned letter, exactly the sort of thing she had come to expect from him in the short time they had known each other. They quarrelled over it and then made up. But in the end it was the letter and her determination to prove him wrong which, more than anything, made up Diana Dill's mind about going to Hollywood.

The rail line to Hollywood was a well-travelled route by hundreds of thousands of aspiring actors and actresses. They took the Twentieth Century out of New York to Chicago and then changed trains to the Super Chief, which would ferry them along with their hopes and aspirations to the Dream Factory. Like all of those others Diana Dill arrived in Los Angeles with grand hopes and schemes and, like most of the others, they were dashed. She was, however, fortunate in that hers would not be dashed quite so quickly, for she did after all have a contract at Warners. Contract players were studio cannon fodder in the movie industry's version of indentured servitude. The standard contract was for a year, with an annual option which the studios used on a whim. It provided a steady salary but anyone who stepped out of line could be put on suspension. This only increased the length of the contract, making it effectively impossible to escape. Naturally if it suited the studio you could be dropped like a stone and taken off wages at a moment's notice. When she arrived in Los Angeles Diana Dill found that she was simply one of dozens of others who were all in the same boat. The studio had no more idea of what to do with her than they had with any of the others. So, for most of her first few weeks at Warner Brothers, Diana Dill spent her time hanging around waiting for something to do, other than the endless round of cheesy glamour shots organised by the studio's publicity department.

She did, however, have a guardian angel in the unlikely shape of Errol Flynn, then one of the world's biggest box office draws, who had taken an interest in the newcomer and took her under his wing. Diana was aware that, like Kirk Douglas, Flynn had a reputation as a notorious Lothario. He was married at the time to Lili Damita, although he insisted to Diana that the marriage was over and they were in fact separated. Diana managed to resist Flynn's advances and they enjoyed a relatively platonic affair during which, presumably with his help, she was screen tested for the role of his sister in *They Died With Their Boots On*. This stirring and highly romanticised version of the life of George Armstrong Custer of the 7th Cavalry would give Flynn one of his most memorable roles and spectacular successes. The role of flamboyant and brash Custer was tailor-made for the equally flamboyant Australian. Even though he was a huge star Flynn unselfishly coached Diana Dill through the test and she won the role. Sadly for her, the part was written out of the next draft of the script and all of their work amounted to nothing. She did later have a brief affair with Flynn, but it was short-lived and ended one night at a dinner party when Flynn, who was Diana's date, buried his face in the ample cleavage of a blonde starlet at the dinner table. Diana left and the relationship was over.

Her relationship with Warner Brothers ended soon after, when she was abruptly told that her option was not being picked up. It would be easy to assume that she had been dropped at the instigation of Flynn as a consequence of ending their affair. This would be a harsh conclusion to reach since, despite an inevitable tension, they remained friends after she left the studio and Flynn seems to have been genuinely fond of her. More likely Warners had simply lost interest, and there was nothing sufficiently special about the young Diana Dill to elevate her above all the other contract players. In any event, in all her time at Warners she had done nothing of substance other than those publicity shots and the screen test. Work was generally hard to come by and after a small role in the MGM film *Keeper of the Flame* with Spencer Tracy and Katharine Hepburn, and a couple of roles in undistinguished 'B' movies Diana decided she and Hollywood had had enough of each other. She returned to New York where she found work with a modelling agency and also trained as a nursing auxiliary.

The photograph that changed her life came in April of 1943 when she went out on a modelling assignment for *Life* magazine at the Brooklyn Botanical Gardens. Diana did not expect to be used much on the assignment, since she was working with Lisa Fonsigrives who was then the highest paid model in the business, but a job was a job. She was as surprised as anyone to see her photograph on the cover of the 3 May 1943 issue of the world's most famous photo-news magazine. She looks elegant in a checked blouse and matching parasol as she gazes dreamily – she describes it as 'rather sulky' – into the middle distance. The cover was a sensation. It turned her into a celebrity in modelling circles, her fees began going up, and suddenly she was much in demand. She even started getting fan mail sent to her care of *Life* magazine and her modelling agency. One of these fan letters came from an unlikely source.

While Diana Dill had gone to Hollywood to pursue a fruitless career, Kirk Douglas had continued to learn his craft. Without any representation it was difficult and he had drifted around in various summer stock companies. Finally he had managed to find a job as a second assistant director in a production of *The Three Sisters*, which starred the legendary Katharine Cornell along with Judith Anderson and Ruth Gordon. This also included a walk-on part as a young servant bearing a samovar of tea, a role Douglas made the most of on a nightly basis. *The Three Sisters* opened on Broadway on 21 December 1942. When its run was over Kirk Douglas left the theatre, temporarily, to go and join the Navy.

It was while he was at Midshipman School at Notre Dame that Kirk Douglas noticed the copy of *Life* magazine. He told his class-mates that he knew the girl under the parasol but no one believed him so he wrote to her at *Life* to prove his point. The letter was eventually forwarded to the Powers Modelling Agency, who passed it on to Diana. She quickly wrote back to the man she had known as Doug, brought him up to speed on her abortive career in Hollywood and told him she was now working in New York, modelling and completing her nursing auxiliary training at Bellevue Hospital. Douglas wrote back suggesting they get together the next time he was in New York. The first date didn't work out because she had gone back to Bermuda to see her family. Then he was posted to Miami for further training, but after several more weeks he wrote again. This time he would come to New York on a Saturday so that he knew she wouldn't be working and she agreed to meet him at his hotel at lunchtime.

They had lunch and Diana was instantly taken with the sheer energy and brio which bristled from this man whom she hadn't seen for two years. He announced that he had tickets for a matinee of *Show and Tell*, starring Richard Widmark, and after that it was dinner and champagne at the Penthouse Club, an up-market restaurant overlooking Central Park. It was a whirlwind day and Diana found herself catching her breath as she tried to keep up with Douglas. They had seen each other for barely ten hours in the past two years and she had no idea what to expect when he announced he had something to tell her.

'Let's get married,' he said as they drank champagne. 'As soon as possible.'

. . . REPENT AT LEISURE

Kirk Douglas's proposal may have taken Diana Dill by surprise, but it had not been a surprise to him. Since they first met that day during the rehearsals of *Bachelor Born* he had, apparently, been telling everyone that Diana Dill was the girl he was going to marry. Obviously he had managed to keep it secret from the one person who really counted, the putative bride. Equally obviously, he had not been keeping himself celibate while carrying a torch for his one true love. While they were stationed in Miami, for example, Douglas had been involved in a passionate relationship with a local divorcee in which he had proclaimed himself perfectly content.

Diana Dill and Kirk Douglas spent the rest of his two week furlough in New York scarcely out of touching distance of each other. Like so many other wartime romances it was a passionate whirlwind affair in which both were swept off their feet. Although she did not agree to his proposal straight away, Diana was plainly not violently opposed to the idea and she confided in her oldest sister Ruth. The older woman was touched but urged her not to rush into anything, suggesting they wait until after the war so they could organise a ceremony in keeping with the style to which Diana's family was accustomed. By this stage Kirk Douglas's leave was over and he had reported back to New Orleans to await commissioning orders for his ship. She, meanwhile, had gone to Arizona on a modelling assignment. They wrote every day and there were frequent phone calls. As events transpired, a heady mixture of passion, separation, and his impending posting to the thick of the war in the Pacific made their decision for them. They decided not to wait but to get married straight away. Diana took the train from Arizona to New Orleans, writing to her mother on the journey to tell her of her plans, and they were married at the Algiers Naval Station on 2 November 1943.

The newlyweds had three weeks together in New Orleans, during which time they were married again, this time in a Jewish ceremony with Kirk Douglas's sister Marian able to travel down to attend the service. Douglas had been assigned to Patrol Craft 1139 as communications officer and also officer of the deck, and the ship was sent on a shakedown cruise to Miami before being assigned to potentially hazardous anti-submarine duties in the Pacific. Since they did not know how much time PC 1139 would spend in Florida before sailing there seemed little point in Diana Douglas remaining in New Orleans. She travelled to Miami and rented an apartment so they could have at least some time together before he shipped out. His ship finally sailed in January 1944 and Diana moved out of the apartment and back to her sister's home in New Brunswick. On the way she stopped off at Schenectady to meet her new mother-in-law for the first time. She was welcomed with open arms by her six sisters-in-law and by Bryna herself. Bryna and Diana bonded almost instantly, and that bond was strengthened when Bryna was the first person in whom Diana confided something she had suspected for several weeks. She was pregnant with a baby she felt had been conceived on Christmas Day.

Diana Douglas was again living at Merriewold, this time in the gardener's cottage which her sister Ruth had moved into with her second husband Phil Crockett. It was from here that Diana sent long, loving letters to her husband as his ship headed through the Panama Canal towards the South Pacific. The letters took some time to catch up with him and arrived in a bundle. Diana wondered why there were was no reply and began to fear the worst. Then in March she received a phone call to tell her that her husband's ship had been involved in a bizarre but dreadful accident. Out on patrol one day off the coast of Hawaii they made contact with what appeared to be a Japanese submarine. As they pursued their quarry, an order to drop depth charge markers was misheard by the inexperienced crew. Instead of dropping markers they dropped live depth charges and almost sank their own ship. It was blown sideways out of the water. The explosion caused a large amount of damage and Kirk Douglas was among the injured.

He had been thrown against a bulkhead by the force of the blast and had serious internal bruising. This, coupled with a bout of amoebic dysentery, meant that he would be spending his war for the foreseeable future at a naval hospital in San Diego. Diana took the train to San Diego to be with him and after a few weeks in hospital he was allowed out on condition that he report in on a daily basis. Finally, in June 1944, the decision was taken that since the disease could recur Kirk Douglas would be given a medical discharge. The news must have come as a shock to a man who had always prided himself on his fitness and vitality. Diana recalls that he was visibly shaken when he came home and told her the news, swearing her to secrecy about the reasons for the discharge in case people got the wrong idea. He was terrified of anyone thinking he had been discharged from the service for psychiatric reasons, and instead simply said that it was as a consequence of his injuries in the depth-charging incident.

Now that he was out of the Navy Kirk Douglas was determined to resume his career as an actor. Diana too had been keen to return to her former profession. The time she had spent with her new husband had renewed her passion for acting and she had decided to give up modelling and return to the theatre. Her pregnancy put all of these other notions on hold. She was six months pregnant when Kirk Douglas received his medical discharge and once again they found themselves back in Merriewold. Diana began to make the nursery wing of the main building as cosy as she could while Kirk looked for an acting job on Broadway. His medical discharge proved to be a blessing in disguise. There was a desperate shortage of young leading men because of the war and, with Richard Widmark leaving to join *Trio*, Kirk Douglas was offered the chance to read for his role in *Kiss and Tell*, the play he and Diana had seen on their first date. He got the job and for the first time had a steady role in a Broadway play.

Diana's parents had come from Bermuda to give her moral support as she awaited the birth of their first child. They rented a house not far from Merrieworld and Diana had her family about her when she gave birth to Michael K. Douglas on 25 September 1944. Within weeks the new family was ensconced in their comfortable Greenwich Village apartment and it was not long after that when Diana Douglas began to feel that all was not well with her marriage.

On the face of it Diana Dill and Kirk Douglas were a mismatched couple right from the start. He was from a poor immigrant family, she was from a family of privileged blue bloods. The psychological scars of his childhood were deep. He had no satisfactory relationship with his father to speak of, he was determined to escape from his numbing poverty, and he felt driven to make an impression in his chosen career. That in itself is a potent cocktail, but add to it Douglas's near paranoia about anti-Semitic bias, and you have an incendiary mixture. The last thing Kirk Douglas needed was the pressures of fatherhood. Once they were away from the cloistered atmosphere of Merriewold, and once the desperation and panic of wartime had passed, they were left, just the three of them, in a comfortable Greenwich Village apartment. The problem was that while it was big enough for them, there wasn't an apartment in New York big enough for the emotional baggage Kirk Douglas had brought with him.

Like many Russians or those of immediate Russian descent, Kirk Douglas's natural state was one of melancholy punctuated by brief periods of happiness. He would spend his days in West Eleventh street in moods which veered between bouts of depression and sudden rages. He would receive rave notices for his work – which was coming thick and fast now – but then quibble that the reviews were not sufficiently laudatory. In June 1945 he appeared in a play called *The Wind is Ninety* by Ralph Nelson, who would later go on to direct films such as *Soldier Blue*. The review featured his picture with the words 'Nothing short of superb' underneath as a caption. 'What do they mean "Nothing short of"?' he demanded of Diana. 'If they think I'm superb why don't they just come out and say so.'

Kirk Douglas was becoming increasingly unhappy and more and more restless. He spent a lot of time at the theatre, which meant he could not form a relationship with his baby son Michael, who was still a serious and thoughtful child and beginning to bond closely with his mother. In addition his reputation as a ladies' man was reasserting itself. While he was in the Navy, he had enjoyed the dubious delights of a Panama brothel, and according to Diana she had to deliver an ultimatum when he made a pass at one of her girlfriends. The ambience in their apartment was becoming decidedly strained and baby Michael would sit and watch and absorb it all, as his mother desperately tried not to make a scene. Finally, and tragically, her opportunity for change came when Thomas Dill died suddenly. Diana went back to Bermuda with Michael, who celebrated his first birthday in the Caribbean.

Left behind in New York, Kirk Douglas found that Hollywood was beckoning. Lauren Bacall had been a year behind Diana Dill at the Academy of Dramatic Art and, in addition, she had also had something of a crush on Kirk Douglas. All three remained friends after drama school. Bacall had gone to Hollywood and made a huge impression opposite Humphrey Bogart, whom she would later marry, in *To Have and Have Not*. What Kirk Douglas did not know was that she had been lobbying on his behalf with producer Hal Wallis, who called to offer him a role in the film *The Strange Love of Martha Ivers* opposite Barbara Stanwyck. He wrote to Diana and Michael in Bermuda and told them that he was going to Hollywood. He was going to close the apartment in New York and once they were done visiting in Bermuda they should join him in Los Angeles. Diana and Michael returned to New York to pack a few things and oversee the closing of their home then, with Diana's mother in tow, they once again headed for the Twentieth Century and the Super Chief bound for Hollywood.

Diana Dill's first excursion to Hollywood had been far from successful and to begin with, even though she was now Diana Douglas, her second outing did not appear to be any more auspicious. Diana, Michael and her mother arrived in town in the middle of an actors' strike. Kirk Douglas was locked in the Paramount set making his film debut and there was nowhere for his family to stay. Fortunately, his new agent Milt Grossman and his wife were able to put them up in their tiny apartment for a few days until their own place was ready. Kirk Douglas was smuggled out of the studio at dead of night in a limousine to spend a few precious hours with his family and welcome them to their new life in Hollywood. With her mother there to provide child care, Diana was able to keep her promise to herself to resume her acting career. The first thing she did was change her professional name. She would no longer be Diana Dill, now she would be Diana Douglas both on and off screen. The next step took her round the agencies and studios until a screen test finally led to a contract at 20th Century Fox.

But Kirk Douglas was restless again. He had completed *The Strange Love of Martha Ivers* and when the studio could not find another role for him straight away he announced he was going back to New York to find a play. He left for the East Coast in January 1947. Ruth Dill, meanwhile, had found it difficult to settle in Hollywood so soon after the death of her husband and there had been tension between her and her son-in-law, so she had returned to Bermuda for Christmas a few weeks previously. Diana Douglas and baby Michael were left on their own in a town where they were still comparative strangers. To all intents and purposes Diana Douglas was now a single mother – albeit considerably better off financially than most. Nonetheless she still had a living to make and Michael got his first real taste of the movie business as she took him along to auditions, costume fittings, photo shoots, interviews and meetings. He would sit there quietly drinking it all in and saying very little.

Kirk Douglas had been touring with the play *Woman Bites Dog* and had formed a romantic attachment to one of the actresses in the cast. Diana discovered this one night when she phoned and found her call to her husband transferred to the actress's room, where he was allegedly helping her run through her lines. Diana Douglas was instantly suspicious that her husband was having an affair. Her instincts might have encouraged her to end the marriage there and then, but her upbringing had conditioned her against that. Divorce had been anathema in her family. As a young girl she remembered the shock when her sister Ruth announced that she and Seward Johnson were splitting up. She felt that, for the time being at least, her only option was to put this infidelity behind her and try to make a go of the marriage. In any event they had bought a house in Vado Place off Laurel Canyon. This would be their first proper family home, a place where Michael could grow up and enjoy the California sunshine, and perhaps provide a settled domestic environment which would curb her husband's wandering.

For a time things improved, the atmosphere became calmer and more relaxed and the family flourished. Diana even became pregnant again. However the improvement was only temporary. Kirk Douglas was still prone to outbursts of temper and in one of them he accused Diana of having been unfaithful while she was back in Bermuda when Michael was a baby. The row was sparked by the arrival of a gift from a family friend to whom Diana was very close, but with whom she had not had an affair. The argument grumbled on but was never satisfactorily settled. Then he announced that the actress he had been seeing during the run of *Woman Bites Dog* was coming to Los Angeles with her parents and he wanted them all to go to dinner together. This, by any standard, is astonishingly insensitive behaviour. Once more, not wishing to make a scene, the now pregnant Diana arranged for child care for Michael and went to dinner with the woman who had been a rival for her affections. According to Diana, Kirk Douglas behaved disgracefully at dinner making it apparent that the flames of his affair with this rising star were still smouldering if not actively burning.

It was obvious that their marriage was in difficulty but before they could actually do anything about it, their second son, Joel Andrew Douglas, was born in January of 1947. Michael, who was just over two years old when his brother was born, did not take kindly to the new arrival at first. He was angry and anxious and had very little to do with the new baby. Slowly but surely, and with some patient explanation from his mother, he began to warm to baby Joel. So much so that he came to see himself as the child's protector and took his responsibilities as seriously as he did everything else in life. On one occasion he even chided his mother publicly at the beach in Santa Monica because he felt she was not supervising Joel sufficiently.

The arrival of the new baby did nothing to improve relations between Kirk and Diana Douglas. They acquired a live-in nanny, which allowed Diana to go back to work when Michael went to kindergarten in the autumn of 1947, but it was obvious that all was not well. Kirk Douglas was unhappy with the roles he was being offered and when he found one that he did like in *A Letter To Three Wives* he promptly had an affair with his co-star Ann Sothern. Diana for her part took herself off to Santa Barbara to appear in a stage production of *The Hasty Heart*. Shortly afterwards they decided they would take a holiday as a family in Bermuda. Ruth Dill had not seen her new grandson and hadn't seen Michael for more than two years. Ruth and the children enjoyed the trip, but for Diana and Kirk Douglas it was purgatory. She recalled later how they would deliberately flirt with people at parties to try to prompt a reaction from the other and were generally short-tempered with each other for the whole trip. It was obvious that something would have to be done and a late night walk along the beach in Bermuda one night proved to be the catalyst.

Kirk Douglas had been offered two roles which he desperately wanted to play. The first was a major studio project for MGM, the other was a small low-budget picture for Stanley Kramer called *Champion*. Although Kramer would go on to be one of the greats, at this stage he had no track record as a producer. Nevertheless Kirk Douglas was drawn to the story of a boxer who is prepared to sacrifice everything to become a champion. Given his own circumstances it's not surprising that the role of Midge Kelly struck a chord. It was a risky project, but that night walking along the beach he decided to play his hunch and go with *Champion*. He spent many hours at his home with Stanley Kramer, working on the script and developing the project. He was involved in casting and varous other aspects of the production. This is something he would do routinely as a producer on subsequent pictures, but this was his first taste of shaping a role specifically for himself. He made only one request of Diana, which was that she not come on the set while he was shooting. She felt this was strange but he insisted it would make him feel self-conscious, so she went along with it. Later, she discovered that her presence had been unwelcome because her husband had begun an affair with his co-star, Marilyn Maxwell.

Even before it had been released the talk around Hollywood was that *Champion* was going to be a huge success and was going to make Kirk Douglas a major star. This was what he had always wanted, but instead of making him happy it seemed to make him even less satisfied. The rows continued. One day he and Diana were in the kitchen having another argument. They saw Michael coming towards them and stopped fighting before he came into the room. Michael, who was barely four at the time, immediately sensed that something was wrong and burst into tears. His parents knew then that the separation they had been talking about would have to become a reality.

Curiously, the separation was a relatively cordial affair. It was announced by Warren Cowan, Kirk Douglas's newly-acquired press agent, but both parties refused to add to the bald announcement. Neither of them would talk to Hedda Hopper, Louella Parsons, or any of the other gossip columnists of the day. They were determined to maintain as dignified an approach as possible and it seemed to work. With her husband out of the house once again Diana Douglas threw herself back into her work. After a couple of film roles she achieved a notable success with a production of George Bernard Shaw's *Major Barbara* at the Circle Theatre, a small but influential venue in Hollywood. The reviews were excellent and no one was more generous in his praise than her estranged husband. One of those who saw and loved the play was Katharine Hepburn, who had just been offered the lead in a new Broadway production *Second Threshhold* by Philip Barry. Hepburn felt she herself was too old for the part but thought Diana Douglas would be perfect and she personally recommended her for the role. Diana was delighted but at the same time reluctant, since taking the play would mean moving to New York and there was no way she could leave the boys and no way she could take them with her. Kirk Douglas found the solution. He would move back into their old house in Vado Place and look after the boys while she went to New York.

Now that he was separated from his wife, Kirk Douglas had begun another relationship. He had met Irene Wrightsman at The Racquet Club in Palm Springs and become instantly besotted with her. It was a tragic, fatalistic obsession for both of them. She was the daughter of an Oklahoma oil tycoon who was one of the richest men in the country. Her wealth was no substitute for paternal affection and both she and her mother drank to excess to compensate. Like Kirk Douglas, Irene Wrightsman sought approval and approbation through a series of love affairs, each one more ill-suited than the last. She died tragically young as a consequence of her hedonistic lifestyle. It was no surprise that two people as seriously emotionally damaged as Kirk Douglas and Irene Wrightsman would find each other.

By a tragic stroke of ill-luck Philip Barry died suddenly before *Second Threshold* could be produced and Diana Douglas did not get what could have been the role of a lifetime. Before that, while she was still going through the audition process and believing the role was hers, a delighted Diana called home to tell her husband the good news. The phone was answered by a strange woman, who said that Kirk Douglas was out so Diana asked to speak to Michael.

'Who answered the phone?' she asked her five-year-old son.

'That was Auntie Irene,' said Michael. 'She's living here now.'

Moving in his girlfriend and trying to make her part of the family was the final straw. Kirk and Diana Douglas were divorced on 8 February 1950. She was given sole custody of the boys and wasted no time in taking them back to New York.

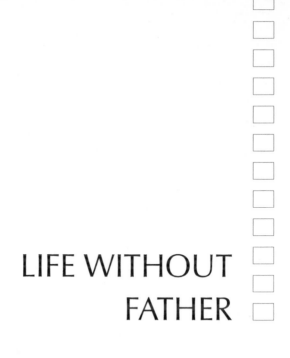

LIFE WITHOUT FATHER

Michael Douglas claims to have been largely unaffected by the break-up of his parents' marriage. Certainly the final split was achieved without rancour. Both Kirk and Diana Douglas claim that while their divorce lawyers once came to blows they themselves seldom rowed, determined to make things as easy for the children as possible. They even watched their own divorce court appearance on television together and critiqued their appearance and performance. Although Michael Douglas insists that it was not as unbearable as one might think, it is hard to believe that he was entirely unaffected. The little boy who spent nights crying in his room as the tension at Vado Place became palpable must have, at the very least, been dreadfully confused by the whole affair.

'People always talk about the effect divorce has on kids,' he said. 'Often the parents suffer more. Kids can handle anything as long as they're loved, and I was always loved.'

As divorces go, Michael Douglas believes his parents' break-up was almost a model of how things should be done, if they have to be done.

'I was very lucky growing up,' he said. 'My mother and father divorced amicably and were good friends and still are good friends. My stepfather and mother and father and stepmother used to get together every couple of weeks for dinner, preferrably without the kids. They just enjoyed each other's company That is a very positive image of what a divorce can be and we were all very lucky. In truth, divorce is not about children. What you are talking about is the relationship with your spouse. Therefore children, at whatever age, as long as they can see their parents speaking amicably to each other, they're fine. I have no patience for the selfishness of wives and husband who put their own interests first and use their children as weapons.'

Michael Douglas made those comments as a grown man after he had had some time to come to terms with growing up as the son of divorced parents. It is undeniably true that both Diana and Kirk Douglas loved their sons more than anything and wanted to spare them any hurt. However, it is immaterial how much Michael Douglas rationalises it later in life, there is no doubt that divorce is still a shattering process for a five-year-old.

The problem with Kirk Douglas was that he simply did not know how to be a father and for that he is more to be pitied than scorned. He had grown up without any relationship to speak of with his own father and had no template on which to base his own behaviour. He knew Harry Demsky had not been a good father and he desperately wanted to be the best father in the world to Michael and Joel, he just didn't have the emotional equipment. Kirk Douglas had always had problems with commitment. His constant womanising can be seen as a search for affection which has been sublimated as conquest. By bedding women he was trying to gain the validation he had never known as a child or a young man. It was the same in his search for a wife. He wanted someone who would act as a hostess for his dinner parties, keep her opinions to herself, and provide admiration for all his achievements. That was not what he found in Diana Dill. It's hardly surprising that the divorce forced Kirk Douglas into therapy – where he remained for some time – perhaps proving his son's point that sometimes it does affect the parents more than the children.

Michael Douglas had become used to shuttling back and forward between the East and West Coasts. Now, however, he was going to have to adjust to life in New York. They moved into an apartment on the corner of Central Park West and 85th Street in which there was a room for Diana and another bedroom which he and Joel could share. There was also a maid's room which became essential because Diana had realised she would have to work and had set her sights on a career in television, which was largely based in New York in those days. A housekeeper named Mrs Doubrava was hired to look after the boys while she was at work. Diana Douglas was horrified when, some years later, Michael told her that the Czech immigrant used to physically abuse both him and Joel. The children would be beaten or have their arms twisted or their ears pinched – always making sure there were never any tell-tale marks or bruises – whenever they infringed Mrs Doubrava's strict code of conduct. Michael said that neither he nor his brother said anything at the time because they were convinced that no one would have believed them.

Although he claims not to have been affected by his parents' split-up, Diana Douglas certainly noticed a change in her oldest son. Joel was barely two and too young to really be aware of his altered circumstances but Michael, who was almost six, knew exactly what was going on. Diana Douglas remembers Michael turning from an amiable, amenable and polite little boy into a difficult and rebellious child. He was stubborn and intractable and defied his mother at every turn. She, in turn, was so concerned that she sought help from a child psychologist, who told her there was really nothing to be alarmed about. Michael had gone through a devastating life change and, according to the psychologist, his mother was probably over-compensating by trying to be too strict. She advised Diana to ease back on the discipline and Michael would return to his old self – she was right.

Nevertheless, Diana Douglas felt that her son needed some sense of order in his life. The Allen Stevenson School impressed her with its academic performance but it also had a strict dress code. The only drawback was that the school was on 78th and Lexington over on the East Side of the city. So every morning Michael, dressed in a white shirt, school tie, and grey flannel shorts in the summer and trousers in the winter, would travel by taxi across the city to his new school. It must have been hugely difficult for a little boy not yet six to be confronted with a strange school, strange accents, and strange customs. On top of that he was, for the first time in his life, facing up to being the son of a famous father. *Champion* may have ended his marriage but it had also made Kirk Douglas a huge star, and Michael was having to deal with being the only movie star's son at an East Side public school. Michael, never the most outgoing child, responded by developing a tough emotional core and withdrawing into it whenever necessary.

'I was not very happy,' he recalled. 'I was an introverted, uptight kind of a kid. I just didn't let anyone rattle my cage. I didn't give out too easily.'

The one thing which their new surroundings did do for Michael was to strengthen his bond with Joel. In later life probably no one would know him as well or be trusted so intimately as his younger brother. Michael had always been inclined to keep an eye out for Joel but now it was very much a case of the two of them against the world. The husky Joel was the exact opposite of the rangy Michael. They would scrap and quarrel like any other set of brothers, but when it really mattered Michael was always there to look after Joel.

The two boys and their mother settled into a routine in their new home in Central Park West. Diana Douglas was quickly making a name for herself and found her skills were much in demand, not only in the new medium of television but also in the theatre. She was so confident that the boys had adjusted to their new lifestyle that she even went off to India for two months to shoot a film called *The Monsoon*, leaving her sons in the tender care of Mrs Doubrava. It's safe to assume that these were not the happiest months of the children's lives. Their father also had regular and unrestricted access to his sons. This turned out to be a source of some frustration for Diana Douglas because, in his attempts to be a good father, Kirk Douglas would either spoil them rotten or discipine them capriciously. The boys did not know what to do for the best. It was the same in the long letters which he regularly sent, in which they would be alternately praised to the heavens or condemned without mercy. On the other hand Kirk Douglas himself was wracked with guilt. He recalls one incident after the divorce when Michael was small and staying with him in Los Angeles. After he had put his son to bed Kirk Douglas was going out for the evening. As he got to the car he looked back at the house and saw Michael, in the open bedroom window, silently sobbing as he watched his father drive off into the night.

Michael and Joel Douglas spent the summer of 1951 with their father. This coincided with an offer to Diana Douglas to join a summer stock company in Ohio, to play the lead in a play called *Light Up the Sky*. Although she did not know it at the time this became another turning point in her life. During the run of the play she met and fell in love with one of the other actors, Bill Darrid. Within two weeks of their meeting he had already mentioned marriage – plainly Diana Douglas had that effect on men. Although she was not going to rush headlong into another marriage Diana Douglas continued her relationship with Bill Darrid. She knew at the back of her mind that the time would come, and probably soon, when he would have to earn the approval of the other two men in her life – Michael and Joel.

Their first meeting came at the airport, when Bill Darrid accompanied Diana to collect her sons after they had flown in from the coast following their summer with their father. Michael Douglas looked at Darrid coldly and simply asked who he was, and where his mother's previous boyfriend had gone. Over the next month or so the boys saw a lot more of Bill Darrid , he had moved to a hotel closer to their Central Park apartment, but that did not mean they had become any more accepting. On one landmark morning Darrid was sitting reading his newspaper in the Douglas's apartment when he thought he smelled smoke. Joel, doubtless encouraged by his older brother, had got hold of a lighter, sneaked up on the interloper, and was trying to set fire to the chair he was sitting in. Darrid's response was measured but direct. He simply picked the boy up, put him across his knee, and paddled his rear.

Diana continued to see Bill Darrid and the boys became more used to having him in their lives. They were not totally accepting of him, at least not according to their father. He tells a story of Diana and the boys visiting him in Paris in the spring of 1952 when he was making a film, *Act of Love*. At the end of their visit, according to Kirk, they were all walking together in the Bois de Boulogne. Michael Douglas who was walking between his parents, took his father's hand and placed it in his mother's.

'Now,' said the little boy, 'the family is together.'

Diana Douglas claims to have no recollection of the incident but Kirk Douglas maintains it broke his heart. If his father's memory is the more reliable in this instance then Michael's behaviour is hardly that of a little boy who was at ease with his new circumstances.

While they were in Paris they were introduced to Anne Buydens who was with Kirk at the time. Although he was unofficially engaged to and somewhat obsessed with the Italian actress Pier Angeli, Kirk Douglas was also conducting a relationship with Anne Buydens. In May of 1954 he called Diana to announce that he and Anne had got married – they remain married to this day. When she broke the news to her sons Joel burst into tears fearing that his father wouldn't want him any more. Michael, who was now nine, on the other hand allowed that Anne Buydens had seemed like a very nice woman.

Other than that his response was to go and stare out of the window for a long time, in an unfathomable mood. This had become his normal response to any problem. He seldom ranted or raved or threw tantrums, he simply locked it inside and dealt with it in his own way.

Michael Douglas was about to have considerably more to deal with in his young life. For one thing there was his film debut to consider. Kirk Douglas had set up his own production company, named after his mother Bryna, fulfilling a promise to her that one day she would see her name in lights. Their first film was *The Indian Fighter* and, for reasons best known to himself, he had offered a role to Diana – which she took. This meant that instead of spending their summer vacation with their father in 1955, Michael and Joel Douglas were babysat in Los Angeles by their now pregnant step-mother Anne Buydens-Douglas, while their parents shot a film together in Oregon. The whole extended family got together in the last few weeks of the shoot when Anne brought the boys up to join their parents. Kirk wanted the boys to be in the film and persuaded director Andre de Toth to give them a couple of lines each. Their performances consisted of running through the set shouting 'The Indians are coming'. Given the amount of time they had spent together playing cowboy games in their New York apartment they were ideally suited for the role. Sadly, they never made the finished film and their debut performances ended up on the cutting room floor.

Kirk Douglas had enjoyed having his sons around him and he asked his ex-wife to consider moving back to California, if only for a year, so that he could see the boys. He felt that now that his own life had settled down with his marriage to Anne, he could try to mend some fences with his sons. For Michael this meant a change of school from the refined atmosphere of Allen Stevenson to Emerson Junior High, which was close to his new home in Westwood. The fine education he had received in New York actually worked against him here. He found himself bumped up two classes because of his academic achievements, which meant that 11-year-old Michael was now in a class of teenagers who were at least two years older than him.

'It was a tough school,' he remembers. 'They had killings. Kids carried knives . . . I had a DA haircut. I remember hiding behind the dashboard of my mother's Ford Crestline convertible so my hair wouldn't get blown in the wind.'

On his own admission Michael Douglas was not a good student. He had no real interest in anything the school had to teach him. His chief concerns were cars and drinking. He claims he got alcohol poisoning once on a quart of gin, the first real sign of the substance abuse which would dog him in later life. He also began his life-long fascination with cars at Emerson Junior High, joining a hot-rod club, taking up drag racing and getting into trouble for stealing parts for cars.

The trip to the coast was not working out as anyone had planned. Kirk Douglas was away working and didn't have the time that he had promised for his sons. In any event he had become a father again with his son Peter being born in November 1955. Michael was not settling at school and Joel had been diagnosed as dyslexic.

The solution to the perceived problem presented itself the following year when Bill Darrid proposed to Diana Douglas. She accepted immediately and they were married in December, 1956. Bill Darrid was increasingly moving away from acting and into writing and producing, so a move back to the East Coast seemed logical. This time they would settle not in New York but in Westport, Connecticut. The boys transferred from their schools in Los Angeles and Michael continued his education at Westport Junior High. There were, surprisingly, more problems at school for Michael Douglas – although they were not the ones which his mother might have anticipated.

It was at Westport that Diana Douglas discovered her elder son's incipient status as a sex symbol. According to a school counsellor he was being subjected to a lot of what his mother refers to as 'aggressive female attention'. As a good looking boy and the son of a movie star, Michael Douglas was turning out to be something of a disruptive influence among the female population. Michael had discovered women at Emerson Junior High although it was not as happy a memory as one might expect.

'I remember the first girl I ever kissed was there (Emerson),' he recalls. 'She had her mouth wide open. Yuuuck! Couldn't believe it. No one told me anything about this.'

Even so his school counsellor at Westport felt that an all-male environment might be helpful for a time and Diana agreed. She and Bill Darrid began to look around for a boarding school for Michael and he, perhaps surprisingly, was not violently opposed to the idea. Diana and Bill Darrid had their hearts set on the prestigious Deerfield but Michael's grades were not good enough. They took advice and placed him in nearby Eaglebrook School, which was designed to improve his qualifications so that he would be able to go to Deerfield the following year. Instead, he enjoyed Eaglebrook so much that he stayed there for three years before finally going on to the elite Choate School.

Life at boarding school was something of an eye-opener for Michael Douglas. He played football at Choate, where he was a defensive end, and was also a member of the track team. There were other aspects of school life which were not so pleasant. He recalls, for instance, being shocked at Choate when he heard a class-mate come out with an outrageously anti-Semitic comment. Helping him through a difficult period was the hugely settling influence of Bill Darrid. Michael Douglas remembers life with his mother and step-father as being almost Victorian in its formality and correctness.

'My memories,' he said later, 'are of how thoughtful he (Bill Darrid) was to her (Diana) and how considerate he was of us.'

Although he was not his biological father, Bill Darrid provided everything that Michael Douglas needed. He was firm but he was also understanding. He appreciated how difficult life could be for a teenager, let alone a teenager in the circumstances in which

Michael Douglas found himself. More important that anything, Bill Darrid made time for Michael Douglas. If the boy had a problem then he could count on his stepfather giving it his full attention. Bill Darrid, he would say later, was the first adult who had ever listened to him and took him seriously. A great deal of what Michael Douglas is today is the result of Bill Darrid's firm but sensitive guidance through his teenage years.

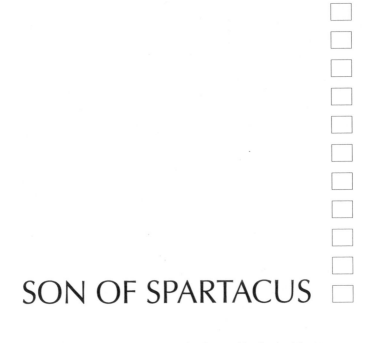

SON OF SPARTACUS

Michael Douglas was now having the best of both worlds. He was living a life of prosperity and privilege and being educated in one of the country's top schools. He did not necessarily know at this stage what he wanted to do with his life, although he was considering a career in law, but whatever he might choose to do he would be well set up for it. Neither of his parents had actively encouraged him to follow in their chosen careers. They had both been bruised by early rejection when they started out as actors, and had discovered first-hand what an insecure and fickle occupation acting could be. They may, in fact, have over-compensated in their determination to let their son make his mind up for himself.

In the summers when he was on vacation from Choate he would head for the west coast to spend a few months with his father. Although they were by no means close, by the time Michael Douglas had become a teenager he had reached some kind of understanding with his father. And what teenager would not be impressed by the kind of cachet that went with being the son of one of the world's biggest movie stars? Despite the best efforts of both parents it was in these summer vacations that the seeds were sown for Michael Douglas's movie career. Since he was out in Los Angeles, his father invariably urged him to come to the set of whatever picture he was working on. This meant that they could spend more time together. It was during this time, for example, that, while his father was shooting at Universal, Michael would take his lunchbreaks in the editing suites. Every day he would slip off for an hour with a brown-bag lunch, and sit absorbed in the craft of the editors as they spliced together the raw footage to create a finished sequence. One of the first pieces he saw being cut together was the famous shower sequence from *Psycho*, which was being edited at Universal while his father was working there.

Eventually he graduated from simply hanging around to being given small jobs. With his own deeply ingrained work ethic, Kirk Douglas plainly felt there was no way his son should be hanging around when he could be doing something useful. One of his first jobs was on *Spartacus* in which he was employed as a gofer, doing all sorts of errands and fetching and carrying on the set. In other films he was employed as an assistant director – a much less grand title than it sounds – and on *Lonely Are the Brave* he was employed as an assistant film editor, this time back in the cutting rooms doing some of the actual cutting.

It could not have been easy making the transition from the Hollywood lifestyle to the discipline of Choate at the end of every holiday. How many other boys at Choate had Hayley Mills as their date for their sixteenth birthday party? Diana Douglas certainly noticed the difference whenever either of her sons returned from visiting their father. There was a marked reluctance to tidy up or do chores, on the basis that Kirk Douglas had a butler and a staff for that kind of thing. The Darrids, however, did not run to domestic staff so there was an often acrimonious but usually brief period of adjust-ment after every trip. Towards the end of his time at Choate the

rebellious teenager who had first seen the light of day at Emerson
Junior High back in Westwood surfaced again. Choate was too close
to Yale to be beyond temptation. On Fridays and Saturdays Michael
Douglas and a few of his friends would sneak out and go to parties
at Yale, where they would do their best in 48 hours to make up for
the strict privations of their single-sex existence at Choate. Douglas
claims he got into a lot of mischief towards the end of his time at the
school, but none of it was too serious. One stunt in his senior year,
however, in which he and some classmates smuggled a live cow
from a nearby pasture into the main reception hall, almost signalled
the end of his relationship with Choate. It seems there was not
enough in student life to sufficiently interest him, but he managed to
graduate before they expelled him.

After he had graduated from Choate, his parents were keen for
Michael to go to Yale. They had even found a relative of Bill Darrid's
who might have been able to pull strings to get him in, despite his
rather lacklustre 'C' average, even though this could have made it
tough for him academically. While Diana and Bill Darrid were
searching for another Ivy League college, Michael had already made
up his mind.

'I wanted the biggest change I could think of,' he says. 'I remember going to this counsellor in high school (who) had all these
brochures on various colleges. And I saw one for this campus by the
sea; a guy walking down the beach with a surfboard, two girls
wearing two-piece bathing suits. This is 1963 and on the East Coast
you hardly ever saw a two-piece bathing suit. So I decided to go to
college out in California and that was my motivation.'

Michael Douglas was heading for Santa Barbara to study English,
but it wasn't just about the girls in their swimsuits. He had become
weary of his stifling, regimented existence and desperately wanted
a change.

'Choate was very conservative, very structured,' he would later
recall, 'and I'd had all of that kind of education system that I could
take so I went to the University of California at Santa Barbara. It was

great. I was just another IBM number as far as the system was concerned and I could do whatever I wanted. I'm not putting upper-middle-class affluence down, it's just that it was the only thing I knew, and going to a school where all the people didn't necessarily have the money to pay tuition was something I wanted to do.'

Turning up in Santa Barbara in the autumn of 1963 gave Michael Douglas a crash course in the spirit of the Sixties and he took to campus life like a duck to water – or at least to certain aspects of it. He was having the time of his life but it had very little to do with his academic work; Michael Douglas was catching up on his experiences at the university of life. The one thing which struck him most forcefully was that for the first time he was part of a community which was dominated by people of his own age. There were no teachers to lay down rules, there was no maternal discipline, and – something which was becoming increasingly important – there was no dominating image of a father to live up to. By now Kirk Douglas had played some of the biggest roles of his career in films such as *Spartacus, The Vikings, Lust For Life,* and *Gunfight at the O.K Corral.* It would have been surprising if Michael Douglas had not started to find it a little difficult to live in his shadow.

'It was hard,' he remembers. 'I saw my father as a gladiator, nailed to a cross, as an artist who cut his ear off and he would be shown doing all of these superhuman things. I'd think: "How can I possibly be a man? How can I be the man that this man was? Jesus! Look at this guy." It took me a long time to get through all that to a sense of myself . . .'

Michael Douglas may have felt that UCSB was a genuine paradise with an ocean view, but even in the climate of free love there was no such things as a free ride. At the end of the spring term both Diana and Kirk Douglas got separate letters suggesting that it might be better if Michael took some time out from college. He wasn't being thrown out, but the academic establishment at UCSB felt that he did not have the right attitude, at the moment, towards his education. They felt he was not showing enough maturity to benefit from the experience, and perhaps a year working somewhere might help. Douglas himself concedes that, looking back, he was immature.

'It was girls, basically,' he says. 'Just the old thing, this discipline formally imposed on you in private schools and then you go to a public university and you have all this freedom.'

Douglas had been so taken by the new-found freedoms of his college life that he had drifted into a commune. Mountain Drive was a counter-culture community on Banana Road in the hills above Santa Barbara. For someone like Michael Douglas it must have been like heaven on earth. Flitting from girl to girl in the free love climate of the early Sixties he only went to classes when he felt like it – which was not often. He was strongly into meditation and equally strongly into marijuana.

'A lot of the members were older people in their thirties and forties who hadn't made it and were attempting to find their own way and go back to natural things,' he remembers. 'It was the kind of thing where you went to school three-quarters of an hour away and when you came back, if you liked, you took off your clothes. I found the hippies supercool, but after a while I realised that the marijuana and the nudity and the acid and all that was a blind alley. It was another way of copping out and I became aware that I didn't want to drop out of society. I wanted to make it on my own.'

That realisation would come later, after Douglas had spent some time in the real world, but as far as his parents were concerned neither of them was too unhappy about him being removed from his temptations at college. Douglas concedes that they must have been worried about him, however they respected his privacy too much to make a big fuss. Kirk Douglas admits that he was very worried about his son's behaviour but he didn't know what to do for the best. And, even though he was living only forty miles away, Kirk decided the best thing to do was to look away and hope things would turn out all right.

Part of that process came when Michael Douglas left university.

This time, instead of bumming around on one of his father's movie sets, he got himself a job. Having had the best education that money could buy, he ended up working in a filling station; Oaks Automotive on Main Street in Westport. This was a deliberate attempt to make something of himself on his own terms. He loved cars, he knew he would be happy working around them, and he wanted to be his own man. It was an illuminating experience. He had a sense of accomplishment that he had never known before, and the young man who had never shown much interest in attending classes or paying attention to his studies suddenly discovered a work ethic he had never known. At the end of his shift, after a hard day of pumping gas, washing windows and checking oil, Michael would go and have a well-deserved beer with the other grease monkeys. He was accepted as 'Mikey', he was just one of the guys. His efforts did not go unnoticed. Over the many years of his career Michael Douglas would pick up many awards, including the ultimate accolade his industry has to offer. None, however, mean as much as that first award, when he was named Mobil's Man of the Month for his efforts in the gas station.

'That was a good summer,' he says. 'I ran the tow truck. It was the first time I had a job on my own and it was really satisfying.'

Award-winning employee or not, pumping gas in Westport's Main Street was not really a proper way to earn a living for a man of his talents or abilities. It was a stop-gap, a pause to give him same sense of himself and some experience of the value of having to work for a living. There were thoughts in his head about what he might really like to do with his life but they had not yet crystallised. The next part of his time out from college was spent, as so many other periods of down-time had been, working with his father.

Kirk Douglas was in Norway making a war film called *The Heroes of Telemark* which was being filmed on location in Scandinavia and in studios in London. Kirk persuaded his son to come and join him in Norway with the promise of a job and the title of 'assistant director'. Even Michael was smart enough to see that this was simply window-dressing to placate a major star. In reality, the job was just another gofer job, running here and there and doing whatever needed to be done. All the same it helped in the decision making process, as did a period spent on his own in London. His father had to go to France on business, leaving Michael with a huge hotel suite to himself. Rather than taking advantage and throwing wild parties, he spent time thinking about what to do with his life. While he was doing that he missed a golden opportunity. On one occasion the assistant director – the real one not an honorary gofer – invited him out to a club. There was a rock band playing whose management were looking for backers and Michael might have been able to get in on the ground floor. Michael declined, preferring to spend the night in his hotel room, and someone else got the chance to make a fortune from The Who.

After *The Heroes of Telemark* was completed Michael followed his father to Israel where he was making *Cast a Giant Shadow*. The film was a biography of the Israeli hero General Mickey Marcus, the American lawyer turned soldier who had helped win the War of Independence. Kirk Douglas was playing Marcus and both Michael and Joel were on the set with him. From being a stocky child, Joel Douglas had grown into an impressively burly young man and found himself working as a *de facto* bodyguard for his father. For the locals it wasn't enough that this was Kirk Douglas, here he was in Israel making a film about a Jewish hero. He couldn't go out into the street without being mobbed by a crowd of people, and invariably at the heart of that mob would be Joel, trying to clear some space for his father. Michael was once again employed on the set as a gofer, but this time he got to make his film debut. There was one scene where an Israeli soldier had to drive a jeep at a furious clip up a narrow mountain path, before braking sharply to stop on a desig-nated mark. The Israeli actor playing the role refused to do it, he thought it was too dangerous. Kirk Douglas, not wanting to miss the shot, told Michael to go and get a uniform and do it. Michael, who had been fanatical about cars almost all his life, leapt behind the wheel, executed the shot perfectly, and hit the mark exactly. His first, albeit uncredited, taste of the big screen.

Being in Israel also gave Michael Douglas a powerful insight into his father. Athough he was circumcised when he was born, and although Kirk Douglas had to promise a rabbi that his son would be brought up in the Jewish faith before he could marry a gentile, no attempt had ever been made to raise Michael Douglas as Jewish. But during the filming of *Cast a Giant Shadow* he gained, perhaps for the first time, some undertanding of the forces which had shaped his father.

'As time goes on I become more and more Jewish,' he would say later. 'I guess there is so little to hold on to that if you're Jewish or black or whatever, the cultural identity you have becomes more and more important because there isn't anything else.'

Years later his father would ask him what religion he was and Michael Douglas would say that he was a Jew. When his father pressed him and asked why, he told him that it was because he felt Jewish. That feeling started on the set of *Cast a Giant Shadow*.

By the time he had finished working with his father Michael Douglas knew what he wanted to do. He was going to go back to the University of California at Santa Barbara and resume his degree. However he would be changing his major. He would no longer be studying English, now he would be majoring in drama. He was going to be an actor and he was prepared to deal with being his father's son.

'I wanted to start school again,' he explained. 'One reason that made me want to . . . was that I found myself interested in dramatics. In acting I began to find my own identity.'

He is the first to admit that there was no burning desire to act, or to be a star. He simply wanted to find out who he was and the best way to do that, for him, was to choose a career in which he would play other people.

STAGE FRIGHT

Michael Douglas claims to have drifted into acting for want of something better to do which may well have been the case. There is no doubt, though, that by following in his father's profession he was, perhaps subconsciously, willing to confront him and willing to confront the label of being the son of Kirk Douglas. If he was to work in his father's chosen field, then what better way to step out of his father's shadow than to be a success in his own right? The beginnings, however, did not augur well. Michael Douglas discovered very quickly that he had stage fright, a condition which would haunt him for years. Whenever he appeared in a student production they would have to keep a bucket in the wings so that he could throw up before going on stage.

Nevertheless he stuck at it and he prospered, slowly but surely. He was still living in the commune in a world of marijuana, maypoles, and velour shirts but this time, after spending some time away, he was better able to deal with it. The commune, he would later realise, at least gave him a strong sense of family and of a genuinely shared lifestyle. This was something which had been missing from his life as a consequence of his parents' divorce and the years spent shuttling back and forth from coast to coast.

'It was a magic period,' he says. 'There was an interesting assortment of people there. I had a friend next door who was a dealer, and he got killed in Mexico. Another guy was a robber who had been in San Quentin for a number of years but had found himself. There was an exposure to different types of people without any sense of fear . . . For me, coming from divorced parents and not knowing who I was, it was a good experience. There was ritual and a family and a cultural feeling that was very secure. It was an extended family. We had an effortless feeling together : being naked together in the pool and having a wonderful ease with women. There was no sense of having to be scared of anything. There was no fear, just warmth.'

Michael Douglas spent four years on and off at Santa Barbara from 1963 until the Summer of Love in 1967, and they were perhaps the most important years of his life in shaping the man he would become. There would be other spells which would shape him as an actor or a producer, but it was college which went a long way towards forming him as a man. From his time in the commune he gained a desire to search for alternatives, whether that be in lifestyle or anything else. As a member of the Meditation Society he would meditate for thirty minutes, morning and night, and so gained a sense of spirituality. But perhaps more importantly, he also learned to search, to be inquisitive, and to be more inclined to see things less as they are than as they ought to be.

College also gave him a sense of political awareness which had been slightly lacking in the cloistered atmosphere of Choate. His father was certainly very outspoken and was seen as something of a radical in some quarters. He was, after all, the man who had smashed the Hollywood blacklist. When he was making *Spartacus*, which he also produced, Kirk Douglas hired Dalton Trumbo, perhaps the most notorious of those punished by the Hollywood blacklist. Trumbo had worked since he had been pilloried for his communist sympathies but always under a *nom de plume*. Kirk Douglas originally hired him as 'Sam Jackson', but became so tired of the charade that midway through filming he dropped the pretence and Trumbo was credited under his own name in the final print. The blacklist was broken. Bill Darrid was also a man of liberal tendencies. His gestures may not have been as dramatic but his fair-mindedness and his strong sense of injustice made a big impression on his step-son.

The West Coast of America was the cradle of the anti-Vietnam war protest movement and, for Michael Douglas like everyone else, it was impossible to be at a California college at that time and not have an opinion. Michael Douglas had a very low lottery number, which meant he was more than likely to be drafted, but he had no intention of fighting what he believed to be an unjust war. There was a momentary but mild confrontation with his father, who reminded him of his duty as a citizen to serve his country. However Kirk Douglas was also opposed to the war and could not find it in his heart to seriously insist that either of his sons – Joel would also be excused on medical grounds – fight in a war which he did not support. Kirk Douglas realised that, perhaps for the first time, his son had made an independent decision and he supported it. Kirk Douglas used his contacts to find a surgeon who would attest to an old but genuine football injury and Michael Douglas turned up at his draft physical with a letter from a doctor and was excused on medical grounds.

'I did some work with orthopaedic surgeons,' he explained, 'and I got letters and a brace. I'm not particularly proud of that now but I did not want to fight in that war.'

Having managed to escape the draft, Michael Douglas still felt a deep sense of resentment against the war, and probably more than a little guilt at not being there. Instead he threw himself into the protest movement and took part in marches and silent vigils and other demonstrations against the conflict. When that wasn't enough he took on a more radical form of protest by joining a guerrilla theatre group. They would burst into classes and disrupt lectures by pelting teachers and pupils with blood bags which splattered fake blood everywhere. Someone from the theatre group would then yell out how many people had been killed in Vietnam the previous day, and they would race out of class before they could be arrested by campus security.

'Sometimes we had to fight our way out,' he remembers. 'The idea was to get a visceral reaction – to make people feel that someone was actually being killed up close, not just on the other side of the world.'

As his political agitation increased so too did his theatre skills. He was still throwing up into the bucket, but he had come to see this as part of a process of testing himself to see if he wanted it badly enough. Both Kirk and Diana Douglas saw him on stage in his first year as a drama student and were impressed, eventually. Since he lived only forty miles away, Kirk Douglas saw Michael more than once. He came to his debut performance in *As You Like It* and thought he was absolutely dreadful. Michael could not disagree, recalling how Shakespeare's dialogue came babbling out in a torrent devoid of either sense or reason. At that point his father felt he would never make it as an actor. However when he saw Michael's next performance in a play called *Escurial*, in which he played an old man, he felt he was marvellous. Diana Douglas, seeing her son for the first time in *Escurial*, did not even recognise him at first. She was mentally praising the elderly character actor until she realised that this old man was actually her son. She felt he was destined for great things and she was so certain that her son could make the grade that she called an old friend, George White, who ran the Eugene O'Neill Foundation Theatre in Waterford, Connecticut, to ask if Michael could work as an apprentice during his summer break. George White agreed and so at the end of his summer term Michael Douglas went, not for a sinecure on one of his father's pictures, but for a chance to further his career in his own right. They were building a new amphitheatre at Waterford and Michael ended up doing construction work. This was perhaps not what he had expected to be doing, and it certainly wasn't what one of the other young people who were there that summer expected either.

Like Kirk and Diana Douglas, Danny De Vito was a graduate of the American Academy of Dramatic Arts. This small, assertive, pugnacious young man from Asbury Park was an unlikely actor. Growing up had been tough for De Vito. His father's sideline as a street corner bookie had kept the wolf from the family door on many an occasion. Like Michael Douglas, he was at best a diffident student, although Asbury Park Junior High was light years away from Choate in every respect. He was, however, an accomplished pool player, thanks to the years spent in the pool hall which his father occasionally managed. Even so, despite difficult circumstances, De Vito discovered and clung on to a desire to act. He had managed to pass the audition for the Academy and found himself in Waterford to appear in a play which was written by one of his teachers at the Academy. The play was being presented at a playwrights' conference being held at the O'Neill Theatre in the summer of 1966.

'I had figured actors would be sitting around bullshitting and stuff,' De Vito recalls. 'But here's Michael and all of these other guys moving wheelbarrows full of dirt and concrete blocks, and pouring cement. I'm from Jersey, I know how to do that stuff, so I came outside and that's how Michael and I met.'

As well as labouring together De Vito and Douglas had also been assigned to the same farmhouse-cum-dormitory. Both were long-haired hippies in the midst of a collection of much straighter, more intense, theatrical types. It was not just their hair styles which united them. They discovered they both had the same warped sense of humour, they shared through their fathers an immigrant sensibility, and they quickly formed a friendship which has lasted for more than thirty years, and spawned a professional relationship which has seen them through four hit films.

As well as acting as an apprentice carpenter, Michael Douglas had also been promised small parts in some of the plays which would be presented during the conference. Having heard his stepson's praises being sung to the heavens by his wife and her ex-husband, this time Bill Darrid, who knew some of the O'Neill Foundation board members, went along to check out this burgeoning talent. Unfortunately he picked the wrong night, since Michael Douglas was again taken with a crippling attack of stage fright. Bill Darrid watched sympathetically before he went home to try to break it to his wife that, no matter how much she wanted him to do well, the boy just didn't have it in him to be an actor. Naturally that injudicious remark became something that Bill Darrid was not allowed to forget in the coming years.

One of the bonuses of being in Waterford that summer was that it allowed Michael Douglas to get to know a number of people who were then budding playwrights but would go on to be major talents. He became friendly with Sam Shepard and John Guare as well as Ron Cowen – most of them based in New York – and meeting them encouraged him to make the decision that New York might be the best place for him to begin his career. Before that he had a degree to finish, and so when the amphitheatre was built and the summer vacation was over Douglas went back to Santa Barbara while his new best friend Danny De Vito returned to the life of a struggling actor in New York. They would remain close and met again in Douglas's final year at UCSB. De Vito was desperate for a role in the screen version of Truman Capote's *In Cold Blood*. The role would eventually go to Robert Blake, but De Vito was so keen to at least be considered that he turned up in Los Angeles looking every inch the psychotic killer, bearing a letter of introduction to the director Richard Brooks. Naturally the first person he called was Douglas, who invited him up to the commune to spend a little time. De Vito was awe-struck. Naked women, drugs, skinny-dipping, free love, free booze; they had none of this in Jersey. But even though his friend was like a child in a sweet shop, for Michael Douglas the attractions of the commune were beginning to pale.

'It reached a point of stagnation,' he explains. 'Everyone was overdosing on hipness. That community became tighter than the society we were trying to get away from.'

He had one more year to do in college but his stint with the Playwrights' Convention had convinced him, more than ever, that acting would be the way to assert his identity and his individuality. The only way to do that was to be in New York at the heart of the American theatre industry. There, away from Hollywood, he might stand a chance of being considered in his own right, with his father – and his reputation – 5000 miles away in California. It looked like he was going to get the ideal start to his career when a former Waterford alumnus almost gave him a huge break. Ron Cowen had written an anti-Vietnam play called *Summertree*, and when it came to casting the lead role he remembered Douglas who had played the part at the O'Neill Theatre. Douglas would play a young man who, while trying to find himself and his way in the world, gets drafted and goes to Vietnam where he is killed. The play was being given a showcase run at the prestigious Lincoln Center in New York and, after five auditions, Douglas genuinely believed he had the part. He had worked out a deal with his college, whereby he could effectively take leave of absence for a term to allow him to go to New York while still technically enrolled at college. As is often the case, that which he thought had been promised turned out not to have been promised at all. Douglas went to New York for one final reading and lost the part to another actor.

'They were afraid I didn't have enough experience and they replaced me,' he explained. 'If I had had a lot of time to sit around thinking about it I guess it could have bothered me but there were other things going on.'

Douglas did as he had always done when confronted with a disappointment or a setback; he kept his thoughts to himself and got on with his life. That meant going back to Santa Barbara, finishing his degree, and spending his final few months at the commune. He left without any regrets and with a certain sense of gratitude.

'The commune did one thing for me though,' he says. 'It enabled me to find my own tempo. Everything's going on in New York, the pace is very frantic, it can really kill you. In the west I learned how to find my own rhythm and keep to it.'

In 1968 Douglas got his Bachelor of Arts degree from UCSB and moved to New York. He studied first with Sanford Meisner at the Neighbourhood Playhouse before continuing his studies with Wynn Handman at the American Place Theatre, while he tried out for the usual round of auditions for off-Broadway and off-off-Broadway productions. He found a place to stay which again re-united him with his friend Danny De Vito. The two of them shared an apartment on West 89th Street and Riverside Drive. When you consider that his last experience of living in New York had him in an apartment overlooking Central Park this was something of a culture shock. Even Douglas admitted that the neighbourhood was more than a little scary, but he also relished the challenge of coping with the bustling urban jungle compared to negotiating the more laid-back ambience of Santa Barbara. He quickly found, however, that he had exchanged one community for another.

'The best thing about my time in New York was that I developed a lot of good friends,' he remembers. 'And it was the first time where I found myself really accomplishing something. In college, I was just irresponsible. So I gained a lot of self-esteem working in New York. And I had all these close friends; Danny De Vito, John Guare, the director Michael Lessac, and we are all still friends. I remember it as continuing that spirit of '67. I lived in a one-room apartment . . . and I was fortunate enough to have a theatre family. As an actor one of the first things you have to face is rejection. So it was easier to deal with that because of this wonderful sense of sharing, whether you were rehearsing or just getting together'.

One of the people who helped him most in that initial period of settling into New York theatre life was De Vito. Again their similarly warped sense of humour provided them with a lot of amusement at other people's expense. One favourite stunt was to use Michael's social cachet to get an invitation to some uptown party or other, to which De Vito would accompany him wearing over-sized stage teeth and disguised as a hunchback. As you might expect they would be treated like pariahs, until Douglas let it slip into the right ear that his unfortunate friend had just been cast as the star of a new movie by whichever director was hot at the time. The mood would thaw noticeably as Douglas and De Vito continued their own little piece of subversive performance art.

Douglas had one other problem to overcome in establishing himself in New York; his name. This time it wasn't because it evoked comparisons with his father, this time it was because it evoked comparisons with someone he had never heard of. Mike Douglas was a TV chat show host and presenter who had prior professional rights to the name. This meant that while Michael Douglas could be billed under his own name in films, he could not use it on television or in the theatre. Since there were no films in the offing, he had to agree to be billed, for the time being, as M.K. Douglas. Ironically this same scenario would happen again about ten years down the line. This time Michael Douglas was the one with pre-existing rights to his name and the newcomer, who wanted to be billed as Michael Douglas since it was his given name, would have to change his name to Michael Keaton.

It was a difficult period for him, whatever name he chose. There was not much work in the theatre and film work was non-existent. But his desire led him to what he probably still considers the most humiliating experience of his professional life.

The cult Italian director Michelangelo Antonioni was holding auditions for what was to be his first American film, *Zabriskie Point.* The film turned out to be a ruinous and almost incomprehensible mess, but no one knew that at the time. In 1969 when Antonioni was casting this was a big deal, especially since he had announced that his preference was to cast unknowns. The auditions were being held in the Cheetah Club and come the morning of the try-outs there were thousands of young hopefuls in a queue which stretched hundreds of yards round the block. Among them, of course, was Michael Douglas. The would-be movie stars were taken in three at a time and made to stand in front of an assistant director in a scene which reminded Douglas of a parody of a line-up from an old Warner Brothers gangster movie. They were asked to talk about some of their previous experiences and Douglas talked about his guerrilla theatre exploits with the blood bags at Santa Barbara. With a nod from the assistant they were then ushered into the presence of the great man, Antonioni. They stood on the stage, three of them in a line, and Douglas was prompted to tell Antonioni what he had just told the assistant.

Douglas takes up the story.

'I'm talking about it and Antonioni's looking at the guy next to me. He's not interested in me at all but he lets me go on talking. So I'm telling him about this one gory time and he's ignoring me, so I said "and of course all Italians eat meatballs". Antonioni didn't even notice. There I was spilling my guts out, so I said "Fuck you" and I walked out.'

For once Michael Douglas had rejected them before they could reject him. But the rejection was about to stop, albeit for a short time.

THE CONQUERING HERO

Although they had become friends during their summer at Waterford, the playwright Ron Cowen was not turning out to be any kind of lucky charm for Michael Douglas. First there was that role in *Summertree* which he missed out on, though he would end up playing the part in circumstances he could not imagine, and now there was another Cowen play called *Saturday Adoption* which brought him no better luck. The play was due to be screened as part of the CBS Playhouse series, which would have meant national television exposure. Once again Cowen recommended Douglas for the part, once again he thought he had it, and once again he missed out on the final reading. Afterwards Douglas said, uncharacteristically sourly, that he thought the finished version had been poorly directed and, all things considered, it might have been for the best that he didn't get the part.

This was a period in Douglas's life where he was basically trying out for everything without a lot of success, it was one of those times when an actor believes that if it wasn't for bad luck he wouldn't have any luck at all. Take, for example, the time when he did finally get a job. He landed a role in an off-Broadway play called *City Scene* but it only ran for six performances and no one of any note saw it, leaving Douglas to pound the pavements from audition to audition once again. Things were about to change and a role that he didn't get would play a big part. Although he had been passed over for *Saturday Adoption*, Douglas had made an impression on the casting team and the producers of CBS Playhouse. They felt he showed some potential and he soon found himself cast in the lead of another CBS Playhouse production, *The Experiment*. In this episode of the series he played a long-haired student radical who was hired by a major chemical company. The play was about how he fitted in with his new establishment life as a college professor but, as the title suggests, the offer had not been entirely serious. It was his big television break and, of course, he was billed as M.K. Douglas

'I hated being billed as M.K. Douglas.' he said. 'It sounds so pretentious, like some old character actor. It was funny though, when we were doing *The Experiment*, Mike Douglas was working at the studio next door and got a couple of calls meant for me. After Douglas answered one of them the caller said "Well it doesn't sound like you Mike," meaning me, and Douglas replied "This is the real Mike Douglas" or something to that effect and hung up. I was thinking of playing a joke on him about it, but I decided not to. He could just have taken a giant eraser and wiped me out.'

The Experiment was well received and Douglas for one was astonished to be recognised on the subway and on the street, however fleetingly, the morning after it screened. Much was made in pre-publicity and then in reviews of *The Experiment* about the fact that Douglas was the son of a famous father. Whether they were impressed by his performance or felt they could get a little more publicity milage out of his connections, after *The Experiment* CBS offered him a movie contract for Cinema Center, the film-making arm of CBS television. These would not be major films but they were films none the less. These were the last remaining days of the double feature and there was still a demand for, if not exactly 'B' movies, product which would support the main feature. His new contract meant that Douglas would have to leave New York for Los Angeles once again although, perhaps as a security, he kept on paying the rent for his part of the apartment he shared with Danny De Vito.

Michael's first role in Hollywood came in *Hail, Hero*, a film which indicated how the powers that be thought of him. In *The Experiment* he had played a student radical, now in this film he played an anti-Vietnam war protester. Obviously, even though his hair was now shorter than it had been in his college days, producers still saw him as ideal to play some sort of activist. Of course, given his own college background, the role in *Hail, Hero* was perfect casting. It was also a very demanding role for a first film, given that he was in almost every scene.

'It's a very sensitive and poetic story,' he explained in an interview when the film came out in the late summer of 1969. 'It's 24 hours in the life of a guy who quits college to enlist in the army and go to Vietnam for all sorts of conflicting reasons. Because there's a military tradition in the family and he wants to please his father. Because he feels guilt about having caused his brother to be a cripple. Because he wants to find out whether he can face the enemy with love and not pull the trigger of his gun. He finally realises that he's human, that the world can only go on if we all love each other. That's all there is left.'

It's easy to see why Douglas, one of nature's idealists and someone who was passionately anti-Vietnam, would want to do this film no matter how trite he makes it sound. Douglas was in almost every scene of the movie but he had an understanding director, which is hardly surprising. David Miller, the man behind the camera on *Hail, Hero*, also directed Kirk Douglas's ground-breaking western, *Lonely Are the Brave*. This film, on which Michael Douglas worked as an apprentice editor, is also – incidentally – Michael

Douglas's favourite among his father's pictures. Michael Douglas has always insisted that Miller didn't know him when he walked into the room to audition. Perhaps he didn't recognise him, since it had been some years since he had seen him, but it is stretching the imagination too much to believe that he didn't renew the acquaintance pretty quickly. Having been frequently paralysed with stage fright, Douglas now also discovered that he was intimidated by the movie camera. He also discovered that, despite those summer vacations on his father's sets, he knew a lot less about film-making than he thought he did.

'I grew up hearing talk about movies all around me,' he continues, 'watching the way my father was handling people. In that sense nothing about making a movie was new to me. But I never knew before, never really knew, how hard it is actually to make a movie. For instance, the way the lights bother you if you have light-coloured eyes. Every time you turn to the camera you are momentarily blinded and have to keep glancing away from the lights so you can see again . . . In a movie you're not really acting. It's not like being on the stage; there you get on and there's nothing anyone can do to you until you are through . . . I have to rely completely on the director. David Miller makes me feel very secure and comfortable . . . When you stop and think that you're playing the main role in your first feature, and you don't really have a grasp of what you're doing, you can't take it too seriously or you would go under.'

Douglas was helped enormously by David Miller as well as the producer, Harold Cohen, who got interested in the story because he was the father of a teenage son. Miller also supported him with two veteran actors in the shape of Arthur Kennedy and Teresa Wright. Yet despite all this *Hail, Hero* was not a success.

His next college type came in *Adam at 6 a.m.* the film he did immediately after *Hail, Hero*. This time he played a 'hip college professor' from a Californian university who begins to question the values of his laid-back lifestyle. He decides he needs to get back in touch with some real people, so he moves to a small town in the Midwest and gets a job as a manual labourer. But, predictably, the real people let him down and he finds out life is not so different there after all. This film was not so well-received, although there were again the inevitable comparisons with his father. Douglas had a few good reviews but most of the attention was paid to a young Joe-Don Baker, who made a big impression in what was a forgettable film.

Although he was working steadily and getting a fair amount of press attention, in which he appeared to revel, life in Los Angeles was tougher than it appeared for Michael Douglas. In college and again in New York there had been a sense of community, first a literal one in the commune then a metaphorical one in the theatrical clique of which he was a member. In Los Angeles, however, it became a case of everyone for himself. Douglas lost the ensemble feeling he had enjoyed so much and began to become more self-absorbed and, at the same time, insecure. His relationship with the girlfriend he had brought out with him from New York broke up. He assumes this was because she just could not stand the fact that he was suddenly more interested in his career than in her. The actor who had never been goal-oriented became like everyone else in the business, just out there hustling for the next part.

This was a period where he was starting to come to terms with what it meant to be second generation Hollywood. On the plus side, he was the wealthy son of a wealthy father, so while he might struggle in career terms he was never going to starve. On the down side were all the normal anxieties and insecurities which face all actors. This time, however, he had some experience of what to expect.

'I grew up surrounded by people in the business,' he explained to an interviewer at the time. 'I can remember nights not believing the accumulation of people in my father's house in Beverly Hills; the Frank Sinatras, the Burt Lancasters, the Robert Mitchums. All these big stars and they were just as awkward and insecure as anyone else. It's a larger than life situation. A friend of mine, John Guare, wrote a play called *The House of Blue Leaves*, and in it he says the stars are the real people and the public are the dreamers. People off the streets fantasise about the stars.

'There's no other business where work and social life are so combined. You're surrounded by people who are attractive and witty and intelligent, and you're flattered, but you have to take it at face value. By growing up in that environment I'm a little better prepared for all the shit that will hit the fan if things start to happen for me. I hope I'll find it easier to cope.'

When he set up Bryna Productions in 1955, Kirk Douglas did so to get a measure of control over his career. He had fought consistently with a number of major studios and had acquired a reputation for being 'difficult' – a Hollywood term usually applied to those who are not prepared to take every instruction from the director or producer as though it were holy writ. By producing his own films that problem would be avoided, since he would be his own boss. The first Bryna film was *The Indian Fighter*, which also starred Michael's mother Diana Douglas, and its most notable success had been *Spartacus*. Bryna, however, served another function in that it also provided a home for what we might now call independent pictures, films which might struggle at a major studio. One such property was *Summertree*, the play in which Michael Douglas had starred at the O'Neill Theatre in Connecticut. He had come close to playing it at the Lincoln Center but missed out, now he would play it on screen.

When it had its premiere performance at Waterford, the writer Ron Cowen had entertained notions of it being made into a film. At that stage, in the summer of 1966, it was just a fanciful notion. The Vietnam war would end soon and the play's major themes would be dated. Not so. By 1971 the Vietnam war was still being fought, public opinion was becoming more and more united in its opposition to the conflict, and *Summertree* appeared more timely than ever. This is plainly what Kirk Douglas saw in it when Bryna acquired the film rights in 1969. Whether he knew it would be a vehicle for his son is another matter. Any allegations of nepotism were somewhat diminished by the fact that Douglas had appeared in two films in his own right before this one. It would have been an entirely different matter if Kirk Douglas had bought the rights to a play for his son to make his screen debut.

At the heart of *Summertree* are a father and son who cannot understand each other. This may appear to foreshadow the Douglas clan's own relationships, although there were definite signs of a thaw between Michael and his father. During the shooting of *Hail, Hero* for example, Michael had stayed at his father's house in Beverly Hills rather than take a place of his own.

The father in *Summertree*, played by Jack Warden, is a blood-and-guts straight shooter who sees situations in simple terms. The son, played by Michael Douglas, is another one of those sensitive young men he had come to specialise in. He is torn between his feelings about the war, the sense of duty to his parents, and his love for his girlfriend, played by Brenda Vaccaro. In the end he pays a tragic price which evoked some comparisons between *Summertree* and *Love Story*, which had been a huge hit the previous year. Douglas, incidentally, was among those actors, including Jon Voight, Michael Sarrazin, Michael York and Beau Bridges, who reportedly turned down the Ryan O'Neal role in the blockbuster tear-jerker.

'A lot of people think that *Summertree* is what *Love Story* should have been,' said Douglas at the time. 'It's a beautiful, unpretentious anti-war story.'

This is typical of the sort of injudicious comment that the neophyte Douglas was prone to make at that stage in his career. Plainly there was no great demand among the tearful millions emerging from *Love Story* for it to have carried a strong anti-war message. Nor should there have been. They loved it for what it was, a hackneyed potboiler with a good marketing campaign which struck a chord with the audience. His comments about *Love Story* came in an interview in which Douglas also went on to be nasty about Ryan O'Neal, Barbra Streisand and Elliot Gould. He has since learned to be a little more diplomatic. Despite Michael Douglas's passion for *Summertree*, the reality is that the film is something of a mess. The play, by all accounts, was a sensitive piece, and none of that transfers to the film. That may have had something to do with the fact that it was directed by Anthony Newley, a fine man for a musical, but not the sort of director who comes to mind when you are looking for someone to handle a family drama.

For Michael Douglas the one positive thing which did emerge from *Summertree* was his relationship with Brenda Vaccaro. She was older, divorced, and more experienced in career terms than he was – she had already appeared memorably in *Midnight Cowboy* which was a huge hit and an Oscar winner – but they were smitten with each other. By the time they had finished shooting *Summertree* they were lovers. Douglas described it as a gradual process over the two or three months they spent together making the film. He couldn't put his finger on what it was that had attracted them other than, as far as he was concerned, she was a 'fantastic actress and a beautiful girl'. They set up homes together in California and New York.

'People loved us,' Vaccaro said later. 'People loved us. Mike was charming, brilliant. Women fell over him, men admired him. And I am, naturally, a good complement to such a man.'

Looking back on his early films Michael Douglas would later admit that perhaps he had been exploited by the system which was cashing in on his name and his celebrity background. On the other hand he was an actor trying to make his way in the business and nowhere near the position where he could pick and choose his work. That would perhaps account for his appearance in *Napoleon and Samantha*, a live-action adventure for the Walt Disney studios.

The young Jodie Foster and Johnny Whitaker star as two children who want to keep a former circus lion as a pet and trek all the way across Oregon to find their friend, played by Douglas, who they believe can help them. It was an undistinguished part but for

Douglas it was an experience of big-budget – or at least bigger than he was used to – film-making. The film also featured a climactic motorbike chase which may or may not have influenced his decision to take the role. It seemed just about every film made around that period had to have a car chase – *Bullitt, The French Connection, What's Up Doc,* to name a few – and Disney, ever a studio with an eye to a trend, were no exception. In *Napoleon and Samantha*, Douglas has to break out of a small town police station and escapes by taking off on a parked motor cycle with the police in hot pursuit. Douglas zig-zags through a lumber camp, specially built for the film by Disney, as he attempts to shake off his pursuers. Disney were proud to boast that Michael Douglas did 90 per cent of his own bike work. The other 10 per cent, which included the scenes in the logging camp, were done by stunt double Everett Creach.

By the summer of 1972 Michael Douglas had now made four films and was still not known as anything more than being Kirk Douglas's son. None of the films had been hugely successful, especially not *Summertree* by which he had set such store for so many years. In an interview to promote *Summertree* in July 1971 he was asked what he would do if the film didn't make it.

'I'll keep on trying for a while at least,' he answered candidly. 'I want to do more plays. You learn a lot more about acting on the stage. There's talk of a movie to be made in Spain so I may do that. But eventually if I find myself beating my head against the wall continuously, I'll take my father's advice. He told me only one thing, "If all else fails – fuck it!"'

Ultimately, Michael Douglas was not about to get the chance to be so uncompromisingly pragmatic. The balloon was about to burst and after *Napoleon and Samantha* it would be almost six years before he would appear in front of a movie camera again.

LIFE ON THE STREETS

Television runs in cycles. Currently the reality show is king. Over the years game shows, science fiction series, variety shows, westerns, sitcoms, and war series have all had their place in the sun. But the one enduring television staple almost since the first cathode ray tube flickered into life is the cop show. It's not hard to see why. In no other genre, except perhaps the western, are the demarcation lines between the good guys and the bad guys so clearly defined. Again, in no other genre, is there the potential for murder, mystery, and mayhem which can all be neatly wrapped up inside a commercial hour.

Fans will argue, but there seems little doubt that the heyday of the television cop show was in the late Sixties and early Seventies, with series such as *Hawaii Five-0* – television's longest-running crime show – *The FBI, Kojak, Starsky and Hutch* and *The Rockford Files* reigning supreme. The man who was the uncrowned king of the genre was Quinn Martin, an unsuccessful actor turned hugely successful producer. Many of the shows he created or has been associated with have gone on to be television classics such as *The Untouchables* and *The Fugitive*, others such as *Barnaby Jones, Cannon, The Invaders,* and *Dan August* have become much-loved cult favourites. In many ways Martin, through his QM Productions, defined the genre, especially in the early Seventies.

It was Quinn Martin who came up with what others came to realise was the perfect formula for the one-hour episodic television drama. He worked out the number of acts, the number of action beats per act, and – perhaps most important – he devised the formula of the cliff-hanging action beat, which would allow you to fade to black and go into a commercial break with the certain knowledge that the audience would be waiting for you on the other side. It was a formula derided by purists as simplistic and manipulative but it worked.

Michael Douglas was about to cross paths with Quinn Martin. After *Napoleon and Samantha* he was surprised to find himself out of work. One minute he was in demand, the next minute no one wanted to hire him. One reason for this may have been that his father had annoyed a lot of people over the years, and this was one way in which those folk could have a small measure of revenge. Douglas always maintained that his father's name was certainly helpful in getting through the door, but it was no guarantee of getting a job. Now perhaps he was finding that in some cases it was an actual hindrance to getting the job. In the short term it wasn't so much of a problem. For one thing there was a chance to go back east and do another play.

Douglas had been asked back to the American Place Theatre in Times Square where he had studied a few years previously. He had been offered the lead role in a limited six week run of a new play called *Pinkville*. Once again it had an anti-Vietnam theme. Douglas played Jerry the Naz, a marine recruit who has joined the Corps but is ideologically opposed to killing. In the course of the play he becomes brutalised and dehumanised by a sadistic drill sergeant and, of course, by the end of the performance he faces the audience as a perfectly programmed, unthinking, unquestioning killer. It was a play which once again reflected how Douglas felt about the war in Vietnam, a subject on which he was becoming more and more outspoken. His view was that we should not blame the men who were fighting – this was around the time of the My Lai massacre – but we should condemn the system which makes them fight without asking themselves what they are doing. As a learning experience *Pinkville* was also valuable to Douglas, who had neglected his stage craft while he had been in Los Angeles. One of the attractions of the play was that it was a guaranteed six-week run, which meant it could not be closed by a hostile review, so Douglas had a chance to develop and flesh out the character. In addition it was done in the round, another new experience for him, and he found the challenge of facing the audience everywhere he turned both exhilarating and immensely satisfying. He and Brenda Vaccaro had moved back to New York for the duration of the run of *Pinkville*, which proved not only to be a commercial but also a critical success. In the end Douglas was rewarded with a Theatre World Award. This was the first official recognition of anything he had done since that Mobil Man of the Month honour back in Westport, and it was no less appreciated.

With no more theatre work in the offing, and no film roles on the horizon, Douglas drifted into television. He had started his career on the small screen, but that *CBS Playhouse* series had been a one-off drama, now he would find himself drifting into episodic television. He started to take guest starring roles on popular television shows. It was around this time that Douglas contributed what he felt was his best performance to date. *Medical Center* was one of CBS Television's enduring hits. The hour-long show, set in the University Medical Center in Los Angeles, starred James Daly as a senior doctor and heartthrob Chad Everett as his dynamic young colleague. Douglas was offered a guest-starring spot to play a retarded boy and he relished the opportunity.

'It was my first opportunity to play something other than a sensitive young man. I was real, real pleased with it,' he says. 'I did my homework, spent some time in hospitals and homes in Los Angeles, getting the voice, the movement and everything like that.'

There was more television work after this, notably an episode of *The FBI*. This was one of the early hits for Quinn Martin, a series based on real-life cases from the Federal Bureau of Investigation with Efrem Zimbalist Jnr as the stone-faced and somewhat humourless Inspector Lewis Erskine. Douglas appeared in an episode entitled *The Hitchhiker* which screened on 28 February 1971. It was a fortuitous piece of casting, because the actor who had originally been due to guest star had dropped out. Douglas got the part at the last minute more because of his availability than anything else. The young actor made an impression on Quinn Martin, and not just because he shot one entire scene with his fly undone.

'I came back to ask the director how it was,' he recalls of his entrance as a gun-wielding robber. 'He said "Well take a look." My fly was open. So the shocked expression when everyone else in the scene looked at me was because they didn't know if I was a bank robber or a pervert.'

Douglas always claims that as a result of his time in the commune he has no inhibitions about showing off his body and indeed would reveal a good deal more later in his career, but that brief indecent exposure certainly helped fix him in the minds of the casting directors at Quinn Martin. The fact that he had contributed an excellent performance at very short notice didn't hurt either.

Michael Douglas now had to make a major career decision. He had gone into television with some modest success in guest starring roles, but was this what he really wanted to do with his career? On the one hand there was no theatre work, his four films to date had yielded no more film offers, and unlike in his parents' day young actors would no longer be put under contract at a studio. The only place you could get a contract these days was on a television series. On the other hand, it was television. Modern actors have no qualms whatsoever about flitting back and forth between television, theatre and films. That was certainly not the case in the early days of the medium. Kirk Douglas was seen as something of a maverick when he used television to promote *Champion* by going on live shows with co-star Marilyn Maxwell and acting out a few scenes from the film. But maverick or not, a major movie star of Kirk Douglas's generation would never have countenanced appearing regularly on television. When Diana Douglas had to go back to work after their divorce she chose television in New York deliberately, for the simple reason that she could get work because film actors were still reluctant to embrace the medium.

Even in the Seventies the stigma still remained and the number of movie stars who had been successful on television could be counted almost on one hand. Clint Eastwood had done *Rawhide*, but had needed to go to Italy and work with Sergio Leone before American audiences would accept him as a movie star. Steve McQueen had also started on television but that was in *Wanted: Dead or Alive* back in the late Fifties. American television in the Seventies had its own generation of stars such as Mary Tyler Moore, Bill Cosby, Bill Bixby, Chad Everett, Buddy Ebsen and Jack Lord. These were all incredibly well-loved and popular actors who, you might argue, could bring a television audience to the cinema with them. Producers, on the other hand, believed that no one would pay at a cinema to see someone they could watch for free at home. It was a fact of industry life that television stars twinkled less brightly than movie stars, and not one of these enormously successful television names would ever be asked to carry a major film. Was this really what Douglas wanted to do? Was he prepared to run the risk of being cast out of Hollywood and into the ratings ghetto which was television?

'I was reluctant,' he confesses. 'I thought I had this image to live up to and there was a stigma attached to television. On the other hand, I was telling myself "Hey asshole, wake up. They're not exactly knocking your door down with movie offers".'

His agency had heard that Quinn Martin was putting together a new cop show and there might be a part in it that would be ideal for Douglas. After some thought Douglas agreed that television might be a reasonable way to move his career along so he decided to allow himself to be put forward. He could, by this stage, use his own name. The M.K. Douglas billing had fallen by the wayside, thanks to the four films he had made which allowed him to petition the union that his career would be seriously hindered unless he could use the same name everywhere. The new show was *The Streets of San Francisco* and part of its unique appeal is that, with the exception of the shots inside the police station which were done in a studio, the whole programme would be shot on location in and around the bay. The show would be the story of veteran detective Mike Stone and his rookie partner Steve Keller. The twist here is that Stone is an old-school, old-fashioned, by-the-book sort of cop, while Keller is a college-educated, liberal-thinking, modern police-man. They would of course distrust each other initially, but in the course of the series each would come to appreciate the other's strengths and they would form an ideal partnership.

By the time Douglas told his agency he was interested the role of the older cop had already been cast. Mike Stone was to be played by Karl Malden, a distinguished veteran of film and theatre and one of America's most respected actors. Malden and Douglas had met by chance when Douglas was filming his guest spot on *The FBI* and Malden was in wardrobe at the same time for a costume fitting. When they were introduced, Malden realised that this was, as he put it, 'Kirk's boy' and thought that any son of Kirk Douglas would be fine by him. Michael Douglas would have known that his father and Karl Malden had been friends, what he may not have known is just how close they had been. For one thing the two men shared an impoverished immigrant background, as Malden comes from Gary, Indiana, a steel town. His real name is Mladen Sekulovich and he became Karl Malden in the same summer that Issur Demsky became Kirk Douglas when the two now famous actors were unknowns at the Tamarack Playhouse in the Adirondacks. Having got Malden for Mike Stone they now needed a Steve Keller.

There is no doubt that someone of Karl Malden's reputation would have had a large say in who his co-star would be, and Michael Douglas makes no bones about admitting that the fact that Malden and his father were friends doubtless gave him an edge. Whatever the reason, he found himself cast as Steve Keller. Kirk Douglas was delighted when Michael called to give him the news but he warned that he would not find it easy. Malden, said his father, worked at a furious pace and set extraordinarily high standards for himself and, by extension, those around him. But if Michael could last the pace, his father promised, it would be the learning experience of a lifetime.

Michael Douglas admits to being aware of the irony of a man who had spent a good part of the past few years railing against the establishment now playing a young policeman. However he realised later that playing a policeman on television made him much more sympathetic to the police in real life. He describes the role of Steve Keller as essentially 'second banana', walking two steps behind Karl Malden and usually in soft focus. As long as he was there, however, he would make the most of it and learn everything he could.

'I will always be indebted to Karl because he really taught me a lot about discipline,' he said. 'He was a workaholic. We got into the habit of working on the next week's script between rehearsals. Meanwhile, I kept my eyes and ears open. I used to stick close to the production manager of the show. When a script came in, I would watch how it broke down. I watched the producers and directors and that's basically where I got all my production experience. After the first year, Karl got the producers to let the kid do what he wanted. In other words he made me much more of an equal.'

The Streets of San Francisco made its debut on the ABC network on Saturday, 16 September 1972. It was in a nine o'clock prime-time slot and its chief competition were half-hour sitcoms starring Mary Tyler Moore and Bob Newhart. The new crime show was not a smash hit but it was successful enough and showed sufficient promise to be promoted to a Thursday night slot at ten o'clock for its second series. The producers were well pleased with the showing of the first series, as was Douglas, especially since he had felt that he was going to be fired before the end of his first show. He and Malden were still at the stage of being polite to each other and getting to know each other when they were required to shoot a scene in their car. Douglas was doing the driving, the car was parked at the top of Nob Hill, and Douglas knew that the traffic light was a short one. When the director said 'action', the two men jumped into the car, Douglas gunned the engine, and they took off down the steep hill at breakneck speed. As the car went over the brow of the hill they were going so fast they became airborne. Douglas is and always has been an expert driver and has several advanced driving qualifications to prove it but, at that stage, Malden didn't know that.

'All I know is that I had enough time while we were in the air to stop and look at Karl,' Douglas remembers. 'He was looking over to me and ready to murder. Thank God, the wheels were straight and we screeched to a stop. I thought I was fired. He was screaming "That's not driving. You call that driving." I only had one accident in four years and I used to drive all the time.'

As the two men became friends, and Douglas admits it took some time, Malden became used to his driving. Latterly when they got into the car Malden would take one leg, being careful to keep it out of shot, and use it to brace himself against the dashboard while his co-star threw their car over the bumps and curves of the streets of San Francisco. Malden had another eye-opener about his co-star's driving style in an episode where Stone and Keller had to use a police computer to run someone's licence number to see if they had any convictions. Once the scene was safely in the can Malden asked to try it for real. He put in his own registration number and came up with a single parking ticket which was more than ten years old. Then he put Michael Douglas's number in and stood back in a mixture of horror and astonishment as the computer threw up pages and pages of violations.

Douglas moved to San Francisco while the series was shooting and loved the idea that the almost continual location shooting meant that the city was as much a character in the show as he or Malden. He always insisted that there wasn't a single bad camera angle in the whole city.

'I love it here,' he said at the time. 'San Francisco is my favourite city. It is so important not to have to be with people in the business all the time. You can drown in LA. Most people here are trying to achieve a sense of balance between work, play, and their private lives, but the social situation there still revolves entirely around business.'

A major part of the success of *The Streets of San Francisco*, which was moved up the schedules to the key Thursday night at nine slot on its third series, was the relationship between Stone and Keller. It was supposed to be paternalistic, with the older man coming to see the virtues of his impetuous young partner, and that reflected the situation in which Malden and Douglas found themselves in real life. In the first year he would occasionally point things out quietly to the younger man, or be there when Douglas asked for advice.

'By year three,' says Malden, 'I didn't say a word. He grew by leaps and bounds. I feel Michael doesn't like it when I feel paternalistic. But I'll tell you why I do. I did exactly the same thing for his father.'

Working on *The Streets of San Francisco* was in effect a finishing school for Michael Douglas who was, to a certain extent, conducting his education in public. He admitted some years later that perhaps the thing to have done in the first place was to stay in New York and continue his training on stage, instead of rushing to Hollywood at the first offer and making four dud pictures. Now, in a situation where he was required to be deeply involved in the process of producing 52 minutes of prime time television every seven days, he was learning just about everything there was to learn about the business.

There were tangible rewards too, apart from a six figure salary. In 1975 he found himself nominated for a Golden Globe in the Best TV Actor – Drama category. The following year he was nominated for an Emmy in the category of Outstanding Continuing Performance by a Supporting Actor in a Drama Series. That was a banner year for *The Streets of San Francisco*, for although no one won the show, Karl Malden and guest star Bill Bixby were both nominated. Douglas also picked up another award in 1974 about which he is less forthcoming. Stunt man Robert Butler was accidentally run over by a power boat during a scene in San Francisco Bay. As he sank bleeding in the water, Douglas leapt in fully-clothed, brought him to the surface and swam to the side with him, where he was given medical treatment. Afterwards Douglas dismissed it as an instinctive reaction, but Robert Butler is in no doubt that he would have died had it not been for his quick thinking. Douglas was later awarded a Presidential citation for bravery.

By the time the show had been running for three years, Michael Douglas was feeling sufficiently confident with what he had learned to have a crack at directing. He had the character of Steve Keller pretty well nailed and Malden, by his own admission, had no complaints about the way the show was going. With Malden's support Douglas asked Quinn Martin if he could direct one of the episodes. So in September of 1975, in the week of his 31st birthday, Michael Douglas found himself doing double duty on both sides of the camera. He was starring and directing in an episode of the show in which the guest star was a young Tom Selleck. Douglas enjoyed the experience and while the episode was not a classic it came in on time and within the budget of $300,000 per show.

Michael Douglas was enjoying the series but he was beginning to feel he should branch out into other directions, there were other things which were making demands on his time. It was also making huge demands on his relationship with Brenda Vaccaro. Making the show meant that he had to stay in San Francisco for eight months a year, while she remained based at the house in Benedict Canyon in Los Angeles which they shared with their pets. It wasn't always easy to find the time to spend together. There were weekends when he would work six days in San Francisco, fly to Los Angeles on a Saturday afternoon and then back to San Francisco on the Sunday night. Equally there were times when she would make the trip in the opposite direction, only to find that the city's notorious mists and fog would prevent her plane from even landing. Douglas went to the extent of arranging for her to be written into the show as a female hitman, but it still didn't work. Just as he insisted they had drifted together in the first place, now they found themselves drifting apart. It was a relationship, he said later, which foundered on neglect.

'I just began to find it boring with Mike,' said Vaccaro perhaps a little harshly. 'I realised he wasn't the man I was going to marry and my relationship changed at that point. I don't think he ever wanted to marry me. Everybody but us seemed to think that marriage was a good idea.'

Michael Douglas left *The Streets of San Francisco* after its fourth series. The show continued with the premise that Steve Keller had quit the force to go back to college and resume a teaching career. Mike Stone found himself partnered by the rather bland Richard Hatch as Inspector Dan Robbins, but there was no chemistry between the two actors. The show lasted for one more series without Michael Douglas before being cancelled at the end of its fifth season.

'I felt that I had given the show all I could give it,' he explained later, 'and I wanted to leave while they stilll wanted me, rather than watching it die in the ratings. I wanted to leave on top.'

His decision to leave the show was a wise one. Increasingly, especially in that third year, he was becoming preoccupied with other things. And, although he had no inkling at the time, one of those other things was about to give him more success than he could ever have imagined.

THE CUCKOO'S NEST

By the time he had made *Spartacus* in 1960, Kirk Douglas was as interested in producing films as he was in starring in them. Not long after the gladiator epic came out he came across two books which made a big impression on him. He acquired the rights to both of them while they were still in galley form, before they had been published. *Seven Days in May* was an anti-nuclear drama in which Kirk Douglas could see the potential for the hit film which it eventually became. The other book was a different scenario. Kirk Douglas didn't see this as a movie at all, at least not initially – he thought this one would be perfect to turn into a play.

Despite his international movie stardom Kirk Douglas hankered after a return, and preferrably a triumphant return, to Broadway and he thought *One Flew Over the Cuckoo's Nest* was just the vehicle to do it. The book had been written by Ken Kesey, one of the heroes of the counter culture and a pioneer of what Tom Wolfe would come to call 'the new journalism'. The central character is Randle P

McMurphy, a recidivist small-time criminal sent to a mental institution. His stay in the asylum becomes a battle of wills between himself and the domineering head nurse who rules the other inmates with her medication tray. Never one to accept the status quo, McMurphy continually rocks the boat at every opportunity and urges the inmates to throw off the shackles of their medication and rebel against the regime of the liquid cosh. Ultimately McMurphy loses his battle in tragic circumstances, but wins the war as a spectacular rebellion finally takes place.

Kirk Douglas immediately saw himself as McMurphy – what actor wouldn't given the potential for scenery-chewing? – and commissioned Dale Wasserman to turn Kesey's novel into a play. Wasserman, who contributed the first draft to Douglas's film *The Vikings*, had been keen to buy the rights to the book for himself but he was more than happy to accept the commission. The results initially appeared to be a spectacular success. As well as Kirk Douglas, they had assembled a terrific cast which included Gene Wilder and William Daniels. The first out of town run in places such as New Haven and Boston produced packed houses and rave reviews. Kirk Douglas had turned down $1.5 million to star in *The Fall of the Roman Empire*, more money than anyone had ever been offered before, in order to do this play. His agents had thought he was crazy but after the first few engagements they were not so sure. Initial reaction was so good that they decided to cancel the rest of the road trip and head straight for Broadway. Audiences, apparently, loved the play when it opened on 14 November 14 1963, but it was slaughtered by the most influential theatre critics. From the opening night the play was dead in the water.

Kirk Douglas was devastated, insisting that the critics were simply out to get him, that they wanted to cut a Hollywood star down to size for having the temerity to forsake Broadway for Hollywood. Michael Douglas also took it hard. He had liked the book himself, he had just started college at Santa Barbara where the book was almost required reading among the student body, and he couldn't understand why the play had been rejected. He had seen it himself and thought it was wonderful. His father was undaunted. If the book had failed as a play then it would succeed as a film. For the next few years he went round every studio in Hollywood pitching the idea, and at every studio, despite his track record and star status, the door was politely but firmly shut in his face. In despair he started to look for someone to buy the rights back from him. It was his son who stopped him. Michael convinced him that this was a great story, not only that but it was a great part for him, and they should not sell it. Michael loved the story too, so he and his father reached a compromise. He would take over the book and he would try to raise the money to get the film made. In short he would become the producer.

This was in 1969 when, without a film hit to his name, Michael Douglas stood more chance of producing a rabbit out of a hat than he did a film version of Kesey's novel. Nonetheless the project stayed with him and, whenever he found himself with some down time, he would dust it off and make another attempt at getting the ball rolling. Michael Douglas had been around the film business all his life. Since he was a toddler sitting in with his mother on costume fittings and make-up tests he had quietly absorbed an awful lot about the business. So, although he was an untested producer, he wasn't exactly a novice. It was not until he moved to San Francisco that all of the pieces of the jigsaw would start to fall into place.

The Streets of San Francisco was an education in itself for Douglas. Not just in the craft of screen acting but also in every other aspect of film making. Working with Karl Malden had helped him overcome his anxiety about the camera so it no longer intimidated him. Working on the set helped him learn about the nuts and bolts of the creative process.

'I developed from this hippie into an actor with a really strong sense of discipline and structure,' he says. 'Karl was the first to really help me in promoting and developing shows that I could star in, bringing me to the forefront . . . I talked to the production manager and I learned about budgeting and all kinds of things. That was all important when we came to put *Cuckoo's Nest* together.'

One Flew Over the Cuckoo's Nest was one of the prime reasons for Douglas leaving *The Streets of San Francisco*. Certainly he felt he could go no further with the show creatively, but he was also consumed by a passion to bring this book to the screen. He was financially secure in his own right – by the end of year four on a hit show an actor tends to be very well paid – and he could afford to take the time off.

'Everybody thought I was pretty crazy to leave the series after four years because it was such a hot show, but I left to produce this film,' Douglas explains. 'I felt really passionate about it. I really loved the project.'

Despite his enthusiasm and drive, for a long time this was a film which resolutely refused to take off. In frustration one day Douglas started going back through the names of people his father had contacted or who had shown an interest in making the film. One name leapt out at him. Saul Zaentz was the head of the renowned Fantasy Records which was based in Berkeley, only a few miles from where Douglas was staying in Russian Hill in San Francisco. It might be worth another shot. Douglas arranged a meeting and found to his surprise and delight that not only was Zaentz as passionate as he was about the film, he also now had money to invest. With $1.5 million from Fantasy Records the new Fantasy Productions was born and the film version of *One Flew Over the Cuckoo's Nest* was officially in development.

Now that they had the money the next thing they had to do was get a script. Zaentz was keen for Ken Kesey to be involved in some capacity. Zaentz and Douglas met Kesey to assure him that they were determined to protect his vision. They also promised him that, whatever happened, they would make sure that he got a share of the proceeds from the film whether he wrote a screenplay or not. If he chose to write a script, which he did, then he would also be paid a salary which, Douglas claims, was larger than the going rate at the time. It's hardly surprising, given those terms, that Kesey was keen to write a screenplay. To their horror, Douglas and Zaentz found that it was virtually unfilmable. One scene apparently had the chief nurse wandering around with a bizarre helmet on her head while the walls of the hospital ran with blood.

It was obvious that Kesey's screenplay would not do. Other writers were commissioned and at the end of the day the final script was credited to Bo Goldman and Lawrence Hauben. One thing of which Douglas was certain was his choice of director. He wanted the Czech director Milos Forman. Although he was well known on the art house circuit for his wry comedies such as *Fireman's Ball*, Forman had made only one film in the United States, *Taking Off*, which had been a critical succes but again barely made it beyond the art houses. Kirk Douglas had sent a copy of the book to Forman several years previously after meeting him on a trip to Prague. Forman never responded and Kirk Douglas assumed he had no interest in the project. It turned out he had never seen the book because the package had been intercepted by government censors. Michael Douglas was determined that Milos Forman should be the man to direct this film. He was determined that it be Forman even before he had his first meeting with Saul Zaentz, but they did agree to look at other directors. This turned out to be a uniformly dispiriting experience.

'Saul Zaentz and I were getting very disappointed because directors were holding their cards so close to their chests,' Douglas recalled later. 'In other words, they'd say they were interested in doing it, so we would say "Well, how do you want to do it?" And they wouldn't share with us. This is one of the key things I've learned in being a producer. You should have an understanding with the director in terms of the form it is going to take. Milos didn't know anything about the success of this book. He just came in and said "Ya, ya, ya, it's a good story, ya. A very good story. I like it." And he sat down, opened up the screenplay on page one, and started talking.'

It didn't take long for Saul Zaentz, the man who was putting up the money for the film, to agree with Douglas's choice. Now they had a director, a script, and all they had to do was convince the man who thought he was starring in it that he wasn't.

The whole *raison d'être* in Kirk Douglas acquiring the rights for *One Flew Over the Cuckoo's Nest* was so that he could give the performance of his career and be justifiably acclaimed in the process. It was becoming more and more obvious in the production process that he was no longer the man for the role. When he first acquired the property he was in his early forties and probably just right, but by the time the film version was actually in production Kirk Douglas was almost sixty. Audiences might have found that a little hard to take. It was Michael who had to break the news to his father who, not surprisingly, was devastated. This was his project, he had found it, he had championed it, he had given it to his oldest son, and now it was going ahead without him. To rub salt into the wound Joel Douglas, who had been acting as co-producer on his father's film *Posse*, announced that he was leaving the project to go and work with his brother on *Cuckoo's Nest*.

A number of actors had been considered for the role of Randle McMurphy once Kirk Douglas was taken out of the equation. The part was offered to Marlon Brando and also to Gene Hackman but both men turned it down. For a time they also considered offering it to Burt Reynolds who, it should be remembered, was then in the middle of a remarkable twelve-year run as one of the world's top ten box office draws. The more they thought about it, the more they were convinced that Jack Nicholson was ideal for the part. His screen image contained enough of the maverick firebrand to encourage an audience to identify with McMurphy, and he was certainly talented enough to deliver the wild and crazy but still delicately nuanced performance which the part required. Their minds were made up when they saw Nicholson in Hal Ashby's film *The Last Detail*. Ashby had been one of the directors linked with *Cuckoo's Nest* in the Hollywood trade papers, but he was never seriously considered. Nicholson was now their main target and Douglas gave him the hard sell to convince him that this could be a career-making film for him. Although he was a fan of the book, one of the things which did finally encourage Nicholson to agree was the degree of openness which Douglas and Zaentz brought to the proceedings. Neither Nicholson nor Milos Forman had come across producers who were quite so collaborative before, and this went a long way to convincing them to sign on.

With Nicholson on board the rest of the cast started to take care of itself. Newcomer Brad Dourif was cast as Billy, the role played by Gene Wilder on stage, while William Redfield played Harding, the role played by William Daniels. Will Sampson played The Chief, Scatman Crothers was the orderly, and there was a role for Danny De Vito as Martini. In fact De Vito had been the first person cast when both Douglas and Forman decided he would be perfect as a cheerful psychotic. The only role remaining to be filled was Nurse Ratched, McMurphy's nemesis. The problem here was that none of the biggest actresses around wanted to play such an unsympathetic character. Those who turned it down included Anne Bancroft, Geraldine Page, Ellen Burstyn, Colleen Dewhurst, Angela Lansbury and Jane Fonda. However, with Nicholson already signed on, Douglas and Zaentz felt that a big female star might actually unbalance the picture dramatically and turn the story into a clash of star egos. In the end the part went to Louise Fletcher, who had impressed Milos Forman with her performance in Robert Altman's *Thieves Like Us*. He had gone to look at Shelley Duval for another part in the film, and came away convinced that he had found their Nurse Ratched in Fletcher.

Both Michael Douglas and Saul Zaentz will now cheerfully agree that *Cuckoo's Nest* was a success almost by accident. They were both debutant producers and were blissfully unaware of how things were supposed to be done, they simply went ahead and did them the way they felt they ought to be done. By luck, they did it right. Since the film has next to no exterior shots, conventional Hollywood wisdom dictates that it should be shot on a sound stage in which an asylum set has been artfully constructed. Not this film. They were going on location to a mental hospital in Salem, Oregon, because that's what the book said. They were always going to film on location, but because of the book's candid revelations about the way mental patients were treated with lobotomies and electric shock therapy it became difficult to find a hospital which would allow them to film. Eventually a hospital in Salem, the town where the book is set, allowed them to shoot there because the director of the institution was another of the book's many fans.

There was a genuine sense of community about the making of this film. That is not to say that it was entirely without incident. There were occasions when Douglas, Zaentz and Forman would be at each other's throats. Douglas maintains that all three of them remember the fights, but they remember them happily because they were for the good of the picture. Ultimately the spirit of the Sixties which Douglas had caught at Santa Barbara, and which Saul Zaentz knew well from Berkeley, infused and informed every aspect of its production. Douglas, for example, thought that if they were shooting in a real psychiatric hospital then they could use some of the genuine inmates. The idea, selflessly, was that it would allow some of the patients to earn some money, gain a sense of responsibility, and with luck contribute to their recovery. It didn't quite turn out like that.

'What I did not realise,' Douglas recalled in a *Playboy* interview some years later, 'was that we were employing patients from the maximum-security ward – criminally insane patients. We had an arsonist working with turpentine with the painters. He had tried to burn the hospital down a year before. We had a murderer working with the electricians. We had a couple of child molesters as well.'

Given that the director of the hospital was so sympathetic, Douglas also enlisted his aid in his quest for realism. He took a copy of Bo Goldman's script and gave it to the director, asking him if he could come up with a psychological profile of the various characters and, if possible, match it to a patient at the hospital. That patient could then spend time with the actor and be on the set and generally add to the mood of realism. It worked up to a point. After rehearsing a group therapy scene Douglas found Nicholson in an agitated state. They had stopped for lunch, all of them – actors and patients alike – had gone to the cafeteria to eat and Nicholson suddenly put his plate down and walked out. Sensing his first crisis as a producer, Douglas followed him out and asked what was wrong.

'Man,' Nicholson said, 'these guys don't quit. I'm eating lunch and nobody breaks character, nothing. What's going on here?'

Since he hadn't been needed for the first week of filming Nicholson had gone on a ski-ing holiday in Switzerland as a break after finishing Mike Nichols' comedy *The Fortune*. He hadn't been around for the first five days of shooting and didn't know about the real patients in the therapy sessions. Douglas gently defused the situation by explaining that it wasn't that they wouldn't break character, it was just that they couldn't. A somewhat embarrassed Nicholson went back to lunch.

Working in a real institution with genuine patients produced exactly the effect that Michael Douglas, Saul Zaentz, and Milos Forman were looking for. There was an intensity and a tension about the set which comes across clearly on the film. The pressure on the cast was increased when, halfway through the film, they discovered that William Redfield, who was playing Harding, had leukemia. The disease was terminal and inoperable but he desperately wanted to finish the film. Douglas respected his wishes and his scenes were all completed. Six weeks after filming finished William Redfield died.

'It was intense,' says Douglas of the filming process, 'but it was also gratifying afterwards, because of the response. There used to be a law in Florida that if someone showed abnormal behaviour, he could be detained or arrested. After the movie came out with the idea, as McMurphy pointed out, that these people were no crazier than the average asshole on the street, the law was rescinded, partly because of the film. There was a heightened awareness about the whole aspect of mental institutions.'

JACKPOT

Having finally got *One Flew Over the Cuckoo's Nest* made, they now had to ensure that it would be seen. Finding a distributor was considerably easier than finding a backer. Michael Douglas and Saul Zaentz had taken all of the risk in raising the $3 million budget – of which $1 million went to Jack Nicholson as a fee – now the film companies were getting ready to take a share of the profits. In the end it was United Artists who won the rights to distribute the film and suddenly found themselves with a gold mine on their hands.

When *One Flew Over the Cuckoo's Nest* opened on 20 November 1975 it was an instant critical and commercial success. Reviewers loved the film and they especially loved Nicholson, whom they were seeing in a new light after his boisterous but tragic performance as McMurphy. The film opened on a limited release but it played to packed houses everywhere it screened. It was bound to be a serious contender for the year-end round of awards. Douglas always felt that they had been making something a little special when they were shooting in Oregon, something to do with that 'spirit of the Sixties' infecting the workplace, but he could have had no idea that the film was going to be quite so successful.

The only cloud on the horizon was Ken Kesey. Even before they started shooting his father had warned Douglas about the writer. Kirk Douglas had known Kesey of old and forecast that he would be trouble. He was dismayed when he heard Michael had given him an opportunity to write the script and told his son that in the long run Kesey would be bad news. The trouble with Ken Kesey had begun in Oregon. When they first met and he was offered the chance to write the screenplay, Kesey told Douglas and Zaentz that there was no need for agents or contracts. It was a handshake deal between him and the men who were producing a film based on his book. Once his script was rejected it became a different story. He sent someone to meet the producers purporting to represent him, and presented them with a whole list of outrageous demands. Douglas pointed out that he had the film rights and he had no obligation to Kesey other than what his father had paid to acquire the property. The bottom line, as he also pointed out, was that there was no need for Kesey to be involved at all. The meeting ended badly and both Douglas and Zaentz felt that they had not heard the end of it.

So it proved. As the film was praised to the heavens the only carping comments came from Kesey and his supporters. In February of 1976, as expected, One Flew Over the Cuckoo's Nest picked up a raft of Oscar nominations. It had nine in all, including Nicholson, Louise Fletcher and Brad Dourif, as well as Bo Goldman and Lawrence Haubert for the script, Jack Nitzche for the music, and of course Douglas and Zaentz as producers. The lustre was somewhat taken off the honours by the fact that Kesey had now gone from sniping to suing. Kesey brought an action in the District Court in Portland, Oregon, claiming that he had been cheated. The defendants in the action were Douglas and Zaentz, Fantasy Films, United Artists, and a Dutch company which had also provided some of the finance. He claimed that they had broken a promise which said that he would get a five per cent share of the film's gross box office take. On top of that, he was looking for almost a million dollars in punitive damages. Kesey was basing his suit on a verbal promise he said had been made in 1972 by both Douglas and Zaentz for him to write the script, in return for that five per cent box office share plus various other payments for additional drafts of the script.

No matter how seriously intentioned Kesey's case was, even a cursory examination would reveal that it lacked merit. Douglas and Zaentz may have been novice producers but neither of them was reckless enough to offer five per cent of gross box office – not gross profits, or even the more usual and generally non-existent net profits – to a writer. Even now this sort of first dollar deal is only given to a star, and then only to the biggest stars in the business. It would have been unthinkable to offer such a deal. Kesey may have felt that, at the end of the day, with their film an Oscar front-runner, Douglas and Zaentz may have wanted to avoid any negative publicity which could have harmed their Oscar chances.

The 1975 Oscar race was a difficult one to call. Hollywood was in a period of transition. The new generation of movie brats led by Steven Spielberg, William Friedkin and Martin Scorsese were beginning to make their mark, while at the same time established directors such as Sidney Lumet, Stanley Kubrick, George Roy Hill and Arthur Hiller were also producing interesting work. This transitional period was reflected in the 1975 Oscar nominations which featured as eclectic a bunch of films and performances as you could hope to find. In the Best Film category *One Flew Over the Cuckoo's Nest* would find itself in contention for the coveted statuette with Kubrick's epic *Barry Lyndon*, Sidney Lumet's *Dog Day Afternoon*, *Jaws* by Steven Spielberg, and *Nashville* by Robert Altman. The directors of four of these films would also contest the Best Director category. The exception was Steven Spielberg, who had endured the humiliation of inviting the television cameras in to his home to capture his reaction on the morning the nominations were announced. The only thing they captured was his horror and mortification when he discovered that, although his film had been nominated, he had not. The fifth directing nomination went to the Italian Federico Fellini for his film *Amarcord*.

Although it appeared to be a tough call, there was a strong buzz in Hollywood circles that *Cuckoo's Nest* was unbeatable. Kubrick's film had been well regarded but was a commercial flop and, tellingly, had no acting awards – which is invariably a bad sign. *Nashville* was discounted by the same token because it had only picked up two minor acting awards in the Best Supporting Actress category. *Jaws* was out of the running because it would be unthinkable for a film to win Best Picture when the director had not been nominated. That left it down to a straight contest between *Cuckoo's Nest* and *Dog Day Afternoon,* and since Al Pacino, the star of Lumet's picture, was not going out of his way to endear himself to the Academy voters then *Cuckoo's Nest* had the edge. Much is made of the popularity contest aspect of the Academy Awards, probably wrongly, but there are occasions when it cannot be overlooked. Although the age profile of the Academy voters has lowered considerably in recent years, in the Seventies it was still very much an establishment gerontocracy. In a situation like this Michael Douglas, whom they would see as 'Kirk's boy' and one of their own, would be inclined to be favoured over someone like Pacino, who, they felt, did not give them the respect they believed they deserved.

The acting nominations in 1975 were nothing short of bizarre. In the Best Actor category Nicholson was facing Pacino for *Dog Day Afternoon* and Walter Matthau for *The Sunshine Boys*. But the rest of the ticket comprised Maximilian Schell for *The Man in the Glass Booth*, and veteran actor James Whitmore in *Give 'Em Hell Harry* which was essentially a film version of his one man show about Harry S Truman. Surely the first instance where the entire cast of a film has been nominated for an Oscar! There was nothing for Warren Beatty, for example, in *Shampoo* or any of Roy Scheider,

Robert Shaw or Richard Dreyfuss from *Jaws*. In the Best Actress category the choices were even more puzzling. Apart from Louise Fletcher, the other contenders were Carol Kane for *Hester Street*, former double winner Glenda Jackson for *Hedda*, Ann-Margret in *Tommy*, and Isabelle Adjani in *The Story of Adele H.* Not one of them from a Hollywood movie, and three of them from outside the United States.

The Best Actress nominations highlighted the increasing paucity of decent roles for women in Hollywood pictures of the Seventies. Some were more forthright in their complaints than others. Ellen Burstyn, for example, urged people to boycott the Academy Awards in protest at this appalling sexism. While probably not disagreeing with her sentiment, Louise Fletcher took exception to Burstyn's tactics. She pointed out that Burstyn should have made her comments the year before, when she herself had been nominated and won for *Alice Doesn't Live Here Anymore*.

This minor spat aside, the 1975 Academy Awards promised to be a relatively peaceful if inevitably long-winded affair. The feeling was that *Cuckoo's Nest* probably had a lock on Best Picture and Best Director. In addition, this was Nicholson's third consecutive Best Actor nomination – he had come away empty-handed for *The Last Detail*, and *Chinatown* in the previous two years as well as *Five Easy Pieces* in 1970 – and he was playing to the Oscar's sympathies by portraying a disturbed character. Nicholson had also been nominated for Best Supporting Actor for *Easy Rider* in 1969 and had been passed over on that occasion too. Missing out for *Cuckoo's Nest* might be more than he could bear. He had already made it clear that he was getting a little weary of talking about his previous nominations.

'After you've been chosen one of the five best actors of the year,' he said, ' and there are only about forty thousand, then people come up to you and ask how it felt to lose. One does not lose an Academy Award.'

The feeling was that this time Jack was going home with the prize and there would be plenty of his co-workers joining him,

Michael Douglas's memories of that Oscar night are a little mixed. He was hugely excited, of course, but the night was tinged with a certain sadness. He and Brenda Vaccaro had split up by now but they attended the ceremony together. She had been nominated as Best Supporting Actress in *Once is Not Enough* in which she co-starred with Kirk Douglas.

'It was a bittersweet thing,' Douglas recalls. 'I had been with Brenda Vaccaro for years and we had just separated . . . So we went together though we were not together. Jack had been nominated (as Best Actor) three times before and had not won. I had to persuade him to go. We had nine nominations. As the night wore, we had lost the first four. Jack was sitting there going "I told you." You try not to place any importance on it but it does get you crazy.'

It is difficult to imagine what Douglas and Zaentz and everyone else must have been thinking of when they sat there in the auditorium watching other people collect trophies. Then Goldman and Hauben picked up the award for Best Adapted Screenplay and things started to look up. Next Milos Forman took Best Director and they knew they were in with a shot. Louise Fletcher contributed the most memorable moment of the night when she won Best Actress and delivered her acceptance speech in sign language for her parents, who are deaf. Despite his pessimism, Nicholson lost his Oscar virginity when he was named Best Actor. Finally, and inevitably, the main award of the night, for Best Picture, went to *One Flew Over the Cuckoo's Nest* and a delighted Douglas and Zaentz went up to collect their Oscar. They had won five Academy Awards – that was the number which Douglas had predicted to the revered *Daily Variety* columnist Army Archerd before the ceremony – and made history in the process. Not since *It Happened One Night*, back in 1934 had a single film made a clean sweep of the five main awards for film, acting and screenplay. It would not happen again until *The Silence of the Lambs* in 1991.

Milos Forman looked at Michael Douglas in the midst of the hubbub and the backstage celebrations.

'Well,' he told him, 'it's all downhill from here.'

He could not have been more wrong. *One Flew Over the Cuckoo's Nest* would launch the careers of both Douglas and Forman and they would never look back from this night on. Indeed, ten years later they would meet again at an Oscar ceremony. This time Douglas, as one of the biggest stars in the world, was presenting an award while Forman, again with Saul Zaentz, was emerging as the big winner for *Amadeus*.

United Artists had gambled on *Cuckoo's Nest* emerging as a leading Oscar winner, although it could not have expected it to have won quite so many awards. The morning after the Academy Award ceremonies the film was re-released in a thousand cinemas in the United States. By the end of its run the film had taken almost $60 million at the American box office and almost $200 million world wide. If he never did another thing Michael Douglas, his children, and probably his grandchildren were set for life.

It will come as no surprise that Ken Kesey was less than pleased about the proceedings. He pointedly ignored the ceremony and the live telecast of the event, claiming that he preferred to go to a regular poker game. His only comment was that he had wished there had been subpoenas inside the envelopes which were being opened on stage that night. In public, no one involved in the suit would say anything for the record. Privately, regardless of what they felt about the merits of the case, they had been exploring avenues for settlement. In the end, according to Michael Douglas, they settled for the amount they had agreed to give him in the first place. However even though the court case was settled, the bad feeling still remained according to Douglas, who claimed that he still loved the book, he just didn't love Ken Kesey.

'It left a bitter taste in his mouth and ours,' he claimed. 'That was unfortunate because I idolised this guy in a lot of ways, not only for his book but for his lifestyle, which I'd read about and had a little taste of.'

*

Michael Douglas was still only 31 years old. He was a failed movie actor, a moderately successful TV star, and now he had hit the jackpot in his first effort as a producer. In the process he had emerged a long way from the shadow of his father. He had chosen the difficult option of trying to make his way in the same field which his father had dominated, but he found a way to succeed in his own right.

'If I had known what a big shot Michael was going to be,' Kirk Douglas would say later, 'I would have been nicer to him when he was a kid.'

Kirk Douglas had started the ball rolling when he acquired the film rights to Ken Kesey's book. But it was Michael Douglas who ran with it and made it work where his father could not. Kirk Douglas made a large amount of money from his share of the film, reportedly as much as $15 million. That's more than he made from *Spartacus*.

'*One Flew Over the Cuckoo's Nest* is one of the biggest disappointments of my life,' he recalled in his autobiography *The Ragman's Son*. 'I made more money from that film than any I acted in. And I would gladly give back every cent, if I could have played that role.'

DIANDRA

As Michael Douglas took stock of his career as a newly-crowned Oscar-winning producer he realised that he owed it all to two men. He had been blessed with two patient and understanding mentors in the shape of Karl Malden and Saul Zaentz. To both men he could have remained simply 'Kirk's son', but they had both trusted him to allow him to develop his potential. Malden trusted him as an actor, Zaentz trusted him as a producer, and with their help he climbed a steep learning curve which ended up with him picking up the statuette on Oscar night. As he points out, neither man had any reason to treat him as well as they both did, and he has acknowledged the debt he owes to them both many times.

After the Oscars *One Flew Over the Cuckoo's Nest* rolled out on an international release buoyed up by the boost of five Academy Awards. For Douglas that meant two things; a year-long round of promotion in foreign markets, and also a year of major partying and celebrating. His constant companion throughout most of this was

Jack Nicholson. The two men, who had barely known each other beforehand, struck up a firm and abiding friendship when they were on location in Oregon. It was here, for example, that Nicholson saw what he describes as a wild and bizarre side of Michael Douglas. Nicholson was impressed when Douglas visited the women's ward in the hospital in Salem where they were filming. The women recognised him from *The Streets of San Francisco* and literally threw themselves at the object of many of their fantasies who had turned up here in their ward. Douglas claims that security guards had to come in to get the women off and get him back to his trailer. That incident in particular amused Nicholson, but Douglas is coy about his friend's description of him as wild and bizarre. This is a description echoed, incidentally, by his former flat mate Danny De Vito.

'You might not know this,' he says not entirely in jest, 'but Michael is one of the sickest people you are ever going to run into in your life.'

Douglas suggests that his friend is only part correct, though he stops short of actually denying anything.

'There's this dichotomy in the way everyone sees me in a very together light,' he says of Nicholson's description. 'Jack sees me otherwise. Our affinity was our sense of absurdity. Up in Oregon we had access to the wards with the mental patients – even the secure units. I used to go up to the wards and then come down with the grimmest stories. The more bent the story about patients, the more fascinated I was. I always liked volatile situations where I thought anything could happen.'

This was a side of himself that Douglas later addressed in another magazine interview.

'I'm a little bent,' he admitted. 'I have a sick sense of humour. It's a little kinky, like things you shouldn't laugh at . . . I have a really bad time at funerals. There's a side of me that struggles for discipline. Sometimes I think the reason I work as hard as I do is that I could go on a binge that could be a lifestyle. So maybe that's the way I release myself.'

Up to and including this point in his career, Michael Douglas had always been thought of as one of the nice guys in the film business, and there is little evidence to contradict that. No one is so nice, however, that they don't appreciate the opportunity of a little payback now and then, and after the success of *Cuckoo's Nest* Douglas found himself in a position where he could settle a few scores, although not overtly. He was given a very hard time by a lot of people in the business when he started, because they felt he was riding his father's coat-tails, and then he was given an even harder time when he tried to raise money for his picture. He admits that what kept him going during the most difficult periods on the film was the belief that one day he would have a hit picture, if only out of sheer spite.

'I think revenge is a very good motivation if you can direct it,' he admits. 'It's healthy. Very healthy. It's like, maybe you happen to be in a restaurant somewhere and you see somebody and you just stop and say "Hi, I'm celebrating passing a hundred million dollars in grosses. Nice to see you again." Revenge is great.'

Douglas also found that five Oscars was a great inducement when it came to getting his calls returned. People who previously would not have given him the time of day were now falling over themselves to get in touch. At this stage, though, Douglas still didn't consider himself a movie producer in the established sense of the word. As far as he was concerned, he was an actor who had made a movie which had turned out to be a huge popular and critical success. It was time for him to take some of his father's advice. Kirk Douglas had always regretted not taking the time to savour the joys of his life and his career. He had told his sons that if they ever did anything remarkable then they should stop and savour the moment. Michael Douglas was more than happy to do what his father had told him on this occasion.

They would be on the road for more than a year on and off, but Douglas and Nicholson started their round of partying in Oregon while they were still filming. They found themselves invited one night to what the invitation promised was a 'Hollywood party'. Not quite knowing what to expect, and Salem not being over-endowed with other diversions, they decided to check it out. Expecting perhaps a fancy dress party they were astonished to discover they had been invited to a wife-swapping orgy, that obviously being how the people of Oregon believed the people of Hollywood spent their time. At this point the schoolboys inside Nicholson and Douglas took over and, guessing this was something they should not miss, they decided to stay without sampling the delights on offer.

'Jack and I aren't wife-swappers but we are major voyeurs,' Douglas said later.

Douglas makes light of this period and claims it was little more than a hedonistic round of partying by two single men in the prime of their life who happened to be representing a fabulously successful film. He claims he was merely milking the success of *Cuckoo's Nest*. There was much more to it than that, there was also the business side of selling their films in territories where no one knew who Ken Kesey was, and no one wanted to see a film about a psychiatric institution. It could at times be a punishing and gruelling schedule. One tour, for example, took them from Hawaii to Australia, Japan, England, France, Italy, Switzerland, West Germany, Sweden, Denmark, and back to New York in the space of 35 days. This was only one of many promotional tours and Nicholson turned out to be the ideal travelling companion. Their visit to Japan, however, left Nicholson somewhat miffed.

When they arrived at the airport the crowds largely ignored him, the star, and flocked to Douglas, the producer. Nicholson was at a loss to understand it until someone pointed out that *The Streets of San Francisco* had been running in Japan for several years and Douglas had a huge Japanese fan base. That apart, Nicholson and Douglas got on famously during their time together.

'He had a giggle in him,' says Douglas. 'Early on we were able to be honest with each other at a time when he was getting a lot of hype, over his career and about him as a person. He was a real twinkle and he thought I was funny. He just got a kick out of me.'

The Nicholson and Douglas version of the Grand Tour was simply a long procession of the best hotels, the best food, the best booze, the most attractive women. It was a time when they had no responsibilities to their families or to their careers. The huge box office clout of their film meant that money was no object and they were determined to enjoy themselves. After a year this was beginning to pale and towards the end of 1976 they began to think about slowing down the partying and getting back to the real world, or as close as the film business ever comes to the real world.

America had changed in the time they had been on the road. In the election of November 1976 President Gerald Ford, who had taken over when Richard Nixon resigned in disgrace, found that he could not overcome the taint of his former boss. The voters rejected Ford in favour of Jimmy Carter, famously characterised as a peanut farmer from Georgia, who swept into the White House with the promise of a new, more liberal regime. A life-long liberal Douglas was, at least by inclination, a Carter supporter. A combination of this and his new-found celebrity status meant that he and Jack Nicholson, along with Nicholson's good friend Warren Beatty, found themselves in Washington DC for the Presidential inauguration in January, 1977.

The night before the ceremony they were invited to the Pre-Inauguration Gala Concert in the Lincoln Center. The concert was followed by a reception to meet the President-Elect, who in a few hours would be the most powerful man in the world. Douglas went along out of interest and curiosity, he was far too jaded by the party circuit to have been attracted by the lure of free champagne and canapés. Suddenly he found himself playing a scene out of a bad movie. He scanned the room with indifference. Suddenly he saw an attractive young blonde woman on the other side of the room and instantly fell in love.

'It was real corny,' he confesses. 'I saw her across a crowded room. She was in a white dress and she looked beautiful, and we started talking over the hors d'oeuvres.'

Diandra Luker was the daughter of a Spanish diplomat. She had been born in Washington but moved to Spain when she was barely two weeks old. The family lived in the town of Deya in northern Spain and her mother's friends included the writer and poet Robert Graves and the painter Miro. Graves, the author of the acclaimed *I, Claudius*, was a particular friend and influence on her career. She was in Washington completing her final year as a student at Georgetown University where she was studying in the Foreign Service programme, as a prelude to a career as a diplomat herself. Growing up in Spain she had had a relatively sheltered life which placed more emphasis on artistic endeavour and academic achievement than anything else. Her television time was limited to an hour a week and the cinema was out of the question. The first film she saw was *My Fair Lady*, by which time she was already a teenager. Consequently, when this man came over to her and started making comments about the state of hors d'oeuvres, she had no idea that he was a famous actor and now a highly successful producer.

'Michael had a beard and he was very handsome,' she recalled. 'I thought he was a painter or a sculptor. I was a little taken aback, a little disappointed to discover that he was an actor.'

Disappointed or not, even though she was there with a date of her own, Diandra Luker found herself enthralled by this dashing and charming man. He had a different take on events from the one she had been brought up with. He was a child of the Sixties, a member of the rock and roll generation. These were things that Diandra had barely heard of, but she was fascinated by this man from a world so completely alien to her own experience. Douglas had been instantly taken with this striking young woman. The reason he had gone across to talk to her straight away was to prevent Beatty or Nicholson making a move on her. He wanted to see more of her, and invited her out after the concert. She said that she couldn't go. She had a date after all, and in any event they were going off to supper at a club. Douglas persisted and offered to meet her there. Diandra told him that it was a private club and there was no way he would get in. This did not bother him in the slightest. Was he not Michael Douglas, successful producer of an Oscar-winning film which he had been using as a calling card the world over for the past eighteen months? He followed her to the club and couldn't get past the door.

Douglas was completely smitten. It was obvious that the attractive 19-year-old was equally taken with him. Before he had to leave the club he persuaded her to come to the inauguration the following day with him and she agreed. Although he did not know it at the time, this was a major step for Diandra to take. Douglas discovered later that she already had a date for the ceremony, with a Congressman who had seats on the podium immediately behind Jimmy Carter. Douglas, on the other hand, had been assigned seats on the main White House grounds, hundreds of yards away from where Carter would be sworn in. As he says himself, from his seats you could barely hear the echoes of the speeches on the loudspeakers.

Nonetheless she decided to forsake her front seat at history to spend the ceremony with this interesting young man. The inauguration was marred by rain and bitterly cold weather against which those on the White House grounds had little protection. Douglas had a hotel room nearby and persuaded Diandra to abandon their seats to the elements and watch the rest of the festivities from the warmth and comfort of his hotel balcony. From then on they were inseparable. He invited her to lunch the following day and they spent hours walking in the Botanical Gardens talking about their lives, their experiences, and their hopes for the future. Their lives were so different they had a lot to talk about. Douglas was still best known as a TV actor and she didn't watch television, so when he eventually told her what he did for a living she had no frame of reference. Then when they started talking about films, she mentioned that her favourite film was *One Flew Over the Cuckoo's Nest*.

Plainly it was a sign. Douglas admits that he fell in love instantaneously, the moment he saw her in that Lincoln Center reception room. It was as puzzling to him as it was to anyone, and he still has never quite worked it out. He had to go to New York for a number of business meetings about new projects, new finance, and the other travails which beset a hit movie producer. He found that his mind was not on his work. Instead of staying at his apartment in New York he kept finding reasons to come back to Washington DC to spend time with Diandra. Nine days after they met, he asked her to marry him. She said yes. They were married on 20 March 1977, six weeks after they had discussed the quality of the Lincoln Center's hors d'oeuvres.

The wedding took place at Kirk Douglas's house in Los Angeles and Kirk gave the bride away. The only member of Diandra's family at the wedding was her mother, who had come under duress. She was violently opposed to the marriage and wanted Diandra to complete her education. However, she would not abandon her on her wedding day. Although Diandra's father was dead, her grandfather was still alive and very much the family patriarch. He was violently opposed to his grand-daughter running off to Hollywood and marrying someone who was not only in the entertainment industry, but was Jewish as well.

None of this seemed to matter to Michael Douglas as he came to terms with his decision to take the plunge.

'This was the last thing I had been thinking about,' said Douglas. 'I had been footloose and fancy free for the previous year and a half, running around savouring *Cuckoo's Nest*. A lot of people showed up for the wedding just to make sure it was happening.'

BACK TO WORK

All those people who turned up for Michael Douglas's wedding just to make sure he would show up may have been surprised at his decision to tie the knot so quickly. There is no reason, however, to have been so shocked. He may have been footloose and fancy free for a year and a half, but this was more a celebration of a rite of passage than anything else. He had achieved something spectacular in his professional life with *Cuckoo's Nest* and perhaps now it was time to get his personal life back into gear. His 18-month tear with Nicholson was really a search for something he may not have known he was looking for, but when he saw Diandra Luker he knew immediately that he had found it.

Not to get too Oedipal he had found, as all men want to in their heart of hearts, a woman who was not unlike his mother. Like Diana Douglas, Diandra was beautiful, intelligent, independent, and not about to become anyone's trophy wife. It was his father's inability to realise this which had gone a long way towards ending his parents' marriage. Douglas, perhaps aware of this, admitted that it would be difficult for Diandra to come and settle in Santa Barbara where he was now living. For one thing she had to finish her degree by transferring to UCSB, where her husband had been such a poor student. She would also have to give up her chosen career in the diplomatic service.

'It requires travelling,' she said, ' and I am . . . married to a man who cannot follow my career without sacrificing his own. However I want my degree and I want to explore how I might remain partly active, especially in the area of international concern for con- servation causes.'

Douglas maintained that marriage was great for him, especially in professional terms. He claimed he felt more centred and more focused and better able to concentrate on the raft of business decisions he would now have to make as a successul producer.

'Just possibly I hadn't realised how insular my life had become,' he said. 'So that when the person closest to you in life comes from a whole other world, literally a continent-and-a-half apart, and from a different cultural environment, you've got an incredibly fresh point of view, a great sounding board, a terrific challenge to expand your scope.'

Michael Douglas may have been wildly enthusiastic but initially marriage was not great for Diandra. Her mother in law was quick to spot it. Diana Douglas could see that the latest member of the clan was not settling in. Her European sensibility – which to a great extent Diana Douglas shared – meant that she was not easily able to deal with the complete lack of privacy or the constant attentions of the paparazzi which went hand in glove with being married to someone as famous as Michael Douglas. It was a transition she made uneasily and uncomfortably and one which she would never entirely accept. She would say somewhat bitterly, not long after they were married, that she liked her her husband more than she liked California.

Douglas, meanwhile, was a little puzzled. He had produced *One*

Flew Over the Cuckoo's Nest, it had won five Oscars and taken $130 million at the box office by this stage. He was also a TV star who had drawn audiences of 25 million viewers a week not so long ago. In spite of all this there was no work coming in. No one, it seemed, was awfully keen to hire Michael Douglas.

'I kept smelling my armpits,' he said. 'The stars and the director (of *One Flew Over the Cuckoo's Nest*) were getting new scripts by the carload but my phone wasn't ringing. I guess people thought I had it handed to me on a platter – somebody's kid who lucked into something . . . I have a long memory and I like carrying grudges. I'm going to remember my friends and I'm going to remember those who weren't.'

So much for the nicest man in Hollywood. Douglas realised that if he wasn't getting any acting offers then he would simply have to develop something for himself. Over the past couple of years, during the long procession from bringing *Cuckoo's Nest* from Ken Kesey's novel to a film which, with the passage of time, would eventually be acclaimed as one of the best films ever made, Douglas had come to realise the joy of producing. He was no longer an actor-turned-producer, he was now a producer who was prepared to do a little bit of acting. The acting was fun, it gave him the chance to play make believe and pick up a big salary, but the producing was what was really creatively satisfying at this stage of his career. He realised also that a hit film like *One Flew Over the Cuckoo's Nest* did great things for careers, but only if you were the star or the director. If you were the producer then you had nothing to do but find something else to produce.

His father outlined much the same argument one day when he scolded him about waiting for the world to come knocking on his door.

'You are an excellent producer,' he told him. 'But why are you producing pictures that have such wonderful parts for other people? How about producing a movie for a wonderful actor named Michael Douglas? Your father's company developed *Spartacus* and there just happened to be a very good role for me. Same with *The Vikings* and *Paths of Glory*. What's wrong with giving a good actor called Michael Douglas a part?'

With his phone remaining metaphorically mute, Douglas was beginning to think his father might have a point. Perhaps it was time to find a movie that he could produce as well as star in. With Fantasy Productions having really only existed for the purpose of producing *Cuckoo's Nest* Michael Douglas had now formed his own production company. It was called Big Stick Productions, a reference to the recommendation that one should speak softly but carry a big stick. In this case the big stick was a handful of Oscars and a nine-figure box office gross. Big Stick set up shop in Hollywood, an easy commute from Douglas's home in Santa Barbara, and started to review scripts.

Mike Gray started his career as an aeronautical engineer in Chicago, who then branched out into being a technical writer. When this began to pall he carved out another career for himself as a successful and respected documentary film maker. While he was working on his documentaries he began to research a disturbing number of accidents at nuclear power plants. Gray thought there might be a film in this, but it might be bigger than his usual guerrilla documentaries. He considered it for a while and started to turn it into a screenplay. When it was finished he sent it out to a number of companies. *The China Syndrome*, as his screenplay was called, turned up at Big Stick in April 1976, not long after Douglas had completed his clean sweep at the Oscars with *One Flew Over the Cuckoo's Nest*. It had been in semi-active development since then, but now Douglas decided that it was time to take it off the back burner and bring it to the front of the stove.

'So many things about it interested me beyond the obvious political issue,' he told *Playboy* magazine later. 'It was a great horror movie, a movie about man against machine, a movie about an individual fighting the system. It had an interesting social message with all the aspects of a great thriller.'

The title of the film comes from a Doomsday scenario in the nuclear industry. If there is a serious accident at a nuclear power plant the greatest fear is that the reactor can go into meltdown. If this happens the theory is that the reactor will simply melt through the crust of the earth. No one is quite certain where the melting reactor will stop on its journey through the planet. When the problem was originally posited someone wryly suggested that China was as good a guess as any, hence The China Syndrome. This is the theory. In practice what is likely to happen is that once the melting reactor reaches the water table, there will be a catastrophic explosion which will send clouds of radioactivity into the atmosphere to drift on the wind. The number of people killed will depend on something as capricious as which way the wind is blowing at the time.

In *The China Syndrome* a news crew is shooting some news footage in a nuclear power plant when there is an incident. They are assured nothing is wrong but they are curious when the panicked behaviour of the plant crew does not match the bland assurances from the official spokesmen. The camera operator secretly shoots some footage of the disturbance and on further investigation there appears to have been a serious accident. To his horror he discovers that the power plant has come close to having its own China Syndrome. The television station errs on the side of caution and refuses to run the item. The camera man and the reporter investigate further and, shaken by the incident, the plant manager agrees to provide them with what they need. When someone delivering the information is run off the road and killed the plant manager snaps and takes over the power station. He is gunned down by a SWAT team and the reporter then goes on air to tell the whole story.

It is a terrific thriller but in Hollywood terms it was a difficult one. Studios are not noted for their willingness to tackle such socially relevant subjects in such a provocative manner. There was also the problem that Gray, who had never directed a feature before, wanted to make his directing debut with this script. Douglas, who was plainly attracted to the challenge of the task involved, had promised he would do whatever he could to ensure that Gray was the director. There were three key roles in Gray's original script: the camera operator, the news producer, and the plant manager. If Douglas was to sell an idea he knew was commercially difficult with an untried director to a conservative film studio, then he would not only need a big-name cast to provide box office insurance, they would also need to cut their fees to keep the budget down. That being the case, Douglas would have to lead by example by cutting his own fee to take what was going to be the best part he would have in some time. He decided he would play the producer, Richard Dreyfuss was to be the cameraman who would be the central character, while Jack Lemmon would play the manager of the power plant.

Lemmon's participation was something of a seal of approval on the project. He had become well known as a narrator of environmentally-conscious television documentaries. Douglas was so convinced that Lemmon was the right man that once he had sent the script he went to Lemmon's home in person to talk him into it. Fortunately, and as he had rather hoped, he was preaching to the choir. When Jack Lemmon saw the script he knew that he wanted to do it. In the end, thanks to production difficulties, he would turn down work and be unemployed for a full year to make sure he could do *The China Syndrome*. Throughout that time his commitment never wavered and he became one of Douglas's staunchest allies.

'What I love about Michael,' he said, ' is that he finally got *Cuckoo's Nest* off the ground and made one of the great, great films. Now, he's the hottest thing in the world. He could have done any one of fifteen things I'm sure. But he . . . waited and waited and waited. He found this damn thing and it was so tough to get off the ground – all the good ones are – and he just stuck with it. He's bright, he's talented, but mainly he cares.'

Lemmon was as passionate about the project as Douglas and Gray, but Dreyfuss appeared less so. Douglas had pitched the idea to Columbia Pictures who were keen, even with Mike Gray directing, providing he could guarantee the casting of himself plus Lemmon and Dreyfuss. In the midst of these negotiations Dreyfuss pulled out of the project. Douglas says merely that he 'fell out' but Gray was quoted as saying that Dreyfuss had reservations about him as a director and took himself out of the running by the simple expedient of increasing his salary demand from $250,000 to $500,000. Whatever the reason, the upshot was that Douglas was looking at a film which was in severe danger of having the plug pulled.

In the early days of the production, Douglas had contacted Robert Redford to see if he would be interested in any of the roles. Redford wrote back politely declining but saying that he thought *The China Syndrome* was the best in its genre, next to the Karen Silkwood story. Karen Silkwood was a nuclear plant worker who died in mysterious circumstances in 1974 when her car ran off the road. In an incident duplicated in *The China Syndrome*, she had been on her way to deliver documents to a journalist which, she had claimed, proved that safety was lax at the Oklahoma plant where she worked. The documents were never recovered from the scene of the crash and no adequate explanation for her death has ever been put forward.

Conspiracy theorists have had a field day with the Silkwood case and it was inevitable that it would attract the attention of Hollywood. In 1983 Mike Nichols eventually turned it into a film, *Silkwood*, which starred Meryl Streep in the title role. Before Nichols had succeeded there were a number of rival Silkwood projects in development at various places. One of these was by Jane Fonda at her production company, which conveniently had a deal at Columbia. Once they had lost Richard Dreyfuss a company executive suggested to Michael Douglas that perhaps they should talk to Fonda and see if something could be worked out.

It was an obvious solution to a problem which threatened to sink a film which was dear to the hearts of everyone concerned. Douglas, perhaps feeling proprietorial, was not initially enthusiastic. What he didn't know was that Fonda had become as discouraged as he had. She was upset not to have got the rights to Karen Silkwood's story and, under the circumstances, his project was a godsend. Fonda read the script and was immediately interested but she had a number of conditions if her company, IPC, was to become involved. First she would play the role originally intended for Dreyfuss, second the film would be told in a more conventional narrative style than the semi-documentary style which Gray had planned, and finally she wanted Gray to be replaced by James Bridges as the director. As she outlined her conditions over dinner in a restaurant on Melrose Avenue, Douglas became increasingly unhappy. The script rewrite was not a major problem, but changing the style of the film would add to the budget. In addition, even though Bridges was a good director with the Oscar-winning *The Paper Chase* to his credit, Douglas had promised Mike Grady he would try to make sure he directed the script he had lived with for six years.

Douglas admits that he did get 'a little bent out of shape' with Fonda's involvement but one of the virtues of being a successful producer is pragmatism. With Fonda on board the film would be given the green light by the studio, and if that's what it took to get it made then he would have to do it. He made his apologies to Grady and Bridges was installed as the director. She felt that this story was so important that it should reach as broad an audience as possible, and believed that audience was used to a specific style of film-making with a certain level of production value. Grady's documentary style, she felt, would only alienate the audience and limit the film's chances of getting out its message effectively.

Fonda's participation meant a shift of character for Douglas. He would have to play the camera man, the role originally intended for Dreyfuss, and while Lemmon could remain as the plant manager, a new character was going to have to be created for Jane Fonda. In the end the new script, which was written by Bridges who is also a gifted screenwriter, had Fonda playing a character called Kimberly Wells. She is a newsreading bimbo, hired for her easy-on-the-eye looks, who suddenly discovers the story of a lifetime dropping in her lap. Douglas's character was essentially the exposition, explaining the story to Fonda and at the same time explaining it to the audience.

Like Fonda, Douglas was equally passionate that this film should reach a wide audience – which meant it had to be accurate. To make sure the film looked as authentic as possible $150,000 was spent on a set which was an exact copy of the control room of a nuclear power plant. In addition he went back to Oregon, where he had filmed *One Flew Over the Cuckoo's Nest*, this time to Portland on a fact-finding mission at the Trojan Nuclear Power Plant. Finally a team of technical experts was hired, which included three former General Electric employees who had resigned from the company because of their concerns about nuclear safety.

Everything was set to start filming but Douglas had one slight misgiving. He had agreed to appear in the film first because he was investing so much energy it would seem foolish not to, and second because he was prepared to reduce his salary as an inducement to the others to work for less. This didn't entirely work out, since Fonda was paid $1 million, twice what Dreyfuss had reportedly asked for when he walked. Now things had changed. The part he would have to play in Bridges' rewrite was much bigger than he had originally envisaged. He hadn't acted since he left *The Streets of San Francisco* at the end of 1975 and hadn't done a film since *Napoleon and Samantha* in 1972. It might be a good idea to make sure he wasn't too ring rusty by getting back in front of a camera again.

Robin Cook and Michael Crichton are both doctors who have turned to writing and in the process frequently terrified readers with their views of where medical technology might take us. Cook's stock in trade is the medical thriller where crusading doctors risk life and limb to expose medical wrong-doing. His white-knuckle books with their trademark one word titles – *Contagion, Shock, Fever,* and *Virus,* to name but a few – have proved worldwide best-sellers, exciting and terrifying their readers in equal measure. Crichton, meanwhile, is the most successful author of scientific cautionary tales of his generation with a range of titles as diverse as *The Terminal Man, Jurassic Park* and *Disclosure* to his credit. In 1979 they were not perhaps at the peak of their powers when they joined forces creatively on *Coma*, which was based on a book by Cook with a screenplay by Crichton, who was also directing.

The medical thriller revolves around a young intern who discovers an abnormally high mortality rate at her hospital among young people who are going in for relatively safe scheduled operations. She investigates and discovers to her horror that the victims are not being killed. They are instead being put into a coma, then transferred to a giant depository where their vital functions will be maintained so that their organs can be harvested and sold to the highest bidder. One of the problems in bringing this story to the screen was that the leading character was a woman and there was a dearth of actresses who could successfully carry a film like this in 1978. It was a fairly short list which included Jane Fonda, Barbra Streisand, Sally Field and not many beyond that. The role of Dr Susan Wheeler, who was eventually played by rising star Genevieve Bujold, would need some support, and in this case it would come from Michael Douglas as Dr Mark Bellows, her love interest, her co-investigator and, in the conclusion to the film, very nearly an involuntary organ donor.

For Douglas it was a relatively painless way of easing himself back into the acting side of the business, and after four seasons with Karl Malden he was well used to playing second banana. Bujold is a talented actress and Crichton and Cook were perfectly correct in their estimation that she and Douglas would be a good fit on screen.

'People could just not see why I would want to take on the insecurity of being an actor all over again,' says Douglas in the publicity material for *Coma*. 'The truth is, just before my first film as a producer, I was beginning to enjoy acting. Besides *Coma* was too good to turn down.'

That last statement is typical of the anodyne commentary which infests studio publicity material and it's debatable whether Douglas actually said it, and even more debatable whether he actually meant it. This is a man who has just produced one of the greatest films ever and is in the middle of producing a film which would prove to be a wake-up call to America's nuclear industry. It is hard to conceive of anything in *Coma*, a satisfactory but nonetheless forgettable thriller, which would have engaged Douglas other than for sheer practical reasons. It enabled him to take time out from many of the problems of producing *The China Syndrome* – now that Fonda was on board Bruce Gilbert of IPC was sharing some of that load – and to hone his acting skills in preparation for the biggest role of his career to date.

LIFE IMITATES ART

When it opened in cinemas on 16 March 1979 *The China Syndrome* was an instant success. Michael Douglas and Columbia Pictures had taken a very conscious marketing decision in their handling of the film. They knew that this was a volatile and contentious subject, so when it came to publicising the film they chose to downplay what one might call the political content and market it simply as a thriller. Again this was an instance where the pragmatism of Douglas the producer won out over the idealism of Douglas, the passionate life-long liberal. It's worth noting at this stage that Douglas claimed he had no position either way when it came to nuclear power going into *The China Syndrome*. As far as promoting the film was concerned, the view was that you would get nowhere by ramming the message down the throats of the audience. The public should be encouraged to see the film on the basis that it was simply an exciting picture with an attractive cast, then once they were in the theatre they could discover the anti-nuclear theme for themselves.

With hindsight their decision may have been the correct one. Going ahead and promoting the film as an anti-nuclear film may have been courting disaster. Douglas had already noted that a Barbara Walters special with Jane Fonda on ABC which was one of the main planks of the film's pre-publicity programme, had run into problems. It wasn't just that Fonda slammed Walters, then America's leading news interviewer, for a show which was 'institutionalised meaninglessness'. The real signs of potential problems came when the General Electric Company withdrew its sponsorship for the Walters special when it was broadcast on 13 March 1979. That small spat made the film something of a hot button and various commentators and energy industry spokesmen lined up to have a swipe at it. One executive from the Edison power company in Southern California claimed *The China Syndrome* had no scientific credibility and was, in fact, ridiculous. In *Newsweek*, George Will, one of America's leading and most influential columnists, wrote a column about the impossibility of a nuclear accident. They were queuing up to have a pop at the picture which was, nonetheless, still finding its audience and was the number one film in the country on its opening weekend. Then the roof fell in on George Will, General Electric, the man from Edison, and all of the other nay-sayers.

Three Mile Island is a small strip of land in the middle of the Susquehanna River near Harrisburg, Pennsylvania. Unless you lived in Harrisburg or unless you were in the power business and knew there was a nuclear power station there, Three Mile Island would cheerfully have passed you by. At four o'clock on the morning of 28 March 1979 there was a problem at Three Mile Island when an automatic valve in the Unit 2 reactor closed by mistake. Nuclear power plants work by heating water in the reactor, the water turns to steam, the steam turns the turbine, and the turbine turns the generator to produce electricity. The closure of the valve in Unit 2 shut off the main water supply to the core, which meant the core shut down automatically, which was supposed to happen as a safety

Michael Douglas and father Kirk celebrate the Oscar success of *One Flew Over The Cuckoo's Nest* – a project that Kirk found and Michael eventually brought to the screen.

King of the world – but not for several years yet. Michael Douglas on the set of *Hail Hero*.

Established star Karl Malden was more than happy to work with 'Kirk's boy'.
Playing Steve Keller on *The Streets of San Francisco* made Michael Douglas a
household name.

Jack Lemmon, Michael Douglas, and Jane Fonda in a tense scene from *The China Syndrome*. Douglas, who was also producing, took over a role originally intended for Richard Dreyfuss.

Michael and Diandra Douglas share an affectionate moment in happier times. Diandra was never happy being a Hollywood wife, which was one reason for the end of the marriage.

Michael Douglas in *Romancing the Stone*. Jack Colton was the sort of role Kirk Douglas would have killed for and Michael was finally starting to step out of his father's shadow.

Greed is good, and lunch is for wimps. Michael Douglas plays Gordon Gecko in *Wall Street*, a role that would win him a Best Actor Oscar.

A chance meeting leads to a fatal attraction. Glenn Close and Michael
Douglas in *Fatal Attraction* – not so much a film as a cultural phenomenon.

Hail to the chief. Having turned down the chance to run for office several years
previously, Michael Douglas finally made it to the White House in *The American
President.*

The second time around. Michael Douglas and Catherine Zeta-Jones step out at a Hollywood function.

feature. But over the next few hours a series of bad decisions, human error, and malfunctioning equipment meant there was a significant drop in the level of water coolant in the reactor which left the core partially exposed.

Leaving aside technical details, what this meant in simple terms was a chemical reaction which produced a huge amount of radioactive hydrogen gas, some of which escaped from the core and into the reactor building. The increase in radiation levels could be detected a mile away. It was the worst accident in the history of the American nuclear power industry and as the world held its breath, waiting to see what would happen in this small town in Pennsylvania, television audiences world-wide watched *The China Syndrome* play out before their eyes. The film, which was already a success, became a phenomenon.

The cast were as stunned and horrified as anyone. Bruce Gilbert, the executive producer, even wondered whether someone had seen their film and, driven by some kind of delusion, had gone and sabotaged the plant to imitate the actions of Jack Lemmon. For his part Lemmon was depressingly proved to have been right all along.

'Every goddammed thing we had in there came true,' said Lemmon of the film's relationship to Three Mile Island. 'But we wanted to make sure that in no way could we use the accident to gain recognition for the film.'

This was a real problem for Lemmon, Douglas and everyone connected with the picture. Suddenly they had a film which was not only a success but was in fact a briefing document for just about every reporter being sent to Harrisburg to cover the story of the year. But it would be churlish, not to say distasteful, to go out on the stump and promote the film on the back of a potential disaster. Douglas cut down his publicity engagements, including cancelling a high profile interview on *The Tonight Show* with Johnny Carson, Lemmon cancelled all of his interviews, but Jane Fonda continued with her nationwide press tour. Some years later, in an in-depth interview with *Playboy* magazine, Michael Douglas finally revealed what he had felt at the time.

'I'm not religious but there was something about it that was uncanny,' he said. 'It was the closest thing to a religious experience I have had in my life. We had educated ourselves about the possibilities of this kind of nuclear accident, and then it was happening in Harrisburg, Pennsylvania. We were terrified. There is a line in the movie when the experts are discussing what would happen in a melt-down, and they turn to each other and say – before the Pennsylania accident happened – that it would destroy an area the size of Pennsylvania.'

Douglas once again found himself the producer of a film which everyone was talking about. There wasn't a television news or current affairs programme anywhere in the world which didn't feature a clip from *The China Syndrome* in the coverage of the Three Mile Island story. Perversely, this seriously affected the film's box office. Douglas insists that people became intimidated by the film. They didn't want to go out for an evening's entertainment and be presented with the story which had the nation on the edge of its seat on the nightly news.

'I think though,' he concluded, 'that along with Three Mile Island, the film did some good, changed some minds about the nuclear issue.'

Certainly the combined effect of the film and the real-life accident did have a severe effect on public confidence in the nuclear power industry in the United States. Seven reactors like the ones at Harrisburg were closed temporarily and there was a freeze – again temporary – on the licensing of new plants. In the end it would be more than five years before any public utility company in the United States ordered a new nuclear reactor. It was 1985 before the Unit 1 reactor at Three Mile Island, which had not been damaged in the accident, resumed operations. Clean-up operations continued on the Unit 2 reactor, which had caused the accident, until 1990. In the end it was decided that with 52 per cent of the reactor core melted down it could not be used again.

Michael Douglas's concerns about the environment had been considerably sharpened, and not just by making *The China Syndrome*. He was now a father. His son Cameron Morrell Douglas was born on 13 December 1978. The birth incidentally cut short another possibly promising acting career. Diandra Douglas, who was still not entirely thrilled with life in California, had been persuaded by her husband to play a small role in *The China Syndrome*. She is seen briefly as a production assistant in the newsroom of the television station where Jane Fonda's character works. Now with her new responsibilities as a mother she had to tear up her Screen Actors Guild card – which would not have distressed her too greatly – but she also had to realise that she had no chance of fulfilling her dreams of becoming a diplomat.

For Douglas, fatherhood was a major step. He knew that his own father had not made a success of it because he had had no proper role model. Douglas was more fortunate in that, although he was not his natural father, Bill Darrid was everything a boy could want in a father figure. For Michael Douglas, the birth of his son was something to be taken extremely seriously.

'Becoming a parent had made me realise that the only threads we have left in society come through the family structure,' he said. 'Hopefully people are getting back into being parents and enjoying it. Besides providing a strong base of love and security for my child, I would like specifically to encourage the development of will-power, stamina, and discipline. Like physical exercise those skills must be attained little by little over the years.'

There is still an element of hippie-dippy naivete in those comments but there is no doubt that Michael Douglas was very sincere in his intention to be the best father he could be for baby Cameron. Certainly, things might be a little better for him than they had been for his own father. In Kirk Douglas's case he was still struggling to establish himself as an actor and was in his first big Broadway role when Michael was born. Michael, however, believed he had his priorties right.

'I wanted to get something going professionally before I would focus on my personal life,' he explained in an interview not long after Cameron was born. 'Suddenly I fell in love and got married within weeks. Now after two years of marriage, including becoming a father, I know that my marriage is of the utmost importance to me.'

For Michael Douglas the success of *One Flew Over the Cuckoo's Nest* followed by the cause célèbre that was *The China Syndrome* meant he had well and truly arrived and had definitely got 'something going professionally'. He was, by any standards, the hottest young producer in Hollywood. Every producer needs to have a relationship with a studio and Douglas was no exception. Big Stick was looking for a housekeeping deal with one of the majors and was being courted shamelessly by all of them. In the end the decision was made to set up office at Columbia Pictures, who had been so supportive and instrumental in shaping the deal with produced *The China Syndrome*. It was a Columbia executive, after all, who had come up with the idea of bringing Jane Fonda in when the film looked dead in the water with the departure of Richard Dreyfuss.

The deal between Big Stick and Columbia was announced to the Hollywood trade papers in May 1979 by Frank Price, who was the president of the studio, and John Veitch who was head of production.

'We enthusiastically welcome Michael Douglas and his company to this relationship with Columbia,' said Price in a prepared statement. 'We are particularly pleased that he has selected Columbia for his production base and that we will have the opportunity to continue the association that has been so successful with *The China Syndrome*.'

In his reply, Michael Douglas, was equally generous.

'From the earliest production meetings and decisions to the overall marketing of the film,' said Douglas of *The China Syndrome*, 'the Columbia team has been significantly responsive, creative, and effective. We have worked together closely as film-making partners and I look forward to the projects we will be doing together.'

Both Price and Douglas were delighted with the deal which called for Big Stick to produce three films for the studio. In the end it would turn out to be a learning experience which would teach both of them a lesson.

A HARSH LESSON

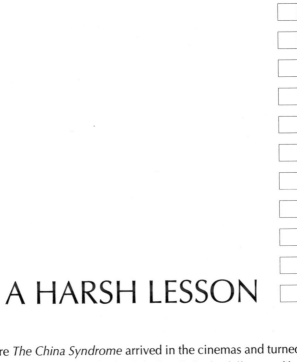

Even before *The China Syndrome* arrived in the cinemas and turned out to be a huge hit, Michael Douglas already had a follow-up film in the can. He was not involved in a producing capacity in this one, this was simply a straight actor for hire job. In August 1978, after he had finished filming the nuclear thriller he went directly on to a film which could not have been more different. Douglas would spend two months in Canada filming *Running*, a film which was supposed to capitalise on the fitness craze which was sending Americans out on to the streets in their millions as they jogged themselves thin. In simplistic terms *Running* was effectively *Rocky* in cross-trainers. Douglas plays Michael Andropolis, a character who is one of nature's losers.

'He's a guy who has never finished anything he started, who has constantly choked in the clutch,' Douglas explained. 'He doubts every damn thing about himself. Andropolis is the guy who I once was.'

This is an interesting observation from Douglas who was perhaps becoming a little more self-analytical with age. He obviously saw in Andropolis echoes of the young man who quit Santa Barbara first time round, and that may explain why he was so effusive about a script which was at best ordinary and at worst downright predictable. When he read it, he claims, he was moved to tears. Andropolis has, as Douglas points out, never seen anything through to the end. His wife leaves him for another man, he manages to lose his dead-end job, and although he was a promising athlete in college when the chips were down he was always found wanting. This is just the sort of scenario that breeds marathon runners, or at least it is in this improbable film. Andropolis decides he will train for a marathon, and despite being hopelessly outclassed and facing insuperable odds he naturally wins the Olympic gold medal.

To get himself in shape for his two months of filming in Toronto and New York, Douglas threw himself into the role. He had never prepared for any part like this. He started to train, he gave up smoking and as a consequence he lost more than a stone in weight. Despite writer-director Steven Stern's assurances that he would never have to run more than a few hundred yards on camera Douglas got himself into the sort of shape where he could run a mile in seven minutes, ideal marathon time.

'I have a wide streak of competitiveness and there is a good bit of the shark in me,' says Douglas of the drive to push himself in this role.

Certainly by the time he got to the end of his fitness programme he looked like a runner. The times early in his training regime when he would collapse with dry heaves, after running what were relatively short distances, were all worth it when anyone watches the marathon sequences in the film. They are far and away the best thing in an otherwise poor film. These scenes are so good that when Stern cuts from Douglas and other cast members to stock footage of the marathon from the 1976 Olympics in Montreal it's hard to work out who are the runners and who are the actors. In the end though it was all for nothing. We cannot judge how satisfying Douglas found the experience or how fulfilled he was creatively, but in empirical terms the film was a critical and box office disaster.

The timing of the release of *Running* was not ideal. The distributors waited until the end of 1979 to put the film into cinemas. By that stage Americans audiences, who were more concerned about the prospect of a US boycott of the 1980 Olympics in Moscow, seemed not to care to have the prospect of an American winning the Olympics against the odds thrust in their face. The distance between *Running* and *The China Syndrome* probably wasn't terribly helpful either. In March and April of 1979 Douglas was being profiled in most of the major magazines – *Cosmopolitan* called him 'The Thinking Girl's Sex Symbol' – but having done all that at the turn of the year there wasn't much more publicity mileage in Douglas for another film six months later. Releasing *Running* closer to *The China Syndrome* wouldn't have made it a better picture or got it more favourable reviews, but it just might have gained a little at the box office from the reflected heat of its star.

By the time *Running* came out Douglas was busy with other things. Big Stick was now comfortably ensconced at Columbia and he was looking forward to making some significant and important pictures. This was a major deal for both of them. Douglas was the hot young producer who had decided to hang his hat at Columbia, while they were the studio who were prepared to invest large amounts of money on his producerial instincts. It was something of a coup for both parties but Douglas may initially have felt he had the better of the deal.

The big advantage for an independent producer who throws his lot in with a studio is that there are no longer those tedious meetings where the budget has to be hand-knitted by scrabbling together money from various investors. Any film maker who is at a studio is fully funded. This was a housekeeping deal which meant that, as a matter of course, Columbia paid all of Big Stick's expenses for accommodation, staff and general development costs. As well as all of those tangible benefits there was also the access to the projects. As a matter of course any new production company coming on to the studio lot is invited to take a look at the inventory of existing scripts to see if there is something they might like to develop for themselves. This was a courtesy Douglas would take advantage of later in his career. If there was nothing there that caught the eye then the studio would underwrite the cost of acquiring something else, or in some cases buy it outright for the production company to make. Lew Wasserman, for example, when he was head of MCA which owned Universal, bought the rights to Thomas Keneally's *Schindler's Ark* – as it was called in book form – as a gift for Steven Spielberg to turn into *Schindler's List*.

For Douglas it was all upside, or so it seemed. All he had to do was make pictures and at the outset he was planning on perhaps one film a year. Given that it had taken him the best part of a decade to produce *One Flew Over the Cuckoo's Nest* and *The China Syndrome* this was perhaps a little more ambitious than it sounded. Going into the deal, however, everything seemed optimistic for all concerned. Although his three year deal was an exclusive producing contract, Douglas was even acting in another film which was to be produced by Columbia.

A Perfect Circle was supposed to be a sophisticated romantic comedy, which starred Jill Clayburgh as a harassed mathematics professor who goes to her father's wedding and falls for the son of his new bride. The stepson, played by Douglas, is a baseball player forced to retire early through injury. Clayburgh then spends the rest of the picture agonising over whether she should choose Douglas or her rather stuffy boyfriend, played by Charles Grodin. Before it was released the film had its title changed to *It's My Turn* but there was no disguising the fact that Douglas was still miscast. He has no real gift for sophisticated romantic comedy, although he would show later in his career that he could comfortably carry off black comedy which was more in tune with his own sense of humour. In films like this, however, he merely looks bland. *It's My Turn* had a higher profile than *Running* and was certainly nowhere near as critically vilified but it was still not a film whose virtues were worth shouting from the rooftops.

There was an awkward moment for Douglas when the film was released. There were stories circulating to the effect that he did not want to promote the film. Bearing in mind that this was a Columbia film and he had a separate deal with the studio the rumour could have proved embarrassing. Douglas, however, was quick to dismiss the stories, pointing out that he had merely said that after *The China Syndrome* he felt he was over-exposed, especially on television talk shows, so it might not be such a good idea to book him on Johnny Carson's couch or anywhere else for that matter. The whole thing turned out to be a storm in a teacup which quickly blew itself out.

By the time *It's My Turn* was released Douglas was almost half-way into his three year deal at Columbia without a single film of his own to show for it. His prediction of making one picture a year was turning out to be wildly optimistic. He had high hopes for his films and had even identified a number of projects that he wanted to make. There was a film about the inspirational American football coach Pop Warner which he had been preparing for two years, for example, and there was another science fiction story called *The Star Man* which he was also keen on. Columbia, for their part, were keen on this one too. It is the story of an alien who comes to earth after he picks up a message from a passing satellite. He meets a young woman after assuming the form of her late husband, and uses his time on earth to discover what it is like to be human. In the end, as she drives him to the staging point where he can return to his planet, they fall in love. He goes back to space but not without impregnating her, leaving her carrying his star-child.

Douglas dislikes science fiction more than any other genre. He has no interest in it and has never made a science fiction film, nor is he likely to. This one was different, for it was essentially a deeply human story which worked without any need for special effects or computer-generated imagery. Douglas liked this film a lot and Columbia seemed to share his enthusiasm for it – this was the studio, after all, which had backed Steven Spielberg when no one else would on *Close Encounters of the Third Kind*. The first thing they did was change the title from the clunky original to the more poetic and evocative *Starman*. The next thing they did was to pass on *E.T.* when Spielberg brought it to them because they were so high on *Starman*. This would be their *E.T.*

Although nothing had been done yet, Douglas remained confident. The studio boss, Frank Price, would remind him that good pictures take time. Price would often point out that *Tootsie*, which went on to be a colossal hit for Columbia, had been in development at the studio for four years. Douglas was suitably mollified, at least temporarily, and in January, 1981, he even signed another deal with the studio. This time it was an exclusive television production contract because he had it in mind to produce a mini-series based on Cortez and the Spanish conquest of the Americas.

Nevertheless the lack of progress on *Starman* frustrated Douglas. He had another adventure script which he had bought from a waitress-turned-screenwriter which he wanted to make as well, but this was moving forward even more slowly than *Starman*. Eventually *E.T.*, the film on which Columbia had passed in favour of *Starman*, was released and became the most successful film ever up to that date. Still there was no sign of *Starman*. The project was intriguing more than just Michael Douglas. The directors who considered it and all had various passes at it were a virtual Who's Who of hot young Hollywood talent. Adrian Lyne tried and failed, so too did John Badham. Michael Mann took a pass at it without success as did Tony Scott, but none of them could apparently make it work. By this stage Douglas was beginning to feel that the studio system might not be for him after all. Producing was taking up all of his time, he could not concentrate on any acting jobs, and the monolith which was Columbia Pictures was rapidly turning into an immovable object against which Douglas was a far from irresistible force.

Douglas had thrived on the spirit of the Sixties, that feeling of comradeship and togetherness on which *One Flew Over the Cuckoo's Nest* had flourished and become so successful. *The China Syndrome* was a little different in that it was his first introduction to big studio pragmatism. Now, the more he became involved in studio film-making, the more he was finding that this way of making pictures simply did not suit him at all.

'What has happened to the movie business is market research,' he said. 'You would think, and I did think, that here I am, I've produced two big movies, and I go to a studio with a new thing that I want to do. I've got a track record, but it turns out that it doesn't matter.'

Douglas was feeling bitter and frustrated and with good cause. This was not an experience he was used to. He was used to having a gut instinct and going with it, not having legions of junior executives give you notes on a project they had no vested interest in sponsoring because they had not generated it. The plain fact was that Douglas and Big Stick were simply one of many producers on the Columbia lot. He did not have the clout of, for example, Rastar Productions which was run by Ray Stark, the effective king maker at the studio. The Oscars and the box office grosses meant nothing, Douglas was merely a cog in the corporate wheel which was turning out movies like cars on an assembly line. His projects, no matter how dear or important they seemed to him, simply fell through the cracks and got lost in the system. In the end Douglas did what so many other producers and directors with development or first-look deals with studios have done. He let the clock run down. When the three-year deal was over, he and Columbia shook hands and parted company without a foot of film having been produced.

'My father taught me that a good business deal is one that is beneficial to both parties,' Douglas said after the Columbia deal had run its course. 'In that sense the Columbia deal was not a good business deal. I discovered that I work best in a funky little office somewhere with just a reader and a secretary.'

That was the way Michael Douglas liked to produce films and that was the way he would produce them from now on. He had been playing with the big boys and hadn't much enjoyed it, from now on it would be his ball, his playground, and his rules.

MICHAEL WHO?

The kind-hearted would describe Michael Douglas's three-year deal at Columbia as a disappointment for both parties, those inclined to be more blunt would call it an unmitigated disaster. Douglas left Columbia with two things. The first was a sense that he would never produce films for a big studio again, the second was Jack Brodsky who had been head of marketing at Columbia. Douglas and Brodsky had met on *The China Syndrome* and poaching Brodsky to come to Big Stick as its executive vice-president was one of Douglas's first tasks at the studio. Douglas also left something behind at the studio in the shape of *Starman*, which was slowly but surely inching its way towards the cameras. Although his deal had lapsed, Douglas was still and would remain the producer of the picture.

The effect that the Columbia deal had on Douglas's career can be gauged by an article in the April 1984 issue of *Esquire* magazine. It asked simply 'Whatever Happened to Michael Douglas?' pointing out that in the time he had been at Columbia he had gone from being a hotshot producer to one whose projects got swallowed up by the system . On the other hand, just some eight months later the same Michael Douglas would be named Producer of the Year by the National Association of Theater Owners who run America's cinemas. After several years of inactivity, things were about to start happening and fast.

Evidently hog-tied as a producer, Douglas was equally unable to find work as an actor. He has at several stages in his career taken a break from acting, insisting that producing is more satisfying. On this occasion, however, the decision was not his. A ski-ing accident and a resulting serious blood infection provided a combination sufficiently potent to keep him from appearing in front of the cameras. A frustrated Douglas spent his time cooling his heels with Diandra and Cameron while he looked around for something that was worth producing. He admits that after *The China Syndrome* he found himself being sent 'every wacko off-the-wall script about every problem there was in the world'. Frustrated and depressed, he increasingly found himself turning to that adventure script which he had bought while he was at Columbia and had taken away with him. Perhaps this would be the moment to spend some time developing it further?

Before that, however, he did finally manage to squeeze in another film as an actor. In *The Star Chamber*, which was released in the summer of 1983, Douglas played a young judge who was becoming increasingly dismayed by the judicial system. He is obliged, because of a technicality, to free a murderer even though he is convinced beyond doubt of his guilt. Sensing his frustration Douglas is tapped by a shadowy organisation of elder judges called The Group. They convene in secret to review such cases and pass the appropriate sentence. Douglas is at first an enthusiastic convert but when a genuinely innocent suspect is convicted by The Group he turns whistle-blower. The Group then hires a hit man to eliminate Douglas so they can continue their institutionalised vigilantism. Naturally Douglas survives and The Group is exposed.

The Star Chamber was directed and co-written by Peter Hyams and while it was not the summer hit that everyone was anticipating, Hyams was impressed with his star, even if he does give the lie to Douglas's carefully cultivated nice guy image.

'He's one of the smartest guys in Hollywood,' says Hyams, 'an extraordinary producer, very perceptive. And by no means a pussycat. We had a couple of trailer-rattling fights . . . but never ever about anything other than how to make the movie better. Never ego. He's just really bright, he understands material.'

Hyams was not the first director with whom Douglas had crossed swords nor would he be the last. But, as Hyams says, it is seldom about personal status and invariably about the picture.

'I try to be diplomatic but if it gets ugly I'll mix it up with anybody,' Douglas said once. 'I've got no problems with that at all . . . I didn't get this far just by being a nice guy.'

Although it wasn't a box office hit *The Star Chamber* still turned out to be a significant film in Michael Douglas's career because it cemented his professional relationship with Sherry Lansing. Over the next few years these two, and her co-producer Stanley Jaffe, would make Hollywood headlines together. Lansing had spotted Douglas when he made *Coma* when she was an executive at MGM. She was vice-president in charge of production at Columbia when *The China Syndrome* was being made, before moving to Fox which made *The Star Chamber*. Lansing was convinced that Michael Douglas had some rare qualities on both sides of the camera and she had very definitely taken an interest in his career. In a few years Lansing would play her part in the film which would establish Douglas as a star and a producer to be reckoned with.

Diane Thomas was a waitress in Los Angeles in the late seventies. In a city where almost every waiter, waitress and bus boy is waiting to be discovered it was no surprise that she too wanted to be in the movies. She had no dreams of stardom, instead she wanted to be a writer. Whenever she had any time off after her shifts she would plug away at a script she had been writing. It was an action-adventure story laced with comedy and romance, about a bookish writer of bodice-ripping romances who is sent a treasure map and winds up on the adventure of a lifetime with a man who is the spitting image of the roguish heroes of her books.

In 1979 the script was doing the rounds of agents and studios, none of whom had seen any potential in it. Eventually it ended up at Big Stick where Jack Brodsky finally read it. He liked what he saw and recommended it to Douglas. Within weeks Diane Thomas had a cheque for $250,000 and Michael Douglas had *Romancing the Stone*. The film would go on to be a huge international success, a crowd-pleasing hit in almost every country in the world, so naturally it took Douglas almost five years to get it off the ground. The major difficulty was that when the script came to him *Raiders of the Lost Ark* was still two years away and people could not grasp the concept of a story which mingled high adventure, belly laughs, and sweeping romance all in the same two-hour picture. After Spielberg's spectacular hit it became a much easier prospect to pitch to studios. In the end *Romancing the Stone* was a roaring box-office smash hit. The budget was less than $10 million and it took $117 million at the box office. It made movie stars of Michael Douglas, Kathleen Turner, and Danny De Vito, and no one who saw it could have believed that it would have been so difficult to produce.

The first problem came in the casting. The actress playing Joan Wilder, the romantic novelist who desperately wants romance in her own life, would have to carry the picture. She would, by turns, have to be strong, smart, funny, vulnerable, and sexy. The audience would have to care for her when she was in peril but at the same time be convinced that she was strong enough to look after herself. Douglas's first choice for the role was Debra Winger who was intrigued by the character, but Douglas apparently didn't think she would be up to the physical and emotional stresses of filming for months in the jungles of Mexico. Others were considered but finally it was Joe Wizan, the then-president of production at Fox where the film had ended up, who recommended Kathleen Turner.

Like almost everyone else, Douglas's perception of Turner was as the sultry Barbara Stanwyck style man-eater from Lawrence Kasdan's *Body Heat*. However, he was also aware that she had proved to be a wonderful comic foil for Steve Martin in *The Man With Two Brains*. As a producer he was sensible enough to put the good of the film over his own misgivings. He was uncertain but the minute he saw her screen test he knew that he had found his Joan Wilder. If only it had been so easy finding Jack Colton, the dashing adventurer who drags her halfway across Colombia.

Colton is, in essence, a swaggering cross between Indiana Jones and Kirk Douglas with a touch of Burt Lancaster thrown in. They approached the usual suspects and both Harrison Ford and Clint Eastwood declined, so too did Sylvester Stallone. Douglas even went to his old friend Jack Nicholson who also politely decided this was not for him. As a producer who was also an experienced actor Douglas was smart enough to know why they were turning it down. There was nothing wrong with the picture, the problem was that it was Turner's picture. *Romancing the Stone* is not Jack Colton's story it's Joan Wilder's story, which is why a great many major male stars passed. In the end Douglas decided that the best thing to do was to play the role himself. It was the best decision he could possibly make, both for himself and for the film. Douglas was perfect in a role in which he was just starting to define what we would come to recognise as his screen persona. Colton was edgy and rascally and downright dishonest, a refreshing change from the roles Douglas had played in every film except *The China Syndrome*. Colton had an edge to him which Douglas relished playing. In addition it was the first time on screen that he had confronted his father's image, and actively invited the comparison by appearing in a role which would have been meat and drink for Kirk Douglas.

The key supporting role of Ralph, the diminutive and luckless gangster who pursues them across the jungles of Central America in their search for a giant emerald, was tailor made for Danny De Vito.

In the years since *One Flew Over the Cuckoo's Nest*, De Vito had established himself as a major TV star. The character of Louie De Palma, the irascible despatcher in the hit comedy series *Taxi*, was not so far away from the corrupt, venal, double-dealing Ralph. Putting all three of them together was a casting marriage made in heaven. Handling this serendipitous bundle of talent was neophyte director Robert Zemeckis. He would go on to direct huge hits such as the *Back to the Future* trilogy, *Forrest Gump* and *What Lies Beneath* but, up till this point, he had one film to his credit, the cult film *Used Cars*. Douglas, however, had no problem with someone who was so relatively inexperienced. No matter who the director is, Douglas subjects them all to the same litmus test, but more so if he is also the producer.

'What you do is, you just talk it out,' he explains. 'You talk it through as an actor. I do a lot of my producing unofficially as an actor. I just make a point and I make the point to a director as an insecure actor, whether I'm insecure or not. I say "I really need to talk this all out." We take the script and I force him, even if it might be a lazy director who has not thought about it, I make him talk before we start shooting the movie. I say "Let me hear the movie through your eyes" and it forces the director to have to talk it out. Obviously in many cases they always know but it allows you to know exactly what the director is planning, what he wants, number one. Then, number two, it gives you a sense of the pace of the picture, the dramatic pace and where it's got to be picked up. And, number three, it gives you a sense of what he needs from you, where he needs conflict, where he needs humour. I analyse all these things, I'm used to doing it now informally.'

Douglas does concede that he is more inclined to work with younger directors who are less likely to be autocratic and less likely to be threatening. That, he insists, is not because he wants a director he can intimidate, but because he has a lot to say about the outcome of the finished film, he is keen to strike a balance as early as possible in the proceedings. Once that tone is set and demarcation lines are established then the collaboration can proceed to the benefit of everyone involved. One thing which Douglas does dislike is the double duty of producing and acting; he would rather do one or the other. Doing both is a distraction and there is no doubt that in *Romancing the Stone*, his character is under-developed. Good and all as he was, an actor with less on his mind might have made more of the role. The film was always Kathleen Turner's but Douglas delivered it to her on a silver salver. Turner concedes that Douglas was less than fair to himself as an actor and he agrees that he was more concerned with her character than his own.

'We were doing a scene, Kathleen and I,' he remembers, 'and as producer I made certain concessions. This is where you hurt yourself as an actor. I said "Okay, get Kathleen's coverage because we are going to lose it. Let's be sure we get her coverage and then we'll pick up mine some other time." That's not the way you'd like to do it as an actor, but that's the way you've got to do it as the producer.'

This was one of those situations which would occur several times in Michael Douglas's career. It was an internal argument between the practicality of the producer and the vanity of the actor. It is to his credit that whenever he has these rows with himself Michael Douglas the actor generally finishes second to Michael Douglas the producer.

'We're all vain, so sure you care,' he told *Rolling Stone* not long after the film came out. 'Do I think in hindsight that I should have protected or developed my part more in *Romancing the Stone*? Maybe yes. *Romancing the Stone* made Kathleen Turner's career. She's a big star now. But the picture was about her character, so if you're going to wear both hats you've got to be a producer first. *Romancing* was about the growth of a woman, a young woman going from this to that, meeting this guy, and the adventure that she had. If we had screwed around with that I wouldn't have made myself a star because maybe the film would have been a turkey. Stars are made out of pictures which are successful. I've got a healthy ego. And we all have our own ways and styles of approaching things. The best, the most satisfying way, for me is to make the best picture.'

The conditions under which they were filming on location in Mexico were appalling. Torrential rain dogged almost every day of the shoot to the point where they were beginning to have problems in matching the shots in continuity terms. It was a nightmare but if Douglas the actor was being pushed to the side, Douglas the producer was about to come of age. According to Turner, the rain was so relentless that the roads to the set were in constant danger of being washed away. A determined Douglas was not going to lose a foot of film which he didn't have to. If there was no road then he would build one. His solution to the problem was a fleet of eighty trucks loaded with gravel, which were standing by from the early hours of every morning to repair the roads when they washed away.

'We called it "Douglasland",' says Turner. 'He made roads wherever he thought we had to go. I mean, this is the man's indominatable spirit. He'd just say, "Oh, is the road gone? Then we'll make one."'

Romancing the Stone was shot in Mexico in the middle of the wettest weather the country had seen in more than thirty years. As well as washed-out roads, they had to contend with tropical storms and landslides. On one occasion the crew came close to death when they were hit without warning by a storm in the middle of one sequence. They were shooting on a road on the side of a mountain when suddenly the mountainside simply gave way. A huge boulder – Douglas describes it as being as big as a car – came plummeting down and landed exactly where the camera crew had been standing. As it was, one man had his leg broken, Turner still has scars on her knee from cuts she sustained, and another crew member broke an arm. But as Douglas points out, had it happened five minutes earlier, when they had been filming with a full crew, they could have lost perhaps seventy people. This was a nightmare and this was only the first week of filming.

The scene they were shooting was the one in which their rickety old bus comes careering out of control down the mountain and collides with a jeep. Having lost their transport Jack and Joan are forced to walk. They only take a few paces when the road slips away from them and Joan slithers down a giant mud-slide, closely followed by Jack who ends up with his head in her crotch. It is the most famous scene in the film and, appropriately enough, Douglas told *Playboy* magazine how it had come about.

'The slide was in there as a sequence in the script,' he explained, 'but the ending – my landing face-first between Kathleen's legs – came up on a story board. Stunt guys did most of the slide, but we had to do sections for close ups. I did the last part of it in one take but there was a lot of preparation – lining Kathleen up with her legs spread, taking careful aim – that needed my classic mud-diving expertise.'

The stunt was a classic. Jeannie Epper who doubled for Turner won the award for Most Spectacular Stunt of the Year, and that one single shot did more than anything to promote the film. It was used in commercials, in trailers, on television shows, on chat shows. If ever a movie generated a must-see buzz on the strength of one sequence it was that one. Audiences loved it. *Romancing the Stone* was a phenomenal success and in the movie-making climate of the mid-1980s that meant only one thing; there would have to be a sequel. Douglas could see their point.

'People just loved *Romancing the Stone*,' he says. 'The mix of action, adventure, comedy and most of all the romance between those two characters. People really wanted to know what happened to the characters Kathleen and I played. *Romancing* opened very nicely and just kept going on and on and on, and all of a sudden people started screaming "Sequel!"'

Douglas had no real problem with a sequel. Where he did have a problem was with a studio, which wanted a sequel in the cinemas barely eighteen months after the original had been released.

JEWS IN DENIAL

The clamour for a sequel to *Romancing the Stone* began within weeks of it being released. It opened in American cinemas on 30 March 1984 and Douglas remembers having a break at home when people started asking him what had happened to Jack and Joan. As a producer he has always acted on instinct and his radar started to tell him that there might well be another picture in these two. He floated the idea to the studio in June as a possible project and they came back to him in August. Twentieth Century Fox, who had by that stage counted up their share of the picture's $77 million American box office, thought a sequel would be a good idea. Not only that, it would be a good idea for the holiday season at the end of 1985.

At that stage Douglas had absolutely nothing. He had no script, he had no stars, and he had no screenwriter. Dianne Thomas had shown such promise with that first script that she was now under contract to Steven Spielberg and could not write the sequel. In any case Douglas really had no idea about what the sequel should involve except that as well as himself and Turner it should also involve Danny De Vito. He felt De Vito's comic talents were part of the 'X factor' which had made the first film so successful. The only other idea he had, for obvious reasons, was that it should not involve jungles or rain forests. He knew it would be tight but he felt that, if everything went right, he could just deliver the picture on the schedule Fox wanted. Even so, he did not commit himself straight away.

One of the reasons for resting up after the rigours of filming and publicising *Romancing the Stone* was that Douglas had another job lined up, a straight acting job this time. He was to appear in Richard Attenborough's screen version of the hit Broadway musical *A Chorus Line* in which he would play the autocratic Zach, the voice in the darkness who has the power to make or break the dancers. Douglas took neither star billing nor a star salary in the film but even so Attenborough had to fight for him.

There was a great deal of resentment towards Attenborough directing *A Chorus Line* in the first place. American directors including Bob Fosse and Mike Nichols had said it could not be done, so he was automatically seen as some kind of upstart immigrant Brit for trying to muscle in on their territory. It didn't matter that he was a multiple-Oscar winner for his previous film *Gandhi* – indeed that may have added to the problem, for there was still a simmering resentment in some quarters because *Gandhi* had beaten *E.T.* on Oscar night. Nonetheless Attenborough was going to do *A Chorus Line* and he was going to do it with Michael Douglas.

'I don't know that Dick thought of anyone else but Michael for the role,' remembers Diana Hawkins, Attenborough's long-time producing partner. 'He said to Embassy, who were funding the film, "'I want Michael Douglas to play Zach" and they said, "Michael Douglas couldn't act his way out of a paper bag." Not only is that patently untrue but it is a horrible thing to say about anyone. I think that . . . we got to a point where Dick said 'If I can't have Michael then we can forget the whole thing.'

In the end Attenborough won the battle and Douglas was cast. The fact that he wasn't taking a big salary and would provide some sort of name recognition, even without star billing, may have played a part. This was a role which meant a lot to Douglas for a number of reasons.

'Earlier in my life,' he recalled, ' I was strongly influenced by my father. I reacted to that by shying away from a lot of his mannerisms and characteristics and typical kinds of parts – the stuff you'd expect to see him play. I did censor myself a lot early on ... That censorship ended with *A Chorus Line*.'

In Attenborough's film Douglas had, for the first time, the chance to play someone who was really not terribly pleasant. Jack Colton definitely had echoes of his father's swagger, but Zach had strong undertones of the sort of driven obsession which Kirk Douglas could bring to roles such as *Champion*. All those bland self-righteous characters he had played in the early days of his career were definitely a reaction against his father. He was almost 40 now, it was time to embrace the fact that he was his father's son rather than fight against it. Even though he favours his mother more in looks, he was reaching that stage where in certain angles he looked like his father. Certainly there are times when if you close your eyes and just listen, you could be hearing his father's voice. The acorn, as it turned out, had not fallen terribly far from the tree but it was time surely to celebrate that rather than resist it. Douglas had long since forgiven his father for his absenteeism when he was a child, they were now even talking about doing a picture together. He had shaken off any suggestion of advancement in his career through nepotism and it was time to come out and be Kirk Douglas's son and be proud of it.

Having got the part that he wanted in *A Chorus Line*, Douglas finally committed himself to filming a sequel to *Romancing the Stone*. It would be called *Jewel of the Nile* and it would have to be shot back-to-back with his film for Attenborough if it was to meet its projected release date. Douglas later claimed he was a glutton for the sort of high-stakes gamble which this entailed.

'I guess it's the adult equivalent of what I liked to do as a kid – high diving, racing motor bikes,' he said.

A Chorus Line was shot in the Mark Hellinger Theatre on Broadway. To make things a little easier, Douglas took a dressing room which was not being used and converted it into a production office for Jewel of the Nile. Although vital, the part of Zach was not a large one and he had time to put one film into production while he was acting in another. That may be why he was so happy to be simply acting for Attenborough. Whenever Attenborough, who also produces his own pictures, ran into a problem Douglas would of course be sympathetic, but at the same time he was just an actor so it didn't really concern him too much.

'Everybody else was running around dealing with crisis after crisis, the way I usually do,' he explained. 'But because I was only acting I sat around sucking on this big old cigar, looking at the beautiful ceiling, and enjoying every minute of it . . . Compared with the sort of sensitive, morally righteous characters I had played in the past – except for Jack Colton – here was a chance to play somebody obsessed and not very nice. It was also an interesting acting exercise. Ninety per cent of the time I had to concentrate on a bunch of cement bags on stage, pretending the dancers were actually there.'

While Romancing the Stone was being a big hit Starman finally went in front of the cameras. Douglas had hankered after the lead role himself, suspecting that it could be a significant departure from the roles he had played in his Coma, It's My Turn and The Star Chamber. The blandness of those last three pictures had contributed to their lack of success at the box office and this was too big a film for someone without a track record. In the end Douglas stepped aside for the good of the picture and the part was played by Jeff

Bridges, who received an Oscar nomination for one of the best performances of a distinguished career. The woman whose dead husband the alien imitates was played by Karen Allen, and by the end of the film there wasn't a dry eye in the house.

Starman was also a departure for its director. Although names such as Adrian Lyne, Tony Scott and Michael Mann had been bandied about, in the end the man behind the camera was John Carpenter. A veteran of genre movies such as *Dark Star, Assault on Precinct 13, Hallowe'en* and *Escape From New York*, Carpenter showed a sensitivity with this film which both captivated and astounded critics as well as endearing itself to audiences. *Starman* took almost $30 million at the box office in December 1984 but it was never the hit it should have been, for films which have such a troubled production history tend to be tainted by it when they finally arrive in cinemas. His involvement with other projects meant that by the time *Starman* finally shot, Douglas's day to day responsibilities as a producer had diminished significantly. Nonetheless it was still his picture and one of which he could be proud.

From his office in the Mark Hellinger Theate, Douglas was slowly but surely pulling together the threads of what would become *The Jewel of the Nile*. Fox had left him to his own devices until such times as he had a script. He had outlined some ideas to screenwriters Marc Rosenthal and Lawrence Konner and by November he finally had a first draft. As he had promised this one did not involve jungles but it did involve deserts. The story takes up events six months after *Romancing the Stone* finished. Jack and Joan have sailed off in the yacht from the end of that picture and have pitched up in the South of France. They are still together, they are still in love, but they are bored. Jack hankers after more adventure, Joan wants to write another book – a serious novel this time. Eventually, through a shady character called Omar, they hear of the Jewel of the Nile. Instantly imagining untold wealth they set off in search of this fabulous gem, closely followed by De Vito's Ralph who has got word of their plans. Instead the Jewel of the Nile turns out to be a guru whom they end up shepherding across the Sudan and through a holy war.

Now that he had a script Douglas felt that the movie was do-able and told Fox they could have their Christmas release. Over the holidays he took a break and went back to Santa Barbara with Diandra and Cameron to work on revisions and rewrites. By January 1985 he was ready to start production on an epic film which would be the tent-pole of a major studio's holiday line-up less than eleven months away. It was an act of uncharacteristic hubris even for a gambler such as Douglas, and it would very soon backfire on him.

Douglas had lost his screenwriter to Steven Spielberg and now he had lost his director too. Robert Zemeckis had been snapped up after *Romancing the Stone* to direct *Back to the Future* for Spielberg. Instead Douglas chose Lewis Teague, whose previous films were the modestly successful horror films *Cujo* and *Alligator*. Douglas claims to have chosen him because he liked the quirky black humour Teague had brought to his films. Locations were chosen – Morocco rather than Egypt or Israel which didn't really offer the right facilities – and Teague and the production team were despatched to sort out specific locations. It was now January and filming was due to begin in April.

The Jewel of the Nile quickly became a troubled production. Almost from the word go there were serious problems. Once they finally got on location there were so many difficulties with weather, props, crew, and almost everything you could think of, the cast and crew started to refer to their film as 'Jews in Denial'. The first hint of difficulties came in March when Douglas, who had by now finished *A Chorus Line*, decided to go and check out progress for himself. On that last night on the Attenborough picture they had shot all night before Douglas said his farewells and left the *Chorus Line* set to head straight to the airport.

The *Jewel of the Nile* production team had based itself at the Victorine Studios in Nice, which they decided would be their jumping-off point for Morocco. But, with six weeks to go before shooting began, Douglas himself got to Morocco and found that nothing had been done. He also found out that since it was almost a four-hour flight from Nice to North Africa, the Victorine Studios wasn't much of a jumping-off point to anywhere. Almost eighty per cent of the filming would have to be done in Morocco, yet less than two months before they were due to start there wasn't a single location confirmed and they didn't even have a location production office.

Douglas's reaction was surprising. There was no bluster, there were no tantrums, there were no recriminations. He simply went to his hotel room and wept. He cried and cried and cried as the enormity of the situation descended on him. He realised he had made a terrible mistake and he could end up squandering millions of dollars. Everything he had done up to now, the reputation he had won, the battles he had fought, the successes at the box office, could all be poured away as if they had never existed.

Romancing the Stone was a nightmare but it was one which he had overcome. That success made him think he could handle whatever came at him, but instead he found himself facing a different kind of nightmare. The only option it seemed was to phone Fox and pull the plug on the picture. If he called it off now they would have to wait three or four months because of the weather before they could film again – which would mean Fox would have to wait until summer 1986 before they could release it.

'If the filming had spilled over into the summer, in Morocco, it would have meant a 100 degree plus nightmare,' he recalls. 'That was when I heard this screaming voice inside me shout "Here you go. Life's been real good. You've been waiting for someone to do something really bad to you and this is it."'

A man of fierce competitive instincts, Douglas was reluctant to throw in the towel just yet. He took a metaphorical deep breath and stepped back from the situation. One phone call to his brother Joel, a co-producer on the picture, brought him out on the next plane to Casablanca. When they were younger Michael had always been the stronger and more resilient of the brothers, he was the one who had looked after Joel when he needed it. Now they were grown it was Joel's turn to repay the favour.

'He covers my back, especially when I'm tied up acting,' says Michael of his professional relationship with his brother. 'There's a lot of financing going on, deals being made, kick-back arrangements happening, especially in a place like Morocco. So you have to have somebody you can trust.'

Together the brothers Douglas took the production in hand. They were less than six weeks away from the start of filming on a $20 million production. People were fired, locations were sorted out, contracts were nailed down as they raced around Morocco to set everything else in train. Michael Douglas had to return to Hollywood where he was presenting at the Academy Awards, but Joel stayed on site to make sure everything was done.

The next blow came while Douglas was back in California. A week before the Oscars, Joel had to call him to tell him that there had been a plane crash and the production designer, the location manager, and a unit pilot had been killed. They had been scouting locations in the Atlas Mountains when they ran into a storm. They were missing for four days before rescuers found the wreckage of the plane and the bodies of the passengers. The storm had forced them down and they had crashed into the foothills of the mountains barely 30 miles from the airport at Fez. There was a growing feeling among the local crew that the production was cursed and Douglas concedes he was just starting to believe it himself.

The deaths of three crew members blighted the production and no one could muster any enthusiasm for what was after all only a film. Then came another blow. Not a tragedy in human terms, but a potential disaster in terms of the film. Two weeks before they were due to start filming Kathleen Turner announced that she didn't want to do the film. She claimed she was unhappy with the script, which rendered her character a stereotypical female and put all the attention on to Jack Colton.

Turner felt strongly that the script was nowhere near as good as *Romancing the Stone* and she felt they should wait until it was. There was also for Turner the added incentive of Steven Spielberg, rapidly becoming something of a stalking horse for this picture, who had offered her a role in *The Money Pit* which would clash with *The Jewel of the Nile*. Douglas intervened. He reminded her that she had made a lot of money from the first film and he also pointed out that she wasn't the only one missing out on opportunities. He and De Vito and everyone else were missing out on jobs while they were committed to this film. Having played the moral card without success Douglas got tough. First he let it be known that he would replace her rather than postpone the picture, and both he and Fox followed this up with the threat of a lawsuit for breach of contract. Finally the situation was resolved. Douglas persuaded Diane Thomas, who was busy with other things, to punch up the lead characters and resolve some of the problems.

Filming began on schedule in Fez in Morocco in April 1984. It was a shoot which succeeded in spite of itself. There were constant problems with missing materials, deliveries going astray and endless bureaucratic nightmares with local officials.

'My motivation on *The Jewel of the Nile* was the hysteria of the producer,' says Michael Douglas. 'We had customs problems, and lost equipment, and we couldn't get permits and on and on. We were there during Ramadan, which is an Islamic religious holiday. So you don't get a lot of preparation time between producing and acting. As a matter of fact I take my hat off to Kathleen Turner. There was many a time when we would be doing a scene and someone would say "Excuse me but the teamsters are about to go on strike." And I'd have to go. She was always wonderful about that. She could get back into it. But, it's good for concentration and that's where my *Streets of San Francisco* training really came in handy for me.'

Eventually *The Jewel of the Nile* finished its location shooting on schedule. The cast and crew toasted the final scenes with champagne, there were fireworks, and then they came back to Hollywood to finish the picture.

There was one final desperate blow for Michael Douglas. In October, as the finishing post-production touches were being put to *The Jewel of the Nile*, Diane Thomas was killed in a car crash. She was driving a white Porsche which Douglas had given her for her uncredited work on fixing his picture.

'She was a close friend and she gave me a lot of insight into stuff I wouldn't otherwise have known,' says Douglas.

Douglas was devastated. As a mark of his respect and regard for her talent he would later endow a screenwriting fellowship with her name at UCLA.

A MAN ON THE EDGE

As luck would have it *A Chorus Line* and *The Jewel of the Nile* were both ear-marked by their respective distributors as their major holiday releases and appeared in cinemas within days of each other in December 1985. Although it had originally been slated for a smaller release, the Attenborough musical was opening on almost 1000 screens. *The Jewel of the Nile*, on the other hand, would open in 1200 cinemas with a further 400 added on Christmas Day. Michael Douglas was more than a little concerned about two of his pictures showing such dominance in the marketplace. Basically Americans going out to the movies over the holidays were faced with more than 2500 screens showing Michael Douglas films.

Douglas himself knew which was the riskier project.

'I hope *A Chorus Line* does as well as it can do,' he said at the time. 'I think successful movies only help breed other successes. It becomes a Christmas of movie talk, and that helps everybody out.'

Perhaps as expected *The Jewel of the Nile* was the more

successful of the pair. Although some critics carped, it was generally well received and audiences loved the film. They flocked to see Douglas, Turner, and De Vito back in harness and the film was a major box office success in its own right, as well as making more money than the first one, which is rare for a sequel. *A Chorus Line* was not so fortunate. Not only did it not do well at the box office, it was also slaughtered by the critics. Richard Attenborough would have been wounded by the comments but he was old enough and experienced enough to take them in his stride. He felt particularly hurt for Douglas, but especially for the rest of the young, and largely unknown, cast.

'I knew that the reviews would not be good,' says Attenborough, 'but what I had not anticipated was the degree or the extent . . . I knew it was a terrible risk but I didn't think they would be so vitriolic and, of course, they were wrong . . . I think you could perhaps argue that the concept of shooting *A Chorus Line* as I did was wrong, you should never have done it that way, you should never have stayed in the theatre. But to say it was badly executed was just not correct. The kids were wonderful and Clive Barnes, the man who was known as "The Butcher of Broadway", wrote an article defending them which ran on the front page of his newspaper. He rode in and crucified all of the film critics, he said they knew nothing about it. He said "I am a dance critic, I know" and I think he even said it was the best dance movie he had ever seen . . . But by this stage the film had been on for two weeks and the damage had been done.'

With both films opening in America at the same time, Douglas then had another six months promoting *The Jewel of the Nile* around the rest of the world. By the summer of 1986, when he finally had the chance to lift his head, he was exhausted. He promised himself he would never again act in a film on which he was also the producer.

'I enjoy the challenge of producing,' he said, 'since you're required to stretch in all directions and it allows me to understand the whole of the film-making process. I enjoy being involved in all of it, while as an actor you are one small part of the picture. But producing is a challenge in which you never get off, really. It's always a struggle to complete another job. So it's essential to pick projects you are absolutely in love with since it takes so long to get a film made. You have to wake up in the middle of the night thinking about the project, as you would with a woman you've just got to have. You have to think about it all the time, taking notes beside your bed when you wake up at night. That's the only thing that will carry you through the amount of time it takes to make a movie. *Cuckoo's Nest* took six years, *China Syndrome* four, *Romancing the Stone* five years. That's a long time knocking on doors.'

There was one final happy note as far as the disaster-stricken *Jewel of the Nile* was concerned – it made Douglas a pop star of sorts. Douglas, Turner and De Vito formed a Motown style backing group for Billy Ocean in the video for the film's theme song *When the Going Gets Tough*. None of their moves would cause The Temptations to lose any sleep, but they are plainly all having the time of their lives. The song was a big hit and even gave Billy Ocean his first number one hit in the United Kingdom.

Once he had finished with his foray into the pop charts, Michael Douglas's next priority was to spend some time away from it all with his family. He was aware that Diandra was unhappy and that life in Hollywood was far from ideal for her. So the two of them went off to Mustique with young Cameron to spend some quality time together.

'When you're wearing both hats as actor and producer you don't have enough hours in the day to spend with your family,' says Douglas. 'The only way we've found is to work and then call it off for three or four months. Basically I'm a very lazy guy. It's easy for me to hang around the house.'

Having sworn never again to produce and act at the same time, Douglas was concentrating on his production work for a large part of 1986. Although *Starman* was not a big hit, it had proved popular enough on video to interest the television networks in a spin-off series. Douglas, as a legacy of his television deal at Columbia, was the executive producer on the short-lived series in which Robert Hays took the Jeff Bridges role. There were other television projects which Douglas was keen to develop, especially that Conquistador mini-series. As for films, his political instincts led him to a property called *Zoo Plane* which was written by his friend the political cartoonist Gary Trudeau, creator of the newspaper strip *Doonesbury*. The film, which would be about the journalists who follow the campaign trail, was to have been directed by Richard Lester. Douglas was also, as he would do from time to time throughout his career, making noises about directing a film himself. So far his experience was confined to a couple of episodes of *The Streets of San Francisco* but there is no doubt that the idea of making a feature film tempted him.

There was one project which interested him more than the others. Several years previously Douglas had acquired a book called *Virgin Kisses* by Gloria Nagy, which he thought would make a great movie. He enthused about it to anyone who would listen, including Lynn Hirschberg in a *Rolling Stone* interview at the beginning of 1986.

'It's about a bored Beverly Hills psychiatrist who has seen everything,' he told her. 'I think he cheated his way through medical school, he's got the right wife, got a good practice. And a woman comes into his office. A pleasant-looking woman, but not your normal Beverly Hills-type thing. And there is something about her that makes this man crazy. It's about lust. It's about how a man destroys all of his ethical practices and codes and starts hypnotising, and his practice falls apart. And he's just gone.'

Douglas also confessed to Hirschberg that, even though he had acquired the property many years ago, he was unable to get anyone interested in making the film. Perhaps the time had come to try again. Certainly by this stage his five films as a producer – *One Flew Over the Cuckoo's Nest*, *The China Syndrome*, *Romancing the Stone*, *Starman* and *Jewel of the Nile* – had taken more than half a billion dollars at the box office. In addition he was now an established star. His performances in 1985 had led him to be named the fourth most popular star of the year, behind Sylvester Stallone, Eddie Murphy and Harrison Ford, by *Box Office* magazine. This might well be the time to have another attempt at *Virgin Kisses*.

As it happened a short time earlier Douglas had met his friend Stanley Jaffe, the producer, on an aeroplane. Making small talk they brought each other up to date on what they were doing. Douglas mentioned *Virgin Kisses* and Jaffe, interested, said that he was developing a similar property. He and Sherry Lansing were now independent co-producers and they had acquired a script called *Fatal Attraction* in which a man's one night stand with a psychotic woman almost destroys his life and his family. The men commented on the similarities of the projects, the talk turned to other things, and when the flight ended they went their separate ways. Jaffe, however, had not let it go at idle chit-chat. When he and Lansing next met to review their various projects he suggested that Douglas would be perfect casting for *Fatal Attraction*. Not surprisingly Lansing, who had been following his career with interest, agreed.

Lansing felt that Douglas was perfect for the part of Dan Gallagher, the luckless adulterer. She knew, from having seen his work , that he was capable of making the audience feel sympathy for the character he was playing, and if the audience did not sympathise with Dan Gallagher then *Fatal Attraction* just wouldn't work. Lansing also felt they would be getting a bonus with Douglas who was not only emerging as a leading man, but also thought like a producer. Throughout the long process of shopping the project around from studio to studio Douglas helped in re-tooling it, rewriting it, and generally boosting morale. He would always remind them of how long it had taken to find a home for *Romancing the Stone* and point out that the delay was not necessarily a bad thing. By the time that film was finally made, according to Douglas, he had aged into the part and was a much more convincing Jack Colton than he would have been to start.

There is no doubt that, as it was written, *Fatal Attraction* was a difficult project not least because the audience is being asked to sympathise with a man who is cheating on his wife. It becomes a question of the audience seeing that a psychotic woman threatening his family must be of greater concern to them than his infidelity. The script was re-written several times once Douglas came aboard with him specifically in mind. Nevertheless there were still directors and studios who did not believe that the audience would get Dan Gallagher. Brian De Palma, for example, was briefly attached to the project but left because he could not see Douglas as someone with whom the audience would sympathise. Columbia, who had originally been interested, decided they didn't want to do it but not before slipping the script to Richard Gere and Jeff Bridges. To their credit, Lansing and Jaffe were showing the same faith in Douglas that he was showing in them. He was a deal-breaker as far as they were concerned. Other actors may have begun to question their suitability in the face of this rejection but not Michael Douglas. He has found himself in this sort of situation before and since. When it happens he always deals with it the same way.

'I'm basically instinctual,' he explains. 'I read something whether it's for acting or not. I read it and it scares me, gets me hot, whatever. Then I go back a second time and I analyse it. I'm an old-fashioned structuralist – three acts and all of that, I have a theatre background, theatre training – so I go back and make sure I was not fooled or seduced. I break it down and analyse it, whether I'm acting or producing. I think that's why the nicest compliment I get, or the one I hear the most, is not so much about me as my roles. They say: "When I see a movie with your name, I don't know what it's gonna be but I know it's gonna be good." That's what I get a lot and that makes me really proud. There is an unexpected feeling, they know it's not going to be easy, I don't know what it's going to be exactly. I think that's what separates me from a lot of movie actors. Most movie actors have a certain image or a certain look or a certain type of role but they allow me to make movies and fit into those movies.'

Having broken it down and analysed it Douglas was convinced he had not been falsely seduced. This was a good movie and the audience would once again see him in something different. When Glenn Close was cast as Alex Forrest, the wronged woman, and Anne Archer was cast as his screen wife he was more convinced than ever that the film would work. The only problem for Douglas, as well as for Lansing and Jaffe, and Adrian Lyne the director, came from the film's moral tone. It had to get it right or risk alienating the audience. On the one hand we have Dan Gallagher who is an adulterer but surely does not deserve to have the lives of his family threatened for his indiscretion. On the other hand we have Alex Forrest, a desperate, needy woman who is more to be pitied than scorned, but once she starts to threaten Gallagher's wife and child then she must lose the audience's sympathy. In the middle of all of this is Anne Archer as poor, wronged Beth Gallagher who seems to be paying the price for her husband's sins.

There were nine different endings in various drafts of the script but basically it came down to two solutions to the problem. There was an ending which was shot in which everyone loses. The point of divergence is in the scene near the end of the film where Dan visits Alex in her apartment for the final confrontation. During their conversation he picks up a carving knife. In one version of the film once he leaves the apartment Alex picks up the knife, which has his fingerprints on it, and kills herself. He is convicted of murder, he goes to prison and his wife and child are left desolate.

This version was shot but it simply did not play well. Douglas rationalises it as an ending which does not give the audience any sense of release, an ending in which no one really gets their just desserts and the innocent Beth Gallagher and her child are punished extravagantly. Instead one of the other endings was shot, which is a more conventional barnstorming finale. After Dan visits Alex's apartment he leaves without incident. She then comes to their house in the country where she boils his son's pet rabbit and then takes the child away. When she returns there is a pitched battle between all three of them and ultimately it is Beth, the one innocent in all of this, who kills her. The audience is then left with the prospect of Dan and Beth saving their marriage, or perhaps not. This ending is much more hysterical, much less reasoned, and – given the time Glenn Close spends submerged in a bath of water – almost unbelievable. The important thing for the film is that audiences loved it. Interestingly the suicide ending was used in some territories, particularly Japan, and the film played just as well in those territories. It seems to have been a question of horses for courses.

Fatal Attraction was a huge hit. It went to number one on its opening weekend in wide release and stayed in the top ten box office charts for months. It established Douglas as a box office draw and it made Glenn Close's career, as well as giving a significant boost to Anne Archer. Both women were nominated for Oscars – Close for Best Actor, Archer for Best Supporting Actor – but there was no nomination for Douglas. The real impact of the film, however, came when people got out of the cinemas and started talking about it. It was more than a hit – it was a *bona fide* phenomenon. Suddenly the film was the single subject of conversation in bars, at dinner parties, on radio phone-ins, on newspaper op-ed pages. Everyone had an opinion, not just in the United States but all over the world.

The debate was heightened by the new climate of sexual con-servatism which was being felt in America in the wake of the first cases of AIDS being reported. Douglas claims he goes on instinct and that his first gut reaction is usually the right one. In this case he was completely and totally correct. It would be the first time, but certainly not the last, that he would catch the mood of the audience. *Fatal Attraction* was the beginning of a series of choices for Michael Douglas which would see him create a whole new persona for himself. He was a man on the edge, a man on the brink of self-destruction. It was a characterisation too which found favour with audiences in the uncertain Eighties.

No movie in recent memory had pushed buttons the way *Fatal*

Attraction had and Michael Douglas was delighted.

'The movie touched a nerve,' he believes, 'an undeclared war between the sexes. There's a lot more hostility out there than we knew about. And nobody knows the answers. If the situation ever occurred . . . I'd like to think I would have told my wife, especially after the ante got raised. But I don't know what I would have done. That's what made it fun to play that guy.'

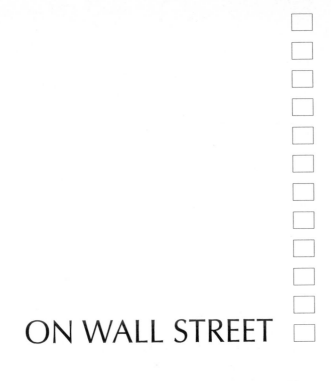

ON WALL STREET

Michael Douglas is always reluctant to characterise himself. At heart he is a private man, there is a part of him which is never given away, a part which he hides even from – or perhaps especially from – the cameras. He was always camera shy as a young actor, possibly because he feared being exposed completely on the big screen. He first started to relax on screen when he played Jack Colton in *Romancing the Stone* where he learned to be comfortable from watching his co-star Kathleen Turner. Jack Colton was also the first character he played where he was able to let himself go. This was the beginning of the end of the self-censorship which had produced so many nondescript performances, which served the film better than they served Michael Douglas. Now with *Fatal Attraction* he had found a way to better express himself on screen. He had found a character type which was worth exploring and for the next ten years he would make this sort of part his own; the role of the shadowy, flawed white male. His good friend Jack Nicholson often jokes that the middle-aged white male is the last oppressed minority on the planet, but in Michael Douglas they were about to find an eloquent spokesman.

Although reluctant to characterise himself, he has always had an easy answer to anyone who asked the question. He would cheerfully describe himself as a late bloomer. He did not achieve anything in college without having three shots at a junior year, he was 31 before he established himself as a producer, and he was in his forties before he found fame as an actor. Even late bloomers have to flower sometimes and for Michael Douglas 1987 was the year he chose to blossom. *Fatal Attraction* opened in the cinemas in the United States on 18 September 1987. It was the number one film at the box office and remained so for several weeks. As the year drew to a close *Fatal Attraction* was still the most talked-about film in the country, but it was about to be replaced by another film and once again Michael Douglas was the star.

Oliver Stone had been a thorn in the flesh of the American establishment for several years. It seemed to be his mission in life both as a screenwriter and a director to be a professional gadfly, always there to prick the conscience of middle America. The son of wealthy parents with a cultured and privileged upbringing, Stone had seen action in Vietnam and undergone a life-changing experience. His film *Platoon* was an attempt to recreate his feelings of that period. The film was essentially the story of the battle for the heart and soul of a naive young recruit played by Charlie Sheen. The two factions were represented by the two platoon sergeants, on the one side there was the demonic Tom Berenger and on the other there was the saintly Willem Dafoe. Sheen was caught in the middle and finally had to decide which way to go. The Oscar-laden *Platoon* was the beginning of a series of films in which Stone would examine the American experience in Vietnam while exorcising his own personal demons.

Stone was the son of a stock broker and like almost everyone else he was astonished and appalled at the amount of money which was being made on Wall Street in the Eighties. Developers like Donald Trump and bond dealers like Michael Milken and Ivan Boesky were as well known to the man in the street as sports stars. These were the Masters of the Universe as characterised by Tom Wolfe in his timely satire *Bonfire of the Vanities*. Stone chose to examine and expose that world in his new film *Wall Street*. Once again Charlie Sheen would be the innocent abroad – an anxious young trader called Bud Fox – and the seemingly omnipotent Gordon Gekko would be the Master of the Universe who would take him under his manipulative wing. Gekko was a hot role and the prime contenders were Warren Beatty and Richard Gere. Stone, however wanted Michael Douglas, and to those who expressed surprise at the choice, the director explained it quite simply. This was a movie about high finance and this was a world in which Douglas had moved for many years. This may have been the only time that Michael Douglas's experience as a producer got him a job as an actor.

Gordon Gekko was the ultimate corporate raider who bought and sold companies and stripped their assets like a jungle predator culling the weakest from a herd. Douglas himself described him as a shark and in his characterisation he came up with a look which brings to mind a Great White. Gekko is sleek with his gelled-down hair, his tailor-made clothes, and his hand-made shoes. He moves through the fim inexorably, constantly maintaining forward momentum because he knows, like the shark, that if he stops he will die. Trailing in his wake, feeding from the scraps is the impression-able Bud who, despite all his own certainties about Gekko, is merely being groomed to take a fall.

'For me the wardrobe was the key – the hair, things like cuff-links, suspenders, immediately gave me a costume,' says Douglas of his portrayal. 'Gordon was what you might call a counter-puncher – he'd always give the jab while the other guy was winding up, so he was always in your face one beat before . . . Anything that's in the way just go through it. His idea of being really well-dressed is probably a little flashy. He didn't come from a well-to-do family.'

Stone was absolutely correct in his instincts about Douglas. In his business dealings as a successful producer he had met men like Gordon Gekko and he knew intuitively their strengths and weaknesses and he could put that up there on screen. In addition, as he was preparing for the role, Douglas spent some time with major real-life Wall Street players to get the feeling of them and their world. Bringing this to the screen was not a pleasant experience for either Douglas or Stone, as it turned out. Where other directors had felt Douglas was not sufficiently sympathetic for previous roles, Oliver Stone felt that for this one he was just too soft. Stone felt Douglas's acting was formulaic and would not work well with his chosen technique for *Wall Street*: long speeches delivered with hand-held cameras only inches away from the actor's face.

'I don't think he had ever worked with anyone like me before,' said Stone at the time. 'Michael has to be pushed sometimes; he can get lazy.'

Douglas acknowledges that there was not a lot of fun on the set, and that he and Stone did not get on especially well. Douglas had taken the chance to seek out Charlie Sheen and get some inside information on what Stone had been like while shooting *Platoon*, which prepared him somewhat for his director. Even so, straight from the first day there were difficulties. One of Douglas's early scenes was a long monologue, and even though he was struggling he felt he had it right. Stone was plainly not happy and Douglas confronted him. If he was so unhappy then why didn't he just re-shoot it. Stone only replied that John Ford never had re-shoots. So Douglas kept at it and kept at it, trying to get whatever it was Stone was looking for. In the end he decided he would go and look at the dailies and see what his performance was like, something he never does unless he suspects there is a problem. As it turned out, the performance was fine, better than anything he had done. Just as Charles Jehlinger had done with his father all those years ago at the American Academy of Dramatic Art, Stone had been deliberately provoking a performance out of Michael Douglas.

'In hindsight, I think what he was probably doing was toughening me up for the kind of role I was playing,' says Douglas. 'He's not outwardly supportive, but he believes in you very strongly. His style is "Let me see whether you can cut it." He's brutally honest.'

One thing you can guarantee about having Michael Douglas on a set is that there will be an extraordinary level of professionalism. There may not be the practical jokes or larking about that you get on some sets, but everyone will be well prepared and know exactly what is expected of them. It is a tone which is set by Douglas who, and this is probably from the producer in him, takes his responsibilities as a leading man very seriously. Whatever his critics may say of him, no one can fault him for his professionalism. He knows every line, he shows up on time, he behaves impeccably. For *Wall Street* he had researched the world of Gordon Gekko meticulously. He knew this man inside out, upside down, and backwards. It was as much a safety net as anything else because having to handle speeches which were longer than anything he had ever come across before, Douglas had to know Gekko intimately as a character. It was important to concentrate on what Gekko was saying without worrying about whether he looked convincing while he said it. That would have come as second nature and that's where the preparation came in.

Wall Street, however, presented a set of unique difficulties. This was a film about corruption and double-dealing and corporate theft. That caused problems with the script because all of the names of companies used in the film had to be cleared legally to make sure no one was libelled by accident. Douglas became increasingly frustrated when these names were not cleared sufficiently early. He would memorise a long speech, several sides of screenplay, only to find at the last minute that the name of the company had been changed for legal reasons.

'You've got this whole long rhythm of these speeches,' he explains, 'just throwing these names off the tip of your tongue, and now in the back of your mind all that you are trying to remember is the name changes.'

One speech more than any other stands out from *Wall Street*. It is one of the dramatic high-points of the film. Gekko stands up in front of a stockholders' meeting of the myhtical Teldar Paper to explain why they should vote for his proposals even though it means their company will be asset-stripped. He is accused of acting out of no other motive than greed. In what became known as the 'Greed is Good' speech Douglas delivers a scalding defence of why the need to make money is more important than anything else, of why without greed there would be nothing else, and why without greed none of them would be sitting there today.

'Greed – you mark my words,' he tells them, '– will save Teldar, and that other malfunctioning corporation, the USA . . . Greed captures the essence of the revolutionary spirit.'

It was ironic that in that one speech, the lifelong liberal had become the most vigorous defender of Reaganomics anyone had ever seen. Gekko became a hero to the wannabe dealers and traders, and 'Greed is Good' became their mantra. In 2000, when Ben Younger made his debut feature *Boiler Room* about illegal junk bond dealers, he had some of his more avaricious characters repeat Gekko's speech from memory.

'I could not believe it,' says Younger. 'When I was researching this picture I came across these guys and they could quote that speech by heart. *Wall Street* to them was like *The Godfather* to gangsters and Gekko was their idol. When I heard it I just had to have that in my picture.'

Wall Street was released in the States on 11 December 1987 just in time to qualify for the Oscars. Once again external events played a part in the success of the film. Just as *The China Syndrome* became a hot issue because of the accident at Three Mile Island, the stock-market crash in October 1987 had made the real-life versions of men like Gordon Gekko big news. Suddenly the public, who could see these people on television every night and read about them in their papers every day, wanted to know more about them and the world they inhabited. Douglas himself had again touched a nerve. In *Fatal Attraction*, the audience had identified with Dan Gallagher because they felt they might act the same in similar circumstances. Now in *Wall Street* they found in Gordon Gekko's cold-hearted ruthlessness an amorality which many of them wished they possessed, and others wished they had the nerve to act on. The film was an enormous critical and commercial success and on its opening weekend Douglas had the rare distinction of having two films in the box office top ten. *Wall Street* was at number one and *Fatal Attraction* was still, three months after its release, in seventh place.

About a year earlier, Michael Douglas had been having a conversation with his father. Relations between the two men were now almost completely normalised and they were spending a lot of time talking to each other and catching up. Kirk Douglas had tried to convince his son that it was time he played darker, more heavyweight roles as he had done himself in *Lust for Life*, for example.

'I'd like to see you play a sonofabitch,' said Kirk

With *Wall Street* doing terrific business and knowing his father was going to see the film, Michael Douglas called him.

'Dad,' he laughed down the phone line. 'You're going to love me. Boy am I mean.'

Once again Douglas had not censored himself and had played Gordon Gekko as he should be, drawing a large part from himself and equally from his father. It was also the first time, on screen, when Michael Douglas had allowed himself to look and sound so much like Kirk Douglas.

'I was talking with Dad,' Douglas said at the time, 'and he paid me the greatest compliment. He said "Son, I noticed the resemblance between us straight away but five minutes into the picture I forgot you were my son. I was watching Gordon Gekko. You really nailed that part."'

Kirk Douglas was not the only one impressed with his son's performance. Michael Douglas's portrayal of Gordon Gekko won him his first Oscar nomination as an actor when he was one of the five nominees in the Best Actor category.

After he had made *Napoleon and Samantha* back in 1972 and the movie offers started drying up, Michael Douglas found himself in something of a quandary. With no serious theatre work in the offing the only real option was the ghetto of television. In those days television was, as we have already explained, a literal wasteland in movie terms. No one who went there ever came back. These days of course, such a theory would be absurd. The rise of premium cable stations such as Home Box Office, TNT, and Showtime means that television now frequently makes films which are more challenging and difficult than in the mainstream cinema. Stars such as John Travolta, Michael J. Fox, Danny De Vito, Eddie Murphy, George Clooney and many others have moved successfully from the small screen to the big screen. Michael Douglas, however, was one of the first. Now, here he was at the 60th anniversary Academy Awards and two of the five nominees in his category owed much of their film success to television.

The other television alumnus was Robin Williams, who had finally managed to find a film role that showcased his enormous comic talents with *Good Morning Vietnam*. Williams had made his way to the Oscars through the West Coast stand-up scene, a smash-hit TV series *Mork and Mindy*, and finally, after a series of forgettable film roles, he had found the right one. The rest of the competition that night came from Douglas's close friend Jack Nicholson, nominated for *Ironweed*, William Hurt for *Broadcast News*, and Marcello Mastroianni for *Dark Eyes*. The screenwriter William Goldman, himself an Oscar winner, famously said that in Hollywood nobody knows anything, but even he would allow that when it comes to Oscar night you can at least make an educated guess.

Mastroianni, for example, was nominated not so much for a

lovely performance in a bittersweet romantic comedy as for his long and distinguished career. The nomination was his Oscar in itself and he would not trouble the Academy voters unduly. Nicholson was king of the hill as far as nominations were concerned – this was his ninth – but his strike rate was not high. In addition only he and his co-star Meryl Streep had been nominated from *Ironweed*, acknowledging two exceptional performances in an otherwise neglected film which not many Academy voters would have seen in the days before they were deluged with video cassettes. Williams too could be ruled out of the running. Not only was he newly-arrived from television, he was perceived as a comedian rather than an actor, and comedy is a genre which has been dealt with more harshly by the Academy than any other – with the possible exception of the horror film.

To most informed observers the contest was a straight race between Douglas and William Hurt for *Broadcast News*. There were pros and cons for both men. Hurt's performance was exceptional in a film which had been a popular success. In addition he was in the middle of a remarkable run of three Best Actor nominations. He had been nominated the previous year for *Children of a Lesser God* and had won the year before that for his marvellous performance in *Kiss of the Spider Woman*. On the other hand he was suffering from what Hollywood insiders call the 'full trophy case' syndrome; giving him two Oscars in three years might seem a little excessive at this stage of his career.

Douglas, on the other hand, was a first time nominee, which might usually count against him. He was also nominated for a performance in a film which had received no nominations in either the Best Director or Best Film categories, which again is something of a demerit. On the up side, his performance in *Wall Street* was exceptional, audiences genuinely had the feeling they were seeing the emergence of a major talent. In addition it was his second great performance that year when *Fatal Attraction* was taken into account – Glenn Close, Anne Archer, Adrian Lyne and Sherry Lansing and

Stanley Jaffe were also all nominees that Oscar night. Finally, and perhaps sentimentally, leaving aside a terrific performance Douglas was one of their own. He was, in Hollywood terms, royalty and that must count for something.

Certainly the handicapping made Douglas a firm pre-Oscar favourite that night. No one was really surprised when his name was announced when the envelope was opened. It was a sentimental moment for all concerned. Douglas was careful to acknowledge the debt that he owed to Oliver Stone in helping to shape the performance which had won him his Oscar. But there was someone else, someone much more important, who needed to be thanked.

Kirk Douglas is one of the legions of great Hollywood stars who have never won an Oscar in their own right. His first nomination came in 1949 for *Champion*, since then he has had two more for *The Bad and the Beautiful* and *Lust For Life*. But still the Oscar eluded him. Now his son, who had already won an Oscar for Best Picture at his first attempt as a producer, had won a Best Actor Oscar on his first nomination. Michael Douglas did what any son would do, he dedicated his precious victory to his father.

'For helping a son step out of the shadow,' he said emotionally. 'I'll be eternally grateful to you, Dad.'

TOGETHER AGAIN

As a rule of thumb it's estimated that winning an Oscar can add an extra zero to an actor's fee. Generally this applies to supporting actors who go from five figure fees to six figure fees, or from six figures to seven. In the case of leading actors such as Michael Douglas, who are already through the seven figure barrier, it can often double the fee. Certainly that was not literally the case for Michael Douglas, but he did admit to American critic Gene Siskel in January 1988 that he was one of the 'top five or six actors in the business'. He was making somewhere between $4 million and $6 million per picture and was in the same category as Harrison Ford, Tom Cruise, Mel Gibson, and Arnold Schwarzenegger. In addition to his fee there would have been a very healthy back-end profits-sharing deal. There is no doubt that winning the Academy Award for *Wall Street* is the defining moment of Michael Douglas's screen career, and not just in terms of further boosting his considerable salary. The Oscar meant more to him than mere money.

'Winning the Academy Award for *Wall Street* really helped me to overcome that "second generation" thing,' he said. 'It's hard for people, no matter how generous and gracious they are, to really allow you any slack. They say "Oh it must have been really hard to be Kirk Douglas's son", but they don't really want to accept it. You grow up in this business and all it means is that you don't get the joy of succeeding. If you succeed, it's expected . . . If you look around you can see that there are hardly any second-generation people that have succeeded at all. It's a minefield of disasters, of broken careers and self-destruction out there.'

Douglas had promised himself he would take one of his intermittent breaks from acting. For one thing he had done two films back to back and they were both tough shoots, and for another he wanted to take some time to consider his options. There was also the very real consideration of once again taking time to re-acquaint himself with his family after such an intensive period of work. The first hints that all was not well in the Douglas marriage were starting to leak out into the media and although they were seldom commented upon, Douglas was keen to mend fences.

Having concentrated for so long on his acting to capitalise on the meaty roles which were finally coming his way, Douglas was also keen to return to his work as a producer, which was always his first love. Big Stick had been his production home for more than a decade, but now he phased that company out and formed a new company called Stonebridge Entertainment. Again he signed on with Columbia Pictures – the studio management had changed since his last spell there – for another three picture deal. The first of them was *Flatliners*, a horror story about young medical students who find a way of crossing to the afterlife. Other Stonebridge properties included *Radio Flyer*, a dark fantasy which dealt with the serious subject of child abuse.

There was more than enough here to keep him busy, but within six months of saying that he was going to take a rest he was back in front of the cameras. It appears in this case there was a combination of loyalty to his friends Sherry Lansing and Stanley Jaffe, who were producing, and a hefty fee involved in getting him to renege on his decision. In *Black Rain* he played Nick Conklin, a corrupt New York policeman who goes to Japan along with his partner to repatriate a Japanese criminal arrested in New York. The prisoner escapes and his partner – an under-used Andy Garcia – is killed by the Japanese gangsters. Douglas is then teamed up with his opposite number in Osaka to infiltrate the gang and recapture the escaped prisoner.

The role of the villain in *Black Rain* could have provided Jackie Chan with his first showcase role in a major American film, but Chan turned it down. He felt that he had built his image in Hong Kong on playing heroes and he would be breaking one of his own rigid rules by playing a villain. The part was eventually played by Yusaku Matsuda. Another established Eastern actor, Ken Takakura, was cast as Conklin's Japanese counterpart. Takakura's character is everything that Douglas's character is not. He is scrupulously honest while Douglas has been on the take. By the end of the film Takakura's decent qualities have rubbed off on Douglas, who shows signs of reforming.

Douglas plainly saw Conklin as another in his expanding range of tragically flawed characters, although the fact that he got to ride a lot of top of the range motor bikes in several sequences may also have played a part.

'I was looking for a tougher action-type picture,' he explained. 'In choosing roles I look for something to which I can bring an essence of myself. In this one I was angry and paranoid. Not a lot of fun to be around.'

Douglas and director Ridley Scott both claim to have enjoyed their time together in Japan shooting the film, which carries an unusual credit. Although Lansing and Jaffe are credited as producers, there is also mention that the film was made 'in association with Michael Douglas'. Apart from this being somewhat self-evident, in that it would be hard to make a film in which he has the starring role without him, it is also an indication of the role Douglas played in the production. He was in effect a consultant producer. At the end of each day's shooting he and Lansing and Jaffe would sit down over a drink and discuss the day's problems and look ahead to the rest of the shoot. He had, it seems, all of the benefits of being a producer with none of the responsibilities.

It was inevitable, given the box office success of *Romancing the Stone* and *The Jewel of the Nile*, that there would be some pressure to turn a sequel into a franchise. None of the participants involved had any strong objections providing the script was right. Curiously, it was Twentieth Century Fox who decided in July 1988, that a third instalment was not for them. The studio balked at the thought of paying $5 million each to both Douglas and Kathleen Turner. This was all the odder considering that they were paying the same amount to Bruce Willis for *Die Hard* and, at that time, he was a television actor who had not made a successful film. *Die Hard* of course turned out to be a colossal success but no one knew that when the deal was cut; Willis was a huge gamble, Douglas and Turner seemed like a sure thing. What was even more curious still was that three months later Douglas, Turner, and Danny De Vito would be back at Fox on another picture.

Although he had forged a successful career as an actor, Danny De Vito had always wanted to be a director. When he was struggling in New York he made dozens of short films on a Super 8 movie camera which, for a time, became his obsession.

'The earliest Super 8 movies you don't want to hear about,' says De Vito. 'My early films were documentary images that I just cut together. One night, for example, I came home late from the movies to my very small narrow apartment in the Village on Thompson Street. I walk in the door and I turn the light on and there is the biggest cockroach you have ever seen and instead of running away he attacks. I filmed the hunt, finally I caught the bastard and I killed him and that was one of my favourites . . . I lost another one of my favourites, which was made for my father. He was born in New York and lived in New Jersey and I just cut together a series of images for him.'

De Vito's first sound film was made in 1973 and called *The Sound Sleeper*. It was a 15 minute black and white film that he and the actress Rhea Perlman, who is now his wife, made together. As De Vito describes it, this is a dark tale of a suburban housewife who dresses as a hooker and kills someone while her husband is asleep. Even De Vito admits it's a sick notion. De Vito was always convinced that he could make it as a director, perhaps more convinced than he was that he would make it as an actor. Sick or not, it was *The Sound Sleeper* which was his passport.

'*Sound Sleeper* cost me 1400 bucks and I applied for a grant at the American Film Institute,' he continues. 'At that same time in 1974 I got the job in *One Flew Over the Cuckoo's Nest* and it was a big hit, so I went out to California with a movie which was a big smash hit and also a grant from the AFI to make another short film which is called *Minestrone*. I play an Italian film maker who finds a tiny diver in his soup and he thinks he's stealing his ideas and he eats him. Then I got an occasional movie like *Goin' South* or *The World's Greatest Lover* and then *Taxi* comes along, which is great. One day I walked into the office and said I wanted to direct a show. They said if you want to direct one then everyone will want to direct one and I said "So what." So they said "Let him direct a show" and I did three. I had fun, I liked working with my friends.'

Taxi turned out to be De Vito's entrée into Hollywood in a number of ways. The success of the series made him a household name and enabled him to be castable in *Romancing the Stone* and *The Jewel of the Nile*. But it also provided him with the directing credits and experience to make his feature film debut as a director. *Throw Momma From the Train* was a black comedy which affectionately borrowed from Hitchcock's classic thriller *Strangers on a Train*. De Vito and co-star Billy Crystal meet at a writing class and Crystal finds himself an unwitting part of De Vito's plan to kill his domineering mother, played by Anne Ramsey. The 1987 film was very funny, very well directed by De Vito but – more important – it was a huge hit. Overnight De Vito had become that most precious of Hollywood commodities, a hyphenate. He was now actor-director Danny De Vito with a certain amount of clout. That clout enabled him to develop another project dear to his heart.

'My involvement with this started almost a year before I did *Throw Momma from the Train*,' De Vito recalls. 'Michael Leeson and I were working on another project, I had always liked his work since his days as a writer on *Taxi*. We were going to lunch one day and there was a script in the car, I saw the title page and it was *The War of the Roses*. I asked if I could take a look at it and I loved it, I also said I would love to throw my hat in the ring as a director. Jim Brooks, the producer, and Michael also thought it was a great idea but Fox wasn't so keen. They were on the fence. There was a lot of stuff going on and finally *Throw Momma* came along and I did that. In the middle of that I guess the people at Fox heard I was coming to work on time, and didn't have a lot of extra-curricular activities, so they offered me the job. These guys (Brooks and Leeson) won out. They got who they wanted and they beat the studio.'

It is easy to understand Fox's initial reluctance, not just to hire De Vito but about the whole project in general. *The War of the Roses* was one of the boldest comedies to come out of Hollywood in a long time. It is a dark and disturbing look at the reality of the American dream. Based on the novel by Warren Adler, this is a bleakly comic look at the disintegration of a marriage. It follows the Roses from the day when they meet and fall headlong in love as a young couple, through their wedding, their life together, their growing antipathy towards each other, and finally a divorce which becomes so acrimonious they are willing to die rather than concede an inch of ground to the other. The film's master touch is to tell the story in a flashback, as a cautionary tale told by their lawyer in an attempt to dissuade another client from following the same path.

De Vito knew instinctively that he could play the role of the lawyer. He also knew instinctively that Michael Douglas would be right for the male lead. As for the female lead, surely there could be no one more appropriate than Kathleen Turner. Douglas agreed but there were some misgivings initially, for fear this would be seen as yet another instalment in the lives of Jack Colton and Joan Wilder. Eventually they decided to go with their instincts and Turner was cast.

' I think it actually worked for us in that people are used to seeing them in a very romantic situation,' says De Vito. 'The movie does travel from very romantic to this very, very dark ending, and that was a great feeling to be able to go from *Wuthering Heights* to *Full Metal Jacket* in under two hours. Even though, in the very beginning, we were all pondering and wondering whether this team should be together for this picture and whether it would help or hurt or how it would work. Those were all the decisions that we were making.

'We knew that Michael was great for this role and we really wanted him to play it. I also really wanted to try to get that feeling of old Hollywood where people really did work on many projects together and it was like a little company. The main task was to get people to understand that it's not a sequel, it's not another in the *Stone* and *Nile* series. It's a dark comedy, its another canvas. We were very successful doing that and I guess the back-story of the romance worked for us rather than against us.'

There is no doubt that the sardonic nature of the script would have appealed to Douglas and his self-confessed bizarre sense of humour. One scene in particular in which a vindictive Oliver Rose urinates in the soup course before a dinner party is both shocking and hilarious, and no one was more entertained than Douglas himself.

'You might not know this,' offers De Vito of his former flatmate, 'but in the Sixties I shot some footage of Michael standing naked over a bidet and we built a movie around it. It was my idea to stand him over the bidet but he is really a great guy, he goes with everything. He goes with the flow of the project, he gets in the spirit of it. The only time he'll back off is if there's a Lakers basketball game on, otherwise he's there one hundred per cent.'

Douglas and De Vito formed a formidable partnership on and off screen. Although he was not the producer, Douglas again took it upon himself to set the tone on the set. When Kathleen Turner, whose career had not perhaps taken off as it should, showed a tendency to be late on occasions, it was Douglas who dealt with it. A quiet word, perhaps a reminder of how important this film was to an old friend, and she was back on track and on time every day. Again, however, Turner remembers Douglas being hard on himself as an actor, just as he was in *Romancing the Stone*. She remembers him as being much more single-minded, much more determined, and much more focused as an actor than when they first worked together. Her recollection of the dinner-party sequence is an interesting insight into Douglas as a performer.

'A lot of actors would sort of give a wink to the camera over their shoulder,' she told *Premiere* magazine. 'Just to let the audience know "I'm not really like this." I never saw Michael do that.'

Douglas urinating in the soup was just one of a number of shocking sequences in the film. None however was as shocking as the finale in which, through a combination of circumstances, the Roses are left dangling from a chandelier over a high stair-well. Each has the opportunity to save themselves but in doing so they would also save the other. Rather than do that they both cling on grimly and ultimately both plunge to their deaths.

'Michael and I and Kathleen, we go back a long way, we're really good buddies,' insists De Vito. 'One of the fantasies I had was that I'd someday be able to grease them up, hang them 35 feet in the air and turn to the company and say "That's lunch, a half hour." And I did it the first day I put them up there. I didn't really take 30 minutes, I took an hour. Some of that scene was done with stunt people and dummies but most of it was done with Kathleen and Michael actually on the chandelier. There was only one way to get those shots and that was with their full co-operation. They understood that I needed those angles and I was very careful. We tied them to the chandelier and we got them up there. It took ten days. But hey, if you can't abuse your friends who are you gonna abuse.'

The ending of *The War of the Roses* is resolutely and defiantly anti-Hollywood. It's a film which offers no comfort to its audience. There are no happy endings on offer here to send you out into the night with your faith in the American Dream reconfirmed.

'It is pretty dark and it is shocking,' De Vito concedes. 'It's uncompromising. At one point we were going to have them get up and dust themselves off and say "Come on, we can work this out." Then they would put their arms round each other and walk out into the sunset. But, nah.'

Once again Michael Douglas found himself with two films in cinemas within weeks of each other in the autumn of 1989. *Black Rain* opened in September with *The War of the Roses* opening in December. Both, however, fared differently. *Black Rain* was roundly and justifiably condemned for its simplistic attitude to the Japanese and was accused in some quarters of racism. This was reflected in a domestic box office take of just under $50 million which, in comparison with his two previous films, was a major disappointment. *The War of the Roses*, on the other hand, was universally praised for its wit, its courage, and its invention. The difficulty of the subject matter did not prove to be much of a barrier to box office success and the film ended up taking $83 million, confirming the box office appeal of the combination of Douglas, De Vito and Turner, as well as establishing Danny De Vito as an 'A' list director.

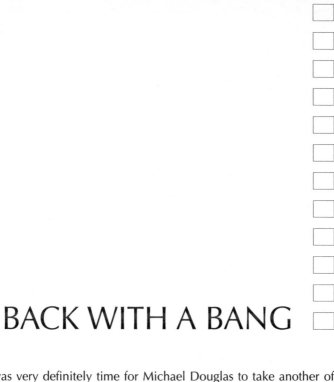

BACK WITH A BANG

It was very definitely time for Michael Douglas to take another of those long breaks with his family. He was more than established now as a top-flight star, his production credentials were second to none and it was time to allow himself to take his foot off the gas. The tough location shoots had been hard on Diandra and Cameron – especially filming *Black Rain* and *The War of the Roses* back to back with only five days in between – and there was a real need to spend some more quality time with his wife and child. He had grown up with an absentee father and he had no desire to put his own son through that particular mill. So, Michael Douglas was marked absent from Hollywood for close to eighteen months as he lazed around at his homes in Santa Barbara, Aspen or Majorca. He read a lot of newspapers, watched a lot of sport on television, and generally let the movie world turn without him for a while. He had taken up golf at the suggestion of Jack Nicholson, as a way of strengthening and exercising his back, which was still prone to discomfort from that old football injury. So he worked on his handicap and generally chilled out.

Douglas's way of relaxing reveals a lot about the man's instincts. He has, almost without exception, been able to identify the controversial and topical issues which enable him to choose the parts that will resonate with the audience. Part of that is instinctive, but there is also a part which is acquired. That's the part Douglas works at even when he's not working.

'I seem to be attracted to contemporary stories,' he says. 'All the movies that I've done, just about every one deals with contemporary people. Probably that's because I don't read a lot of fiction. I read a lot of newspapers and current events and my interests just tend to go in that area, about what's going on in the world in one perverse way or another . . . I'm a news junkie, I get three or four newspapers a day. I watch sports because, unlike movies, you can never guess the end. In movies you can always guess the end. The news, on the other hand, is better than any movie you can imagine.'

Douglas's only involvement in the film business in this period came through reading scripts, few of which interested him, and keeping an eye on his production company Stonebridge. *Flatliners* had been a big hit all over the world, bringing in $150 million on a budget of around one-tenth of that. However the production slate had expanded rapidly to the point where there were now around 40 projects in development. Subsequent releases such as *Double Impact* and *Stone Cold* did not do well, and the other big project, *Radio Flyer*, was showing signs of becoming a troubled production. Douglas was maintaining a watching brief on Stonebridge while maintaining a hands-off position. His partner Rick Bieber was minding the store and Douglas didn't want to step in unless he had to. There may well have been troubles brewing but they could be put off until another day.

He did get one intriguing offer in 1989, an offer which was so intriguing that he didn't even think it was serious.

'There was a brief moment when the Democratic party was in

terrible, terrible straits in California where they asked me to consider running for governor. That was when I considered changing parties because if that was the sort of shape we were in . . .' he laughs. 'It sounds like a joke. At one time three senators and some congress-men – all Democrats – came to me and said "We paid for a study and we understand that if we have to have a chance against Governor Wilson, we need to get a candidate who has a high personal recognition." And I said "Yeah." Then they said, "And who is willing and able to pay for his own campaign." I looked at these guys and asked "How much did you pay for this study? It sounds like a kamikaze mission to me. You mean to tell me that you paid money for someone to tell you that you had to find someone who had a recognisable face who could pay for his own campaign? You guys are in worse shape than I thought." That was the end of that.'

With a political career dead before it ever got off the ground, he was eventually lured back away from his round-the-clock satellite sports heaven for perhaps the most improbable role of his career. *Shining Through* was based on a popular novel by Susan Isaacs, set during the Second World War. Michael Douglas played the role of spymaster Ed Leland who needs to find out what a high-ranking Nazi – played by Liam Neeson – was up to. The most suitable person for the mission turns out to be his untrained secretary, played by Melanie Griffith. Naturally it all goes wrong and Douglas has to go behind enemy lines to face Neeson and rescue Griffith.

This was a bizarre choice for almost everyone concerned and it is hard to think of a recent film in which all the leads have been so comprehensively miscast. Nonetheless Douglas made all the right noises, claiming he was keen to do this old-fashioned action role, and also keen to work with Griffith. Director David Seltzer had sought out Douglas for the role of Ed Leland, believing Douglas had a Gary Cooper quality which he could bring to the role. The whole idea was ill-conceived. The last thing audiences wanted at the beginning of the Nineties was an old-fashioned clichéd romance about the Second World War. *Shining Through* was released in

January of 1992 and the audience voted with their feet. The film barely managed to take $21 million at the US box office. *Shining Through* was shot in England, mostly at Pinewood Studios, and while Douglas was there making his war movie his thoughts were on another film which he had left behind in California.

A few years previously Douglas had admitted to being one of the highest paid actors in Hollywood, earning as much as $6 million per picture. That was at the beginning of 1988. Now, barely two years later, no leading man worth his salt would even consider a film for that kind of money. Hollywood was going through a period of hyper-inflation where fees were concerned, and at the heart of it were independent companies who were determined to become major movie studios. One of the biggest of these was Carolco, run by Mario Kassar and Andrew Vajna, and they had been making the biggest of big splashes.

For their science fiction film *Total Recall*, for example, they paid Arnold Schwarzenegger $10 million and also, allegedly, threw in a jet. Their largesse did not extend merely to the talent in front of the camera. Carolco also paid $3 million for a script written on spec by the mercurial Joe Eszterhas, and they were now offering Michael Douglas as much as $14 million to star in it. In the midst of all this largesse it seemed almost an irrelevance to Vajna and Kassar that Carolco was estimated to be anywhere between $200 million and $500 million in the red. They continued playing a risky game which would ultimately be their undoing.

Their latest high-spending project was *Basic Instinct*, a steamy tale of a policeman investigating the murder of a former rock star. The prime suspect is the rock star's girlfriend, a cool blonde who is bi-sexual and may also be a serial killer. As the case becomes more complicated the policeman finds himself drawn into a web of sexual intrigue which seems certain to see him sharing the same fate as the ageing rock star. As it was written by Eszterhas, *Basic Instinct* was as sexually explicit a script as it was possible to get. This film was controversial from the off, but its problems were only beginning.

The $3 million payment to Eszterhas, as it was intended to do, sent shockwaves through the Hollywood establishment. Carolco had just upped the ante for everyone, especially when it was discovered that this deal also included an additional $1 million for a producer to be nominated by the writer. Eszterhas chose Irwin Winkler, an established producer whose credits included *Raging Bull*. For his pick, Carolco boss Kassar got to choose the stars and the director. He went for Douglas as the star, dangling the lure of that $14 million fee plus the knowledge that the actor was looking for a sexy role after the disaster of *Shining Through*. For the director he went back to an old favourite and offered the job to Paul Verhoeven, the Dutch director who had made almost $300 million world-wide with *Total Recall*.

'The casting of Michael was basically done before I came to the movie,' recalls Verhoeven. 'Mario Kassar gave me the script for *Basic Instinct* with Michael attached and said "This is the script and Michael is going to play this guy. Do you want to do it?" I was asked to say yes or no, but it was not one without the other. Mario made the deal with Michael first and then added the director to it. I thought it was a good idea or I wouldn't have said yes to the project.'

The first meeting did not go well. Verhoeven managed to antagonise both Winkler and Douglas in one fell swoop. Douglas, in particular, was concerned that there wasn't enough going on with his character, Nick Curran, he felt he was being far too passive and that the female character, Catherine Tramell, was gaining the upper hand. Ultimately Winkler and Eszterhas pulled out of the project but Douglas stayed attached to the film. Verhoeven had convinced him he could fix whatever problems the actor perceived, and Douglas agreed to give him until he came back from Europe and shooting *Shining Through*. Verhoeven was keen to accommodate his star because he believed there were few others around who could play Nick Curran. He felt there was something in Douglas which reflected the dark and shadowy nature of Curran specifically and the story as a whole. But the Dutchman also believed that Douglas was willing to join him in the huge risk they were both taking.

'If you look at a lot of the parts Michael has played,' says Verhoeven, 'there is an audacity to a lot of those parts which is very reminiscent of the parts his father dared to do, which are also very audacious choices like *Ace in the Hole*. Kirk Douglas made movies which were not necessarily entertainment-oriented. I think Michael has always been willing to take chances, so I thought he would be able to play a cop who has gone through tribulations and has done bad things in his life. He has done cocaine, he has driven his wife to despair and whatever. I was clear that Michael could do that, what was important in my first conversation with Michael was to be sure that he agreed with the script.'

When Douglas came back from Europe he was horrified to find out that the script had not been re-written and they were back with Eszterhas's final draft. He was furious, not appreciating that Verhoeven had actually abandoned the Eszterhas version and tried, on his own and with another writer, to come up with a different version but nothing had worked. This was the first of several disagreements between the director and the star.

'Ultimately I did a lot of fighting with Michael because I thought the script was good and Michael felt there were a lot of problems with it,' Verhoeven explains. 'I felt there were fewer problems than he perceived. I had been studying the script and had made my own mistakes already by trying to rewrite it with another writer and I failed. I think Michael had to go through the same process that I did, to say "What are the alternatives?" and realise there were none.'

Verhoeven convinced Douglas that he should go ahead with the script as it was written. Douglas agreed but there were several conditions, one of which was a clause in the contract which stipulated that he would show no full-frontal nudity. The other condition was that Verhoeven find another major star to absorb some of the flak. Verhoeven had been inclined to offer the key role of Catherine Tramell to Sharon Stone, whom he had effectively discovered in *Total Recall*. She had made several films previously but none had provided her with the same impact. He knew that there was so much nudity involved that few established female stars would be able to take the risk that Douglas was willing to take. In all the part was offered to fifty actresses including Geena Davis, Mariel Hemingway and Ellen Barkin, but they all decided it was not for them. In the end, after an excellent screen test, Douglas agreed that they should go with Stone.

That was another victory for Verhoeven, whose biggest challenge lay ahead in persuading both Douglas and Stone to perform on screen in the most sexually graphic mainstream film which had ever been released. Douglas had previously said that screen sex is simply a matter of mechanics, it's all about choreography, and technicalities. Not like this it wasn't.

'I think when he saw my storyboards he was taken aback,' laughs Verhoeven. 'Yes and Sharon too. They both looked at the storyboards and were saying "Are you really? . . . is that what we are supposed to do?" But on the other hand when I explained it and presented them with every move that they had to do naked I think they were convinced. It was so choreographed and so laid out that when we started shooting it they didn't feel this clumsiness of "Now we are together we have to have sex" because every sex move – all the moves that you do during sex – be it kissing, licking whatever – was laid out. In general I think Michael is an extremely courageous guy. He did things that I think 99 per cent of American actors would not even have considered, really. What he did with Sharon and what he did with Jeanne Tripplehorn in the date rape scene, in what he does and the way he does it to her, was on the edge of knowing that it was completely politically incorrect and that there would be a lot of animosity because of it. He's not afraid of that, he doesn't care. He's not afraid to be disliked and that makes him likeable anyhow.'

Michael Douglas may have been won over by Verhoeven's arguments but his wife was far from happy. Diandra Douglas did not want her husband to take the part when she heard what it entailed, and she was hurt and shocked when she saw Verhoeven's finished film. It wasn't so much the nudity or the sex that she objected to as an underlying nastiness of tone in a film in which sex was seen as a form of manipulation. Diandra was also concerned that the film seemed to condone violent sex. Doubtless she voiced these concerns strongly to her husband but, as she acknowledges, the final decision was not hers to make. Douglas for his part vehemently denied suggestions that Diandra's opposition to the film had put more strain on their marriage.

'None of that was true at all,' he said. 'I have a very understanding wife. Diandra may shake her head sometimes but she has been extraordinarily supportive. You never want to embarass the people who are close to you.'

For Jeanne Tripplehorn the role of Curran's former girlfriend was her first screen role. She was somewhat nonplussed to discover that her wardrobe consisted of specially-made Velcro breakaway panties for the scene in which Curran brutalises and rapes her. It was a daunting introduction to film-making, but she insists that she could not have done it without Douglas. After every take he would make sure that she was all right and felt capable of continuing, during every take he would whisper reassurance and encouragement to her, and every take was rehearsed scrupulously until Tripplehorn was as comfortable as she could be.

Again as the star Douglas took it upon himself to ensure the welfare of his co-stars. Verhoeven could see what he was doing and he was grateful for it. It wasn't just Tripplehorn who benefited from Douglas's attention, he was equally solicitous of Stone who, even though she was more experienced than Tripplehorn, was still very much in the firing line in this film. Just as he had done in *Romancing the Stone* and *Fatal Attraction*, Douglas was willing to step back slightly to ensure that his female co-star could have the full benefit of a career-making role. Verhoeven was and remains full of admiration for Douglas's generosity.

'Honestly I don't think people even saw the essence of what

happened there, in that film,' he says. 'Sharon was so good because Michael was great. All the attention of course went on Sharon, the discovery of the decade, and that was such an amazing performance of course. I think nobody realised that without the generosity of Michael Douglas this would not have happened to her, because he supported her throughout in every take, even if he was off-screen. Even if he was just talking to her off-camera and not in the frame, he was always going completely for her performance and helped her throughout the whole movie.

'It's not even that they liked each other so much, it was his inborn feeling of being not a producer on this movie, but being experienced as a producer and knowing, as a producer, that he would be only good when she would be good. I think I have never seen an actor being so much aware of that and seeing the necessity to be completely there for Sharon. I think people have never really seen how good his acting is and how much of that comes from him. As I said the attention goes to Sharon and for good reasons because Sharon does a great job too. But I think what has been missed by most of the critics is what Michael did.'

Basic Instinct had begun with an argument and there would be many more throughout the shoot. Paul Verhoeven would be at the centre of what *The Star Chamber* director Peter Hyams described as 'trailer-rattling' arguments. On one occasion the stress got so much for him that he collapsed with a nosebleed so severe he had to be hospitalised for several days, closing down the whole production. But, like Hyams, Verhoeven would be the first to concede that these were never rows about lighting, or close-ups, or whose trailer was closest to the set. These were arguments purely and simply between two men who shared a passionate vision to make the best film they could, but frequently disagreed about how they should go about it.

When Paul Verhoeven finally called 'Cut' for the last time, *Basic Instinct* had been filming for 89 days, well over its scheduled 65 day shoot, but at $43 million it was only slightly over its projected budget. If Verhoeven and Douglas thought their troubles were over now that the film was in the can, they could not have been more wrong.

'I'M THE BAD GUY?...'

Basic Instinct was due to open in the United States on 20 March 1992. In the weeks heading up to the opening the persistent protests against the film gathered strength, as a consequence of gathering strength they attracted media coverage, and as a consequence of the media coverage they simply grew in strength. It was a vicious circle and Douglas, Verhoeven and Eszterhas were right in the middle of it. None of it was entirely unexpected, but it is reasonable to assume that none of the men was prepared for the vehemence of the storm which blew up around their film.

Almost from the very beginning of filming in San Francisco there had been demonstrations and protests about the film from gay and lesbian groups, as well as the National Organisation of Women. The gay and lesbian groups felt the film was homophobic, while NOW believed it was misogynistic. San Francisco had once been Michael Douglas's favourite film location but it was getting to be very trying. Filming in the city became a constant battle of nerves as protesters from various groups tried, whenever they could, to disrupt filming through noisy demonstrations. After getting hold of an early draft of the script the protesters were insisting on a number of changes, including re-writing the character of Nick Curran to make him homosexual. That would doubtless have placated them but it wouldn't have done much for the 'sexy crime thriller' which Douglas thought he had signed on for. Nor would another suggestion that the killer be more even-handed, killing both gays and straight people. In an effort to reach some sort of accommodation producer Alan Marshall, who had taken over from the departed Winkler, decided to hold meetings with the protesters to try to convince them that their fears were unfounded. All they were doing with *Basic Instinct* was making a steamy movie. That may not have been the most laudable of ambitions but they were certainly not trying to discriminate against anyone.

The men behind *Basic Instinct* – Douglas, Verhoeven, Eszterhas, and now Marshall – had agreed on a united front in dealing with the demonstrators. Eszterhas, however, in an astonishing volte-face suddenly jumped ship and started speaking out on behalf of the demonstrators. He attacked Douglas and Verhoeven and the others involved and claimed that he had been working on a script which proposed changes along the lines the protesters were demanding. Douglas was both angry and bitterly, bitterly disappointed. He could, if he forced himself, see Eszterhas's point in that he lived in San Francisco and might not want to have himself or his family be targeted by demonstrators. On the other hand, Douglas also believed strongly that if Eszterhas genuinely felt like that then he should have told them beforehand. At the very least he should have informed Marshall, who had stuck his neck out in organising the meeting, instead of hanging him out to dry. Both Douglas and Paul Verhoeven were bitter in their condemnation of the screenwriter who, after his initial outburst, maintained a steadfast silence. Verhoeven and Eszterhas have since made up and made the film *Showgirls* together, but it is unlikely that Eszterhas figures highly on

Michael Douglas's Christmas card list, or vice versa.

Once they left San Francisco and moved to Los Angeles the protests died down and they were able to finish the film. It was, however, still a hot potato as far as the media were concerned, and it attracted news coverage like bees round a honey pot.

The next controversy came when Verhoeven finished the film and submitted it for certification by the MPAA. The sensible thing would have been to pass the film uncut with the special NC-17 certificate which had been created two years previously for *Henry and June*, Philip Kaufman's film about Henry Miller and Anais Nin. The problem is that the NC-17 classification, which means that no one under seventeen is allowed in to the cinema, is the only mandatory certification in America, the others are all recommendations. In addition the NC-17 still carried connotations of the old 'X' certificate, which was used for sex films. There were a number of cinema chains which, as a matter of policy, would not book NC-17 films, a number of newspapers and television stations which would similarly not carry advertising for them, and some chains of video stores would also not stock NC-17 titles. The NC-17 certificate may have been designed to allow artistic freedom, but in reality it was the most restrictive classification a film could have. There was absolutely no way a film could recover a $43 million budget with an NC-17 certificate.

Columbia TriStar were distributing the film in the United States, Carolco had sold overseas territories in separate deals. After viewing the film Mike Medavoy, the head of the studio, decided that the film would have to have an 'R' rating. This classification would allow young people to see the film if they were accompanied by an adult. Artistic freedom was one thing, but a return to the shareholders was something else entirely. So, not for the first time in his Hollywood career, Verhoeven started trimming the sex scenes between Douglas and Stone. They were cut as carefully as they had been choreographed in the first place. He had, he admits, suspected it might come to this, so he had shot additional footage to begin with which could replace some of the more contentious sequences. Eventually, after being submitted to the ratings board several times, *Basic Instinct* was finally given the desired 'R' rating in the middle of February, barely a month before it was due to be shown in cinemas, and very close to the point where it would have to be shown to journalists to get media coverage.

The final hurdle came when the film eventually opened to the public. There were demonstrators outside some cinemas, some groups carried placards of Douglas's face over-printed with the words 'homophobic' or 'misogynist', others stood at ticket desks revealing the ending of the film to potential ticket buyers. None of this had any effect on the public whatsoever. *Basic Instinct* took a then-massive $15 million on its opening weekend and went on to take $117 million in the United States alone and $352 million world-wide. By any standard the film was a success and Douglas had justified the gamble which Carolco had taken by paying him $14 million.

As the star of the film Douglas was the point man for most of the media attacks. He was the one who had to go on television and be charming and defend the film. He would often insist that he simply could not be politically correct, it was not in his nature. Some may see that as a character flaw but Douglas seems to have intended it to be taken as a plea in mitigation in a positive way. As the fuss died down, however, it was plain that he had been rattled by the strength of feeling which was being shown against this film.

'I got in shape and I just wanted to do a sexy, cop psychothriller. The gay issue really took me by surprise,' he insists. 'I don't see anybody in the movie being upset because anyone is gay or bisexual or anything else. Catherine's bisexuality was just an interesting twist. If you are going to deal in this detective genre, which has been done to death, you have to look for different twists. This is a difficult time right now – a time to get closer. Rather than trying to point out our differences, we should be trying to find out what our similarities are. Be kind to each other.'

Basic Instinct had taken a lot out of Michael Douglas. There had been a great deal of opposition to him taking the role from both Diandra and his son, Cameron. With Cameron, who was now thirteen, and in his first year at his father's old school Eaglebrook, Douglas sat him down and explained that it was just like he did in all his movies, it was pretend. The boy, however, was not convinced that pretending to shoot someone in, for example, *Shining Through* was quite the same as pretending to be making passionate, uninhibited love to them in *Basic Instinct*. Diandra, although she said little in public at the time, seemed with hindsight to be similarly unconvinced and this was another stressful time in their relationship. Douglas appeared to be well aware of this and made a conscious attempt to make an effort. His annual holiday party at Aspen over Christmas and New Year is a coveted invitation on the Hollywood circuit. In 1991, however, after he had finished shooting *Basic Instinct*, he decided to give Colorado a miss and he and Diandra and Cameron went off together.

There were other business decisions to be taken around this time. Stonebridge was just not working out as Michael Douglas had intended. *Flatliners* had been their only real success and things had got out of control once he took his eye off the ball. In November 1991, he and Rick Bieber ended their partnership and Douglas decided that it was time for him to simplify things a little.

'That taught me to be careful of what you wish for, because it might come true,' he said later. 'Stonebridge had forty projects in development and the production deal was so rich that it was almost in Columbia's best interests not to do a picture with me. That creates a situation that works against you. It's a mistake studios make – to have too many pictures in development. I became the producer as prisoner. I would come off an acting role and deal with a large number of projects that weren't in good shape and it was hard to focus on one.'

Just as he had learned a lesson the first time round at Columbia –

that he worked best in a little office with a small development staff, which is what Stonebridge would now become – he learned another lesson this time round. From now on he would only produce films he was in love with.

'Choosing which movie to do is a lot like falling in love with a woman,' he explained, elaborating on a metaphor he had used before to explain film production. 'You are attracted to her, you are attracted to a project. You then, because you are a little older now, don't impulsively go out and get married i.e. commit to a project, but you find out about it. How many times do you find yourself thinking about it? Do you have a paper and pen by your bed at night? Do you wake up thinking about her, about the project? And if she stays with you, that project, and you can't get enough of her, you're hooked and you know you have to do it. You have to go and make that movie. If the initial infatuation wavers and wanders, you know that you don't want to make that commitment.'

Douglas was in love again, not as a producer but as an actor. He had signed on to work with director Joel Schumacher in a dark and interesting film called *Falling Down*. When he was first approached by Schumacher and offered the script, Douglas was intrigued straight away.

The film is set in a single day in Los Angeles. It's the last day on the job for a veteran detective and he is doing his best to stay out of harm's way and make it through to the end of his shift without incident. Meanwhile, on the freeway there is a traffic jam. In the midst of the traffic jam one man simply gets out of his car and walks away. He has had enough. He decides to walk from the freeway, across Los Angeles to his ex-wife's house in Venice where his daughter is having a birthday party. Along the way the man – known only as D-Fens from his personalised number plate – acquires a holdall full of automatic weapons. Feeling empowered he begins to extract payback for the injustices he has been dealt, including recently losing his defence industry job as a consequence of corporate down-sizing. With D-Fens shooting up the town, the cop is forced to leave the safety of his office and go and confront the gunman. They meet face to face on the pier at Santa Monica. D-Fens does not understand why the police are looking for him or what he has done wrong. There is one brief moment of confrontation and D-Fens is shot dead by the policeman.

Michael Douglas loved this script and thought it could provide him with the best role of his career. He had one quibble; he was being offered the role of the cop and he really wanted to play D-Fens. This was the part which was the distillation perhaps of all of the flawed characters he had played up till now. This was everything he had ever wanted to play. Although he may not have recognised it at the time, it would become apparent very shortly that there were strong subconscious forces guiding Douglas in his choice of role in this film. The producers had no problem with him being the bad guy. His presence in the film in any capacity guaranteed that it would be made and they were more than happy to accommodate him. If he was playing the villain then they would get someone else for the cop, in this case Robert Duvall.

They did, however, have a problem with his fee. Whatever an agent can negotiate for his client in terms of a fee is known as that actor's 'quote' and in Hollywood quotes are precedential. Having been paid $14 million for *Basic Instinct*, Douglas was entitled to expect to be offered the same for *Falling Down*, the fee had become a benchmark. Warner Brothers, who were producing *Falling Down*, felt that was simply out of the question. They argued that his Carolco fee was a special circumstance which took into account the high risk nature of the part he played in *Basic Instinct*. They felt that something closer to the $6 million he had received for *Shining Through* might have been nearer the mark. In the end, after some negotiation, there was compromise on both sides and Douglas was paid $8 million for *Falling Down*.

No matter the fee, *Falling Down* director Joel Schumacher certainly felt that he and the studio had got their money's worth.

Douglas submitted to the director's will without complaint. Even when Schumacher told him he was going to have to have most of his hair cut off for D-Fens' severe buzz-cut he did not protest. Not once, according to Schumacher, did he ask for a single concession to make his character more sympathetic or accessible to the audience.

'Michael dares to play what could be considered non-user-friendly roles,' says Schumacher. 'At no point did he come to me and ask if the character could be made more sympathetic. A lot of actors can do rage but they telegraph it, so it's no surprise to the audience when they step out of the car and start to destroy Los Angeles. I think a lot of the controversy surrounding *Falling Down* was caused by people's confusion about whether Michael's character was the good guy or the bad guy.'

Whether he knew or cared about the controversy, Michael Douglas gave the performance of his life in *Falling Down*, and even now he considers it to be the best performance of his career. In the final moments of the film before he is fatally shot, D-Fens tries vainly to make sense of all that has happened to him in the past few hours. How did he come from being stuck in a traffic jam to ending up here in a shoot-out at the end of the Santa Monica pier?

'I'm the bad guy?' he asked quizzically just before Duvall pulls the trigger.

Within a few months it was a question Douglas would be asking himself for real – and not just in the movies.

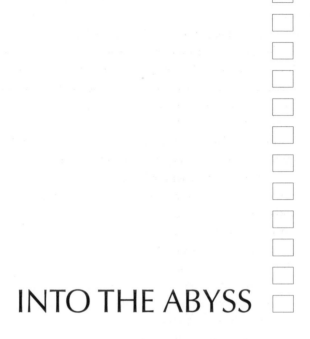

INTO THE ABYSS

Michael Douglas had come into his own as an actor with that remarkable string of performances which began with *Fatal Attraction* and had taken him, so far, up to *Falling Down*. There had been the odd blip along the way – notably *Shining Through* – but the parts had all been characterised by one thing. In each of them, from Dan Gallagher to D-Fens, there was a deep rage and frustration against the circumstances in which the character found himself. Gallagher raged against Alex Forrest, Gordon Gekko was bitter about his own past, Nick Conklin hated himself, Oliver Rose hated his wife, Nick Curran loathed everyone, and D-Fens lashed out at the system which had conspired to bring him to the stage he had reached.

Douglas had no problem playing rage. He had bottled it up for years. The little boy standing staring out of the window when his father phoned to announce he had re-married, the young stage actor who was passed over by Antonioni, the young film actor who had to bear the burden of being known as Little Kirk or Little Spartacus, the fledgling producer who had to watch door after door being slammed in his face by people who wanted to get their own back on his father. All of this was quietly marked by Douglas. There were few outbursts, few tantrums – at least not public ones. Revenge is a dish best served cold and Douglas simply stored it all and bided his time.

'I have anger in me, definitely,' he admits. 'I try to channel it in productive ways. It's a stimulant. It's a way that you keep going longer and harder and further than you normally would. But time will show it can be exhausting, and take its toll. Sometimes there are easier ways to do it.'

Having reached his maturity as an actor he was able to draw deeply from a well of rage and hurt and use it to inform his characters. He has said that he had never spent a day in therapy in his life but perhaps he should have. Douglas would argue that his films provided all the outlet he could possibly need, but there weren't enough films in the world to deal with a lifetime of frustration. As he said himself, acting out of rage and anger as your motivation is a tiring process. All that frustration had to find a channel somewhere and finally Michael Douglas snapped.

A professional to his fingertips he fulfilled his commitment to Joel Schumacher on *Falling Down* and then, in the words of one friend, he 'short-circuited'. Other friends began to be concerned for him. Those who knew him best, like *Rolling Stone* publisher Jann Wenner, could see what was happening. He had been drinking too much and too often. The years of bitterness he had felt towards his father were taking their toll, and also, no matter what he might say in public, the feeling that he would never be the man his father was weighed heavily upon him. In addition his marriage was on the point of disintegration. An intervention was necessary and soon.

It came from Diandra, his wife. She had never settled in Hollywood and never been entirely happy there since the day she got married. Her husband's long absences also played a part. He was frequently as much of an absentee father and husband as his own father had been. No matter how much he tried to compensate in terms of quality time it was never enough. Long stints in Mexico filming *Romancing the Stone*, or Japan filming *Black Rain*, or England filming *Shining Through* had all stretched their relationship to near breaking point. There were also tabloid rumours of Douglas's infidelity, including suggestions in some newspapers that Diandra had caught him *in flagrante*. Douglas has never dignified the rumours with comment, all he has said was that 'a crisis situation' forced him to take responsibility for his behaviour.

In a candid joint interview with *Vanity Fair* magazine they spoke about their difficulties. Diandra made it quite plain that she was the crisis situation to which her husband had referred.

'It's obviously no secret that this marriage has had its difficulties,' she said. 'It hasn't been easy . . . I told Michael he had to look at himself and his life or our relationship would be over.'

There was one other factor waiting to tip Michael Douglas over the edge. On 11 July 1992, Bill Darrid, the man who had been more of a father to him growing up than his own biological parent had been, died after a long illness. Diana Douglas Darrid was devastated but her sons, Michael and Joel, were there to provide support and saw her through the most difficult period of her life. Not only had she lost her husband, a matter of days after she had seen her sister Marge at Bill Darrid's wake, Marge died suddenly. Michael Douglas was a dutiful son who did all he could for his mother in her own time of need but eventually he could take no more. In September 1992, he checked himself into the Sierra Tucson clinic in Arizona, an upmarket clinic which deals with all forms of addiction.

Michael Douglas had always had a good relationship with the press. He had been accessible, friendly, open, and – especially in his early days – more forthright than was occasionally good for him. The producer in him recognised the value of publicity, the actor in him just loved to meet people, to hang out, and to talk. He loved the media and the media loved him. He was one of the nice guys – you'll go a long way before you can find someone with a genuine grievance against Michael Douglas – and he had the added attraction of being good copy.

All of that changed at the beginning of the Nineties, not just for Douglas but for most major Hollywood names. The rise of tabloid television shows and the cutthroat circulation battles between tabloid newspapers all over the world meant that every celebrity in Hollywood was fair game. First of all it was the paparazzi, who would snap away from concealed locations from the security of their long lenses as they captured the indiscretions, real and imagined, of the rich and famous. Later they were followed by the videorazzi, who would frequently go to the extent of provoking a celebrity into a violent reaction, capturing it on tape, then selling it to the highest tabloid television bidder. Douglas, who was good sexy copy with the rows over *Basic Instinct*, suddenly found himself at the centre of a tabloid feeding frenzy. He had gone into Sierra Tucson but, according to the English media where the reports appeared to have started, it wasn't for substance abuse, it was to cure an addiction to sex.

Certainly people who suffer from all forms of addictive behaviour, including sex addiction and drug addiction, are treated at Sierra Tucson. Yet Douglas was adamant at the time and remains so, that he had gone there for treatment for alcohol abuse. To defend himself against the tabloids he was forced to admit publicly that he had a drink problem. The evidence certainly bears out Douglas's version of the story. Even as a young student at Emerson High he had been treated for alcohol poisoning on one occasion. Since then he had frequently conducted interviews at the end of a day's shooting with a glass of vodka not far away. In addition, who would admit to being an alcoholic if they did not have to? The stigma attached to alcoholism in some quarters is far outweighed by the approbation that would come from other quarters for being addicted to sex in the increasingly laddish Nineties. Douglas knows exactly how it happened, but that doesn't make it any easier to deal with.

'It's just been this sort of yoke, it was my first example of a title, like the Scarlet A,' he says, referring to the mark of the adulteress in Nathanael Hawthorne's *The Scarlet Letter*. 'The fact is that I went to rehab for alcohol abuse soon after *Basic Instinct*, but because that is not enough of a story, somehow, somebody, I don't know how it got started – probably in the tabloids – decided this was a great handle for a story. And even mention of it gives more weight to it. It just is boring, it's disappointing because you think as a person you have more things to offer rather than trying to defend yourself about lies. There are things I would love to talk about politics, culture, history, rather than some fact that somebody came up with some late night to sell a weekly tabloid. My family know who I am, my son knows who I am, and I'm sure it causes him discomfort from other people or friends or parents. So your friends know who you are.

'I used to love doing all of this media stuff. I used to love the chance to talk to people because we live such an isolated life making movies and it's a chance to get beyond that. But I do understand why more and more people are insulating themselves because the competition between print, news, and television has got more vicious. Editors are demanding of the writers tougher and tougher things or the writers (are demanding it) of themselves. It's getting out of control, it's unfortunate because I know more and more people are starting to question the balance of promoting movies, to what degree you can. And is it really worth it that your personal life gets so dragged through this medium which gets so much attention because there is so much money involved.'

Michael Douglas never pretended to being a saint but now, like D-Fens, he found himself being categorised in black and white terms as the bad guy. There wasn't a tabloid in the English-speaking world that didn't have him marked down as some middle-aged, skirt-chasing lecher. Douglas, meanwhile, was in Sierra Tucson slowly, surely, and painfully changing his life.

'At Sierra Tucson,' he told *Vanity Fair*, 'I addressed what basically had become a cumulative lifestyle. I knew I was drinking too much. It was 25 years of work, pressure, knocking it back. The pressure started in 1963 when I started college – those good Sixties years of being a hippie – through twenty years of work, a long track record of which I am very proud and which I don't feel is ever really acknowledged.'

That resentment at a career he felt was unrecognised in many ways echoed his father's dissatisfaction at the response to his early career. Michael Douglas was now approaching his fiftieth birthday, which was less than two years away. For half his life he had been the very model of a driven man, and now the wheels had come off. Douglas says he went into rehab to save his marriage but he ended up saving his life. It does seem likely that if he had continued to punish himself in the way he had been doing he would not have made old bones. Even so Sierra Tucson was not a holiday camp. He was forced to come to terms with some unpleasant truths about himself, he had to acknowledge that what he thought was taking care of everything could be seen by others as controlling. And what he saw as taking care of business, others could see as selfish.

'For me,' he said, 'having a famous and successful father and having entered the same field, I identified success in my work. I had two careers, which I pursued strongly and actively. Once you've achieved a certain amount of success, you are used to a certain level of control in other areas of your life. And that doesn't always work well in an intimate relationship. My work took first priority, even beyond my marriage, when I was working. The difference is that when I wasn't working I could focus on my family, but when I was working there was no way to balance them. Most people have an eight-hour job and they go home, and their family and their life are the most important part of their world. I got comfortable working. I got acknowledgement and approval from working. And in relationships you don't get a medal for being a good partner each week.'

Sierra Tucson gave Michael Douglas the chance to talk to people on an individual basis for the first time in a long time. These were people who had no interest in knowing Michael Douglas the movie star, these were people who just wanted to listen and help.

When he left the clinic Douglas wanted to spend more time with his wife and son. There was also his mother to think about, and his brother Joel who had also once again started to drink more than he should. There were no holidays in Aspen again that Christmas, instead they spent the holidays in Santa Barbara. Michael and Diandra had invited Diana to come and spend Christmas with them, which meant she could also be near Kirk and Anne Douglas, who had been close friends for many years. All things considered, it must have been a somewhat subdued festive season.

Diana Douglas Darrid recalls it as being a difficult time for her oldest son. It was obvious to her that there were still unresolved problems between Michael and Diandra and she was especially concerned about the effect on young Cameron. Although much is made of Michael Douglas's resemblance to his father it is really just the hair and the chin, in almost every other respect he resembles his mother. He has her eyes, her smile and her bone structure. He also got from her a sense of determination to succeed and a belief in himself which sustained him through difficult times. Along with his wife and his brother, no one knew Michael Douglas as well as Diana Darrid.

After Christmas Michael and his family went back to Bermuda with his mother. This again was a difficult period for him. Largely because of his own problems he had never dealt with Bill Darrid's death some six months previously. Now in Bermuda, where his stepfather was buried, he would have to come to terms with it. That happened one night when he got up around two in the morning and started to walk. He ended up walking all the way across the island to where Bill Darrid was buried and spent the night at his graveside. When he returned in the morning all he would tell his mother was that he had had a deeply spiritual experience. After Bermuda, Michael remained close by his mother to supervise the New York production of *The Best of Friends*, a play which Bill Darrid had been instrumental in bringing to the stage. It was something of a farewell gift to his stepfather and his association with the play did it no harm at all in publicity terms when it reached New York.

Sierra Tucson also helped to finally change Douglas's attitude towards his biological father. He learned that much of what he was he owed to him. He learned finally to forgive and understand his father, and he also learned to forgive himself for the resentment he felt towards him. From this point on he and Kirk Douglas would form a strong and unbreakable parental bond. It may have taken years to be forged, but the important thing is that it was finally there.

'It just means we are all getting a little older,' he said sometime later of his relationship with his father. 'Kirk is Kirk and I was looking recently and I think I was up to 25 movies and I think Kirk was just finishing his eightieth. It's a different time and a different place and I think we all just age a little bit more and forget that. For my father it's a true sense of immortality. There is nothing more loving than a sense of continuity of generations and the feeling of yourself going on. I think that's the best part of being brought up second generation, it teaches you a little humility, you can't take yourself too serious and life goes on. There'll always be someone else coming after you.'

INDECENT
DISCLOSURE

Michael Crichton is a writer who has a singular talent. In many ways his skill in his books mirrors Michael Douglas's skill in choosing film roles. Like Douglas, Crichton has an almost unerring knack for homing in on subjects which will engage and frequently disturb audiences. The high adventure of *Jurassic Park* contains some hard science about the morality of genetic engineering; the horror of *The Terminal Man* has at its heart the fear of a humanity controlled by machines; and the suspense of *Rising Sun* is deeply wrapped up in fears that the tiger economies of the Pacific Rim will triumph over conventional but outmoded American industrial practice. Similarly his best-seller *Disclosure* was another potentially controversial piece concerning sexual harassment in the workplace. This time, to give the scenario an unconventional twist, the harasser is female and the victim is male.

Everything that Hollywood could want in a commercial film, *Disclosure* has by the bucketful. It has a, literally, sexy subject, there are roles for glamorous movie stars, and the drama will play itself out neatly, with the possibility that the audience might still be thinking about what they had just seen even after they had driven out of the car park. In addition it was a best-seller with name recognition, and it dealt with a subject on which almost everyone had an opinion.

Disclosure is set in the new hi-tech world of the multi-billion dollar computer industry. A senior executive finds that his new boss is a woman who was once his girlfriend. There is a major promotion in the offing and he is obviously keen to get it. She is keen to help him but only if he will rekindle their relationship. The executive by this stage is a happily married man and although he is tempted and initially succumbs, he ultimately refuses to cooperate. He is then in the middle of a sexual harassment scenario in which he is fighting to save his marriage, his job and his career.

It was all good trashy stuff and in many ways it was tailor-made for Michael Douglas. Warner Brothers, who were making the film, were certainly willing to pay him $12 million for the privilege of watching audiences sympathise with Douglas as the victim instead of the villain. The female role was a meaty part and one which many actresses coveted. Annette Bening was originally to have played the role, but she had to pass when she became pregnant. Geena Davis was also reportedly considered until finally the role went to Demi Moore, playing her on-screen villain. She was paid $5 million but the irony of the disparity in salaries in a film about sexual equality went generally unremarked.

There had been almost two years between the end of filming *Falling Down* and the beginning of shooting *Disclosure*. They had been two difficult years for Michael Douglas, but he was now ready to get back into the fray. When he looked around at what was on offer he found that *Disclosure* was the best of the bunch. He had some reservations, which he expressed to his agent, in that he felt that in many ways this film covered similar territory to *Fatal Attraction*. Certainly the central character is a man who is almost undone by one moment of temptation which spins out of control and threatens everything he holds dear. On the other hand he had to remind himself that there was more than ten years between *Fatal Attraction* and *Disclosure* and both he and the audience had moved on by then. Douglas was ultimately intrigued by the role and amused by the possibility of turning audience perceptions of him on their head.

'I love being politically incorrect,' he said echoing the theme of his answers when he was publicising *Basic Instinct*. 'I thought the reverse twist of changing the roles of sexual harassment would give people a way to look at the issue from a different point of view. Reversing the roles stops us from lining up simply on the side of gender, and allows people to see the other side. I don't mean we should start feeling sorry for guys, but I think it helps everybody to look at the other side.'

Once again it was another sexually-charged role following on from Dan Gallagher and Nick Curran in his previous successes. Diandra was beginning to be concerned about his choices.

'I often ask myself why he picked these roles,' she said later. 'And I still don't know the answer. I think they have made it very difficult for me to live my life. I would be lying ... if I said this is every woman's dream.'

The man responsible for bringing *Disclosure* to the screen was director Barry Levinson, a witty and erudite man who could turn in studio hits such as *Rain Man* and *Good Morning Vietnam* or deeply personal independent films such as *Diner* with equal facility. He conceded that a lot would be asked of whoever played the male lead in this film, but he was certain Douglas was more than capable of carrying the burden.

'His role is difficult because he is carrying the movie on his back,' says Levinson, 'but he has the ability to make it look effortless. Having some big bravura emotional scene is easy, but it's very hard to take the audience through this story, to tell this story, without the audience getting tired of looking at him. But Michael always seems to be saying "Watch me. Look at me." '

One of the themes which Michael Douglas had brought to the surface in *Fatal Attraction* was the essential difference in attitudes to sexual morality between men and women. He frequently made reference to the undeclared war between the sexes. For Douglas, the issue of sexual harassment was simply another skirmish on that particular battlefield.

'It's nothing new,' he insisted. 'It goes back to men dragging women by the hair into the cave. It's just that now it's become this issue . . . I think we are in the middle of a gender war. I think guys are confused these days. I think they feel their role has been usurped. Who's the provider? Who's the nurturer? Who knows anymore? It's a big problem . . . if we all followed the rules, we'd all be these sensitive, upstanding, compassionate men – and no women would want us. Women want aggressive guys who lay it on the line. It's really confusing for men these days.'

Certainly with those attitudes no one appears more confused than Michael Douglas, although that perhaps was the point he was attempting to illustrate.

Disclosure was filmed in the spring of 1994 in and around Seattle. It was a tough and difficult shoot for all concerned. This was partly because, having drafted Demi Moore into the role originally intended for Annette Bening, Warners had to make sure that she would be free to take up her commitment to play the lead in a new version of *The Scarlet Letter*. To accommodate Moore's other film, six day weeks became the norm on the *Disclosure* set.

In addition, Douglas was getting back into film production. Stonebridge's deal with Columbia ended on 30 April 1994 and on 1 May, Douglas set up a new production company. This time he had partnered with Steven Reuther, a former president of New Regency Films, to form Constellation Films. Douglas knew and liked Reuther, whose company had produced *The Client, War of the Roses,* and *Falling Down*. Together they had raised a staggering $500 million in finance, much of it from a German financier whom Reuther had brought to the table. This was a tremendous deal for Douglas, who became the first actor in Hollywood with the financial clout to green-light a picture in which he was not starring. In addition to giving the nod to films which he did not appear in, the deal was non-exclusive – which allowed Douglas to go and make films for other companies if he so desired. Douglas had also learned his lessons from his twin sojourns at Columbia. Constellation's films would be distributed in the United States by Paramount, which was now being run by his old friend and guardian angel Sherry Lansing. The idea was that Constellation would produce twelve films in four years. The benefits would be huge if they were hits but, as Douglas himself admitted, there was a lot to lose if they flopped. He knew that his films would have to perform.

'I think I have found a way to marry my two careers, which have always been on separate tracks to a certain degree,' said Douglas. 'When I had my success as a producer, people always wanted to know why I wanted to be an actor. And when I got some success as an actor, people asked me why I still wanted to produce. It's always made some people uncomfortable that I won't be just one thing or the other.'

While he was putting together his production slate with Steven Reuther for Constellation, which he hoped would finally include the long-promised project with his father, Michael Douglas was also considering another couple of film offers. Carolco, who had served his bank balance so royally with *Basic Instinct*, wanted him to headline another of their films. They were hoping to lure him aboard a pirate adventure called *Cutthroat Island*. The film was to be directed by Renny Harlin and would star his then wife Geena Davis as a female pirate plundering the Caribbean. Douglas was being lined up for the role of her love interest and ship mate, who is instrumental in helping her recover the fortune in treasure left to her by her freebooting father. He was also being tempted by *Virtuosity*. Despite his pronounced dislike for science fiction films, Douglas was intrigued by the script for this film in which a futuristic policeman hunts down a virtual reality murderer, who has been programmed with the memories of some notorious serial killers.

Of the two it seemed that Douglas was more likely to do *Cutthroat Island*. He was sufficiently interested to ask for several rewrites to try to improve the balance of the film. However in July, 1994 he decided that he could not do it. He had completed *Disclosure* by now, but the arduous schedule of six-day weeks had left him feeling weary. Since the final rewrite of the pirate script called for him to be in almost every scene of what would, by definition, have to be a rousing, high-energy adventure yarn Douglas eventually declined. Even without him *Cutthroat Island* was still deemed to be a hot project and, initially, names such as Michael Keaton, Kurt Russell and Keanu Reeves were considered for varying lengths of time.

The production dragged on and finally made it to the screen with Matthew Modine opposite Geena Davis. The film was an unmitigated disaster which was reviled by critics and ignored by audiences, making it one of the biggest financial flops in the history of cinema. Carolco had almost been ruined by its failure and Davis and Harlin ultimately divorced. *Cutthroat Island* had been handed the Black Spot almost from the day and hour it was conceived and it is highly debatable whether Michael Douglas could have helped. All things considered he had dodged a bullet, a lucrative bullet to be sure but a bullet nonetheless. Shortly after passing on *Cutthroat Island*, Douglas also decided not to do *Virtuosity*. The film eventually starred Denzel Washington and Russell Crowe but both men would do bigger and better films in the years to come.

Michael Douglas had been sorely tested in the previous two years. He had almost lost his marriage, his stepfather who had been an abiding influence in his life had died, and, of course, he had been forced to face his own inner demons when he checked himself into Sierra Tucson. There was one more blow to come. Peter De Palma had been Douglas's personal assistant and general factotum for eighteen years. He was one of his most trusted friends and closest confidants. In *Disclosure*, Douglas teasingly persuaded him to make his film debut playing a waiter behind a buffet table at a party scene. Shortly after *Disclosure* finished filming Peter De Palma died suddenly of a massive heart attack. He was 68 years old. Douglas was devastated, not only had De Palma died on his fiftieth birthday, once again he had lost another of the dwindling band of men in whom he could truly confide.

All things considered it was a subdued Michael Douglas who celebrated his fiftieth birthday party on 25 September 1994. There had been some terrible trials in the previous years but there was still much to be grateful for. He was still married, he still had his family, he was still alive. He had been tested in the arena and emerged bloodied but unbowed. He knew ultimately who he had to thank.

'I am more in love with Diandra now than on the day I married her,' a grateful Douglas told his friends and family at his birthday celebrations.

Within nine months he and Diandra announced that they could not reconcile their differences and would be separating.

As Barry Levinson was putting the finishing touches to *Disclosure* there were some rumblings of unrest before the film was released. This was not along the lines of the virulent protests which marred the release of *Basic Instinct*, but there was at least what might be termed a feminist backlash. There were those who were less than happy that Demi Moore had been characterised as the villain of the piece.

Michael Douglas was, perhaps predictably, completely unrepentant.

'A lot of feminists are concerned about women playing villains,' he said. 'It's interesting. Male actors love playing villains, it's a big part of our careers. But it's an issue with women. I think back to *One Flew Over the Cuckoo's Nest*. We had five actresses turn down Nurse Ratched because they didn't want to play a heavy. Then Louise Fletcher won an Oscar for it.'

During his interviews to promote *Disclosure* Barry Levinson remarked on more than one occasion how well Michael Douglas worked with women. A lot of actors are insecure around female stars and try to dominate them on screen but not Michael Douglas. His generosity to female co-stars had been one of the distinguishing marks of his career. He had made Kathleen Turner a star in *Romancing the Stone*, he had provided a showcase for Glenn Close in *Fatal Attraction*, and he had provided support and protection on-screen and off for both Sharon Stone and Jeanne Tripplehorn in *Basic Instinct*. Even in *Disclosure* he resisted the temptation to upstage Demi Moore and allowed her the chance to shine in what would be her last major hit for some time.

'Actresses know that I am going to make them feel comfortable,' says Douglas. 'I think almost every actress I have worked with has given one of their best performances opposite me. Why is that? I think it is because they know I am not going to be competing with them. They know that I am not going to try to cut the movie to make it the best movie for me, I am going to cut it to simply make it the best movie it can be.'

Although it was opening in the traditional end of year awards slot, no one seriously expected *Disclosure* to figure in the Oscars race. The reviews of the film were mixed but there was no escaping the amount of publicity it generated as the subject of sexual harassment in the workplace became a hot media topic. In the end the film took $83 million in the United States and almost $120 million internationally, which made it a major hit for Warner Brothers. Once again Michael Douglas had touched a chord with the public and they had responded at the box office. This incredible knack of picking the right subject at the right time is all the more impressive when you consider, on his own admission, that Michael Douglas doesn't go to the cinema much. He's not a great movie fan so his choices are not reacting to industry trends.

'I have made the point about reading lots of newspapers,' says Douglas about his ability to choose successful subjects. 'But you can't make a movie about a topic. So I do read a lot, I get the chance to go round the world, so I have an inherent sense of what's going on, I don't feel out of touch. I always find, I guess, that what triggers me or motivates me might also motivate someone else or be of interest to someone else. Basically I've gained the confidence to realise that if I'm interested in something then there might be another couple of loonies out there interested in it too.'

For Michael Douglas *Disclosure* completed a loose trilogy – the *Los Angeles Times* perceptively called it 'a rough-trade triptych' – which had begun with *Fatal Attraction* and continued with *Basic Instinct*. For Michael Douglas, enough was enough, and he promised that this was the last audiences would see of him in these types of roles in the forseeable future.

'Let's put this in perspective,' he said later. 'If *Fatal Attraction* did not do $350 million and if *Basic Instinct* was not a big success, we would not be having this conversation. The simple fact that the movies did very well – they were good movies – has become the sort of yoke that I carry around with questions here and in my personal life. It has become so ridiculous. I guess that is the price you pay for some successful films. I think I have done my trilogy if you want to include *Disclosure*. Do I think that there is a struggle between the sexes? Yes. There are identity issues involved. I think both men and women have troubles relating in this new period? Yes. I think we are having a tough time.

'But I think I will keep my pants up for a while,' he smiled, 'although I did enjoy it when they were down.'

HAIL TO THE CHIEF

For his birthday in 1994 Michael Douglas gave his father a special gift. It did not look like much, it was slim, not too heavy, generally unprepossessing. Kirk Douglas had been around the track often enough to know exactly what it was the moment his son gave it to him: it was a script. Not only that, it was a script for a film which the two of them would make together. It was called a *A Song for David*, it had been written by Dan Gordon and it was a story about a son and his father and their construction business. Kirk was touched and delighted. They had talked about doing a film together before, but it had been just that, talk. Kirk had wanted Michael to star with him in *Take Me Home Again*, as a way of getting back into the business after his breakdown. This was a television movie about a dying father being reconciled with his prodigal son. Michael was interested but had decided to do *Disclosure* instead. Since the producers wouldn't wait for him to finish Barry Levinson's film, *Take Me Home Again* went ahead with Kirk Douglas and Craig T. Nelson.

A Song for David was different. This time there was a note from Michael with the gift promising that they would make it together in 1995. The relationship between Michael Douglas and his father had improved immeasurably. Michael's spell in Sierra Tucson had helped a great deal and being a father himself also contributed a sense of understanding.

'I started to relax around him,' says Kirk Douglas, 'and he, learning a thing or two about being a father himself, stopped being so hard on me.'

From Michael's point of view, he was more eager and more ready to acknowledge his gratitude to his father. Instead of rather bland comments about the difficulty of following in his father's footsteps, he was prepared to come out and talk about how much he owed to his father. He conceded, however, that this may not necessarily have been what people wanted to hear.

'This is true generally about the press because it is easier to write about conflict than it is about love or support,' he says, 'because for whatever reason that is not seen as such an interesting story. He (Kirk) was very active in those days, he made three movies, four movies a year back then, so there wasn't a lot of time to be around home and he tended to have to push all his fatherhood into short brief spurts. As far as working in the business I have learned my professionalism and also the vulnerabilities from watching my dad and his friends who are movie stars around the house, and you got more of a sense of the reality of this career and this work from that, rather than the fantasy which you get from the press. I think that has been the biggest asset for me in helping me through my failures as well as my successes – because we work as hard on all of them – and that gives you a sense of balance.'

The script for *A Song for David* was the most obvious sign of a rapprochement in their relationship. Michael had come close to losing his father three years previously when Kirk was involved in a helicopter crash. The two young people in the aircraft were killed but Kirk survived. It was an epiphany which turned him towards a more spiritual exploration of himself and his faith. The serenity which Kirk Douglas found was an enormous help to his oldest son in trying times. As Michael told him, he didn't think he would need a father when he was fifty, but Kirk was there for him. Kirk Douglas was touched beyond words and also delighted that, even though it had taken fifty years, Michael saw him finally as a father. The relationship between the two characters in *A Song for David* is a fragile one, and neither Kirk nor Michael Douglas could contemplate making the film unless they were sure of their relationship with each other.

Michael Douglas had promised his father that they would make their film in 1995 and although he intended to make good on it, events conspired against him. However he had at least gone public on his promise. He had spent several months putting together a production slate for Constellation Films and, when it was announced in September 1995, *A Song for David* was on the list. The idea was to make twelve films in four years and Douglas and Steven Reuther were announcing the first four to go into production. Constellation's first foray into production was *Sabrina*, Sidney Pollack's remake of the much-loved Billy Wilder film, this time starring Harrison Ford and Julia Ormond. Constellation and Paramount were splitting the risk on the $50 million budget of the film which was due out in December 1995. Constellation had also paid $6 million for the screen rights to the John Grisham best-seller *The Rain Maker* and Grisham was to write the screenplay. The film would eventually star Matt Damon and Danny De Vito and be directed by Francis Ford Coppola. They were also producing *The Ghost and the Darkness*, an African adventure which was due to start filming in the autumn of 1995 starring Val Kilmer, and of course there was *A Song for David* in which he and his father would appear together.

There were other projects in the pipeline from Constellation apart from the four on which they were going public. At the post-premiere party for *Disclosure* in November 1994, for example, Douglas the star became Douglas the producer as he schmoozed Lou Pitt of the giant ICM agency. Douglas wanted Pitt's client Arnold Schwarzenegger to star in *Face/Off*, a science fiction crime thriller which Constellation were producing about a policeman who swaps faces with a terrorist to uncover his secrets. Schwarzenegger passed and when the film was eventually made, with John Travolta as the cop, Nicolas Cage as the terrorist, and John Woo behind the camera, it would give Constellation its biggest hit.

By the time he announced Constellation's initial slate to the Hollywood trade press Michael Douglas had almost completed another film. True to his word, it allowed him to keep his pants on, he did not play a flawed or tragic character, and he even got the girl. *The American President* is a romantic comedy in which the President of the United States, Andrew Shepherd, is a widower with a teenage daughter. Although isolated from most of the world by his position he manages to meet and fall in love with a lobbyist, Sydney Ellen Wade. Once word of the relationship gets out, she becomes the target of muck-raking political opponents and also the tabloid press. The promises Shepherd makes to her appear to compromise his political survival and in the end he has to decide which is more important to him.

The film was directed by Rob Reiner and owes much to another unproduced film called *The President Elopes*. From its self-evident title, this was another romantic comedy about a president who falls in love in office. That had been a pet project of Robert Redford's which never made it to the screen. The original idea had been for Redford and Emma Thompson to do that film, but by the time Reiner and screenwriter Aaron Sorkin finished their take on it, the parts were perfect for Michael Douglas and Annette Bening. They had been due to work together on *Disclosure*, and now that she was returning to work after the birth of her child they would get their chance.

'There are fourteen different versions of *The President Elopes* by fourteen different writers and I have not read one of them, purposely,' says Rob Reiner. 'Robert Redford approached me in 1989 with this project and described it very loosely as a Thirties or Forties screwball comedy in a very traditional style, about a president who leaves the White House in disguise and elopes and things like that. Frankly I wasn't really interested in that story, I had just made *When Harry Met Sally* and I didn't want to do another comedy. As years went by Aaron Sorkin and I had worked together on *A Few Good Men* and we had talked about doing a political film set in Washington. So I went back to it and asked if he would be interested in taking this basic idea. All we had was a single president and I asked if he would be interested in adding a political reality and he agreed.

'We developed the script and we showed it to Robert Redford but he really had his heart set on a much more traditional romantic comedy without these politics, even though he was aligned with those politics, and we parted the ways. Luckily Michael agreed to do it, and I say luckily because, if not, then I don't know who we would have got to do it. The Sydney character was not based on anyone, we just wanted a major character who would be believable. A number of times during the making of the film Michael asked me "They (Shepherd and Wade) get together very quickly. How is that going to work?" I said if I have been right I have cast the best actress in this country to come in and play this part and you will see what the attraction is right away. Annette brings with her not only her talents as an actress but also her intelligence. She brings a strength, a great sense of humour and all of those come on to the scene. When his character hears that for the first time – he is a person who has shut that part of himself away because his wife has died – all of a sudden those desires percolate to the surface when he hears a certain tone and a certain way this person carries herself and that's what triggers his interest.'

It was another big pay-day for Michael Douglas. His quote was now up to $15 million but Hollywood star salaries were in the middle of an astonishing inflationary spiral which would hit a peak as *The American President* was filming, when Mark Canton at

Columbia Pictures gave the nod to break the $20 million barrier to get Jim Carrey for *The Cable Guy*. Douglas, however, was very sanguine about his big fees, and had already given an eloquent and forthright defence of his salary to *Premiere* magazine when he was picking up $14 million for *Basic Instinct*.

'I defend myself with my credentials and my success in foreign markets,' said Douglas. '. . . For a lot of pictures foreign is larger (than domestic markets) and video is even larger. I spent time promoting my pictures overseas. That's why a company like Carolco knows it can sell its pictures in all of those territories . . . Then why should I give myself away? Just because you have a new austerity programme that has nothing to do with me. Life is not fair. If life were fair, the studios would share the video profits, the largest source of their income, on an equitable basis . . . And why aren't women compensated more? Because their movies have not been that successful. A lot of times they are more interested in how their role is worked out and defined, at the expense of the movie.'

For Douglas, the character of Andrew Shepherd in *The American President* was a character he could admire and even look up. Shepherd, like Douglas, was a staunch liberal. He was also, like Douglas, a fierce advocate of gun control. Douglas and his friend Jann Wenner, the publisher of *Rolling Stone*, had formed an organisation called Cease Fire which campaigns for handgun control. The group was set up in the aftermath of the murder of John Lennon and Douglas does commercials and voice-overs for them to raise their public profile.

Andrew Shepherd was, one suspects, a president for whom Douglas would cheerfully have voted. A supporter of then-President Bill Clinton, Douglas had had some experience of White House society, but not a great deal. However as part of his research he did spend some time with Clinton's staff, as well as some time observing Clinton himself. After a while, he confessed, he started to feel almost presidential himself.

'It took a little while but after we got the hair and make-up test done I looked okay, then I had all those nice words from Aaron Sorkin,' says Douglas. 'I did tend to get to work a half hour early in the morning so that I could get that extra walk around the stage with everyone saying "Good morning Mr President." I enjoyed that part. One of the nice perks of playing the president is that you get to go home at night as opposed to the real guy who keeps on going.'

Douglas was joking about the presidential adulation but he was sincere in his desire to do justice to this part. He was aware that he was perhaps becoming somewhat typecast in these flawed roles he had made his own, and Andrew Shepherd was a chance to break that mould. There were also resonances in a very human way between Shepherd's experiences and his own. According to Rob Reiner, one of the inspirations for *The President Elopes* had been a remark attributed to John F. Kennedy shortly after he was elected President. He evidently turned to one of his trusted aides and pointed out that he would now never make another friend for as long as he lived. He would never know whether anyone was interested in him for himself or because of the office he occupied. As an international celebrity, Michael Douglas had also had some experience of that.

'It's hard in my business to make new friends because you are always suspicious of their motives,' he says. 'While I don't like it about myself, I tend to be a little more cautious about making new friends. The people that you knew either when you were starting out in your career or in college didn't take your success as part of the equation of your friendship. They are the ones you love and trust. I would like to be more open about meeting people, but it's hard.'

The American President is, partly, an essay on the isolation of fame and that is something which Michael Douglas understood perfectly.

'The picture tried to portray that and this is one of the areas where, being a so-called celebrity in show business, you can identify a little bit,' he says. 'There is an isolationist quality, there is a feeling of a certain self-consciousness when you go out in public because you don't know what you're going to be dealing with. People may or may not be looking at you more abnormally than someone else, and you have to plan your moves to some degree.

'There's a total lack of privacy anywhere you go publicly, anywhere in the world. I was with a friend on a boat in the Seychelles and we went to an isolated archipelago where there is no one but a ranger whom they change every six months. We struggled our Zodiac through the surf and this man came out and said 'Ah Michael Douglas, *bonsoir*." I asked how he knew me and he said they had a video on the island with some of my movies. So it's everywhere you go in the world. You end up kind of hanging out with your old friends. It's hard to make new friends, so you know you have people who are either friends from university or friends like Danny De Vito or Jack Nicholson, people you've known for 25 years, 30 years. It's difficult because it's not your nature, but people do act differently around you. You go to Washington and even senators and congressmen there get goofy about celebrities. Everyone gets kinda goofy about celebrities.'

One of the attractions for Douglas in the screenplay of *The American President* was the way in which Reiner and Sorkin had developed their theme and tried to remind people that the Chief Executive is a man too. It was nice, says Douglas, to see a script which reminded people that the president has foibles just as they do.

If he was forced, Douglas would admit to Jimmy Carter as being the President whom he most admires, as much for what he has done since he left the White House as what he did in office. Although the film was released in the United States at the time of Bill Clinton's 1996 re-election bid and the villain of the piece – Richard Dreyfuss's hawkish Republican Bob Rumson – seemed to be very similar to Clinton's opponent Bob Dole, Douglas says Andrew Shepherd is not – nor was he intended to be – Bill Clinton.

'I'm not as tall as Bill Clinton for a start,' he jokes. 'I met him formally on two or three occasions, I was in the Oval Office one day when he did his Saturday radio address to the nation. It was really more a combination of looking at films going back as far as President Kennedy. Rob was very helpful to me in getting hold of a lot of presidential daily diaries of different presidents to give the idea of unrelenting pace, always trying to catch up, always trying to stay on top of something. So I don't think in terms of mannerisms or anything of that area I was really trying to focus on President Clinton. Quite the contrary. His style is actually a more folksy style. Actually because of the liberalism of the piece I wanted a president who looked a little more conservative than our image of the Democratic presidents we've had. Someone who was more palatable to a particular audience.'

With *The American President* in the can, Douglas was back home again. He and Diandra knew that they had a difficult decision to make. Despite all their best efforts it was obvious that their marriage was not working and had not been working for some time. On his birthday the previous September he had told everyone how much in love he was with his wife. Now in July, 1996 – some nine months later – they announced that they were separating, citing irreconcilable differences. It was another blow in a dreadful two year spell which showed no sign of letting up. Although he did not know it, there was much more to come before this run of tragedy and bad luck would end.

Despite all of Michael Douglas's best efforts to find a palatable president, the film was not palatable to large parts of the cinema-going audience. There is no doubt that it is a warm, witty, intelligent romantic comedy. Apart from fine work from Douglas and Benning, there is also excellent support from an outstanding cast which included Martin Sheen, Michael J. Fox, and David Paymer. But *The American President* simply did not find its audience at the box office when it was released in November 1995. Perhaps they were simply too tired of seeing politics on television every night in election coverage to go and pay to watch it at the movies. By Hollywood standards *The American President* was not hugely expensive at $62 million, however in the United States it brought in only $65 million at the box office with about the same again overseas.

As he prepared to go on his own with *The Ghost and the Darkness*, the first fully-financed film from Constellation, Michael Douglas must have been aware that a box office return like that could do his new company a lot of real damage.

INTO AFRICA

The box-office disappointment of *The American President* was followed a month later by another blow for Michael Douglas when *Sabrina*, Constellation's first real production, also under-performed at the box office. *Sabrina* was a remake of the 1954 Billy Wilder film about a rich playboy who falls in love with the chauffeur's daughter. His staid older brother is given the job of breaking up the relationship but instead falls for her himself. In the original version William Holden was the playboy, Humphrey Bogart the older brother, and Audrey Hepburn was Sabrina. In this version the roles were played by Greg Kinnear, Harrison Ford and Julia Ormond. The film was well received critically and should by rights have been a big hit. To this day Harrison Ford is still puzzled that it wasn't. In the event the film, which cost $58 million, took only $53 million at the box office in the United States. Constellation's exposure had been limited by the fact that it was sharing production costs with Paramount, but even so, the hoped for home run had barely made it to first base.

While this may have been a concern for Michael Douglas it was no more than an irritation. In the early months of 1996 he was much more concerned for his father. Kirk Douglas had suffered a debilitating stroke in January which, combined with crippling sciatica, had left him barely able to walk or talk. It was a huge blow for Kirk Douglas, who had been an actor for fifty years. Acting was his life and if he could not walk or talk then what use would he be. He was doubly devastated because the stroke had come only weeks after a production date had been announced for *A Song for David*, which was to begin filming in the spring of 1996. Michael put everything on hold and raced to his father's side, he was the eldest son so he took on a great deal of his father's responsibilities. His greatest task was simply to be there, to encourage his father and to support his indomitable will power. Kirk Douglas was determined that he would walk and talk again and began an intensive programme of physical and speech therapy.

'Michael was very encouraging,' he said later. 'I remember one day when he called me on the phone and said "Dad, don't worry. You keep working with your speech therapist and when you can talk like me, we'll make the movie." And I told him, 'Why don't you go to a speech therapist to learn to talk like me and then no one will be able to tell the difference."'

Apart from *A Song for David*, Kirk Douglas had another target to achieve on his road to recovery. Despite marvellous performances in films such as *Champion, Lust for Life, The Bad and the Beautiful, Ace in the Hole, Spartacus* and many more, Kirk Douglas had never won an Oscar. At the Academy Awards ceremony in March of 1996 he was due to receive a special Oscar for lifetime achievement. At this stage the extent of his speech problem had not been made public, and actor's vanity meant that he asked Michael to accept on his behalf. His son refused. Michael pointed out that this was an award he should have won forty years ago and, even if he had to crawl, Kirk Douglas should go on that stage to pick up what was due to him. On the night there was not a dry eye in the house – including

Michael Douglas – when his father came on stage to accept his award from Steven Spielberg and make a brief but moving speech which earned him his second standing ovation of the night.

The stroke which devastated Kirk Douglas was a bad enough blow in itself for Michael Douglas, but it did not occur in isolation. At almost the same time that his father had his stroke, his mother was diagnosed as having breast cancer. She had gone for a routine examination and a lump had been discovered. A biopsy revealed that it was malignant and there was a fear that the cancer may have spread. However, further investigation discovered that the lymph nodes were clear and the disease did not appear to have meta-stasised. After two months of radiation therapy Diana was finally given a clean bill of health. There was another scare later in the year when she returned for a check-up. Another lump was discovered but this one turned out to be benign.

After those initial few anxious weeks following his father's stroke and his mother's radiation treatment, Michael Douglas was able to return to work. Immediately after the release of *The American President* he was on his way to Africa to co-star with Val Kilmer in *The Ghost and the Darkness*, an epic adventure set in colonial Africa. The film had been written several years previously by Oscar-winning screenwriter William Goldman.

'Our company landed at Paramount Studios with basically a blank slate with no pictures in production or development,' he explained. 'What you do as a production company is that you go and look at a studio's inventory and see what they have. Studios are notorious for developing huge amounts of material which is never made. Obviously a screenplay by William Goldman was worth taking a look at, and I loved the script and could not understand why it had not been made in the six years it had been at the studio before we got there.'

Goldman's screenplay is based on a true story about a pair of man-eating lions which terrorised the workforce attempting to build a bridge over the Tsavo River in East Africa to carry a vital link in a trans-continental railway. These beasts – one was named 'The Ghost' by terrified workers who named the other one 'The Darkness' – hunted for pleasure and not for food and, uncannily, they hunted as a pair. During a nine month period in 1898 they were responsible for the deaths of 135 railway workers. Eventually John Patterson, a railway engineer, who was forced to become a big-game hunter by circumstance, taught himself how to hunt and track and killed them. The lions can currently be seen at the Field Museum in Chicago.

It is an exciting and gripping story. When he read accounts of it President Theodore Roosevelt, himself a famous hunter, called it 'the most remarkable account of which we have any record.' Some-times exciting and gripping is not enough on its own in Hollywood. They want stars and the more the better. Obviously Patterson would be the central figure in the story, but there was a chance for another starring role here. During his nine-month hunt – condensed to three in the film – Patterson was assisted by a number of other hunters who were all unsuccessful in bagging the lions. This assortment of characters was distilled into one white hunter, called Remington.

'Remington is false so let's start with that,' said Douglas. 'They actually tried, there were a number of attempts for people to come and kill the lions . . . and the idea of this white hunter being American, which did exist at that time, was a reach. But since we were telling essentially a British story in Africa we thought that it would add an element in terms of attracting an American under-standing as someone who came out of the Civil War. But from what I can see from Patterson's book, from what we've read, the rest is pretty accurate and pretty true.'

Stephen Hopkins, a young and talented British director, was chosen to direct the film and Val Kilmer was to play Patterson. The fact that Kilmer had spent at least one month a year in Africa for the past twelve years made him something of an obvious choice. Finding someone to play Remington, on the other hand, was becoming problematic. The film had actually started shooting in Africa without the role being cast. Finally, as producer, Michael

Douglas cast an actor he had known all his life: himself.

'I was never, ever thinking about being involved in this picture at all as an actor,' Douglas explains. 'This was simply basically going to be a production for our company. But as I started spending more time on the development of the script, working with Bill Goldman and getting to do a little more research on what was going on in Africa at that time, I got more and more interested . . . I got involved with the casting with Val and Stephen Hopkins, and our production design. And I hadn't found anything I wanted to do as an actor at that time so I thought "What the hell, Remington would be great." I do these pictures where you are in every single scene of the movie and you really have a tremendous responsibility to the picture when you do that kind of movie. I used to always be jealous of these actors who come in for three or four weeks, act their ass off and have a really good time and I'm stuck there carrying the story. I thought this will be great, it has some of the character aspects I like – basically overacting – and the chance to have some fun. So that's how I decided to jump in it was kind of towards the end. But I never thought about playing Paterson, no.'

There were other, more significant casting problems than finding a meaty supporting role for himself. The mood of the audience had changed since William Goldman wrote his original script. When this film was finally in production not only were audiences generally more ecologically aware, this was also, as Douglas pointed out, the age of *The Lion King*. Would audiences who knew and loved the Disney experience relate to Patterson and Remington, or would the simply dismiss them and start mentally cheering for the lions? The tone of the film was very important and the potential drift in audience sympathy had been a major concern for studios over the years. Another significant concern was the cost of the film. Either way, whether you used animatronic lions or took a risk with real ones, this was not a cheap film – the final budget was around $55 million – and if the lions didn't look right it wouldn't matter who else was starring in it. It was a problem of which Douglas was only too well aware.

'We had a man named Sledge Reynolds who was our animal co-ordinator,' Douglas explains. 'He was basically a casting agent who went around the world looking for lions matching up five or six lions to the requirements that these two lions would need. We ended up with two French lions who were the most ferocious and the most violent – you only worked with them with a trainer who had a big whip and a camera crew in a security cage – down to two American and a Canadian lion. There were ones that could run and ones that could jump and Stephen Hopkins worked with Sledge in terms of storyboarding the action sequences and what needed to be done. Sledge then brought the whole animal crew to the location about four months before we started shooting to get used to the lions and used to the environment.

'The other problem he had was that, as in the movie, these two male lions had to work together and they don't like to do that. They have their own prides and they are very separate. What happened, and this was one of the great surprises, was that when the days came to work with them, the lions were the least of our problems and they hit their marks better than some actors I know. They did a really good job. We also had animatronic lions and some computer-generated ones, but the live ones were the most important'.

The Ghost and the Darkness was a difficult shoot in terms of simply getting to the location. Choosing locations had been a problem. Douglas had been keen to make the film in the Tsavo National Park itself, but it had no real infrastructure for a film of this size. Instead much of the film was shot in the Songimelvo Game Reserve, which is on the border between Swaziland and South Africa. There was one other factor which may have tipped the scales in Songimelvo's favour.

'Remote as it was,' he explains, 'there was a young couple from Namibia who had recently moved over there and developed their farm into a nine hole golf course. I just couldn't believe it. I had a great time and that was because I had a lot of producing help and I wasn't carrying a movie. I was reminded of the joy and fun of movie making rather than the overbearing responsibility I am usually involved with.'

As Douglas concedes, the hotel where the cast and crew were staying was remote and involved a minimum 40-minute drive to the location – and that was only after they had built bridges and improved the roads. Two days before the start of filming the rains came with a vengeance. A seven-year drought ended, producing torrential rain which brought with it serious flooding in places. Everything they had built in terms of roads and bridges was simply washed away in the torrent. The only alternative was for the cast and crew to travel to the location on rubber rafts along swollen rivers, with armed guards stationed on the boats to drive off hippos which might capsize them. None of this was a problem for Kilmer. As an old African hand he had eschewed the comforts of the hotel and decided to stay out in the park with Sledge Reynolds and the lion handlers. It is this singular attitude of Kilmer's which has led to him being branded one of Hollywood's more difficult actors. John Frankenheimer reportedly ordered him off the set in *The Island of Dr Moreau* the minute his last shot was in the can, while Joel Schumacher, who directed him in *Batman Forever*, called him 'childish and impossible'.

Michael Douglas would not have been unaware of Kilmer's reputation when he cast him. He would also not have been unsympathetic to Kilmer's emotional state given that his marriage to his wife, Joanne Whalley, was on the verge of breaking up. He was, however, also the producer of the film and he would not take those responsibilities lightly.

'We got along fine, mostly,' says Douglas. 'I arrived four or five weeks after production had started. Val had a heavy load, he was in the middle of a divorce, and I think he had done two or three pictures back to back. He was working a lot. He was also late, and he was getting later. We had a talk about the responsibilities of carrying a movie. I told him my philosophy about how if you're carrying a movie you have to set a tone for that.'

While he was on location in Africa, Douglas was staying in close contact with Kirk and Anne Douglas to monitor his father's progress, as well as staying in touch with his mother to keep an eye on her health. As for Diandra and Cameron, even though he and his wife were now separated they all remained on good terms. They had been married for almost 20 years and there was too much involved to simply throw it all away. Douglas had an idea. With him already being in Africa , why not take advantage of the splendour of the location and take the chance to spend one of their most exotic family breaks together?

'My family came down at Christmas – I'd been there for a month and a half – and I took them to a safari camp,' he recalls. 'They have these open vehicles and they do this night tracking which is pretty amazing, where a guy sits on the hood with a flashlight. What happens is that they pick up the reflection of eyes, like a reflector in a road sign, and they can tell which eyes are those of nocturnal animals, and they tracked a lion who had just been at a wildebeest kill. Some of the people on the safari recognised me, I told them why I was down there – I had been down for a couple of months and I had my whole Remington look – and the driver pulls up in this thing and the lion is only feet away eating the wildebeest. It's looking up and there is a kind of a crunching sound going. I said "Excuse me, should we be this close?" and they all said "Oh sure, big white hunter, here for two months",' he laughs. 'But that was actually the most nervous time I had dealing with all of the lions, when I was on safari.'

'I actually asked the guide if we would be all right being so close to the lions. "Oh it's all right Mr Douglas", he said, "I have seen all your movies. Nothing frightens you."'

ALL IN THE GAME

The beginning of 1996 saw Michael Douglas busier than ever. He was fielding film offers right, left and centre and continuing to produce his own films through Constellation. *Face/Off*, the film for which he had approached Arnold Schwarzenegger almost eighteen months ago, was getting ready to go and would go on to be one of the most successful films of 1997. In the meantime Douglas's talents as an actor were still very much in demand.

He had hoped to follow *The Ghost in the Darkness* with *A Song for David* but his father's illness had put paid to that for the time being. Both men, however, were determined that the project was merely delayed and not abandoned. The time in between was being spent continuing to get to know each other. Kirk Douglas's stroke was turning out to be a blessing in disguise for his oldest son.

'Since his stroke I have been spending a great deal of time with him,' he says. 'We are becoming the father and son that we never were . . . He's inspirational. I really love him to death. He's turned out to be such a super dad at a time when you'd least expect to be getting input from your father.'

Leaving his domestic affairs to one side, Douglas was juggling two equally intriguing and equally lucrative film offers. The film industry is an industry which is dominated by trends. As the century drew to a close the risk involved in the soaring cost of making films meant that fewer and fewer films were genuinely original. Studios felt they had a better chance of getting a return on their money with films that audiences felt comfortable with. The consequence of this is that when one studio got a winning idea it was immediately copy-catted by other studios and smaller film companies. Sometimes they all got their big ideas at the same time, which in recent years has led to two Robin Hood movies with a third left at the starting gate, competing versions of the Three Musketeers, two asteroid movies, and two computer-animated films about insects doing battle at the box office at roughly the same time.

At the beginning of 1996 Hollywood's big theme was volcanoes and there were two projects on the stocks, each desperate to be first into the cinema. Conventional wisdom has it that first one in gets the bulk of the box office, although that did not happen in the race between *Deep Impact* and *Armageddon* or *Antz* and *A Bug's Life*. The two competing projects were *Dante's Peak*, about a volcanic eruption which devastates a small town in the Pacific North-West, and *Volcano*, about a volcanic eruption centred on the La Brea tar pits in the heart of Los Angeles.

This was a high stakes game and to demonstrate their sincerity Universal had offered Michael Douglas the lead in *Dante's Peak*, as a vulcanologist who tries to warn the town of the impending danger. To further demonstrate their conviction they were also offering a salary of $20 million. Within days, however, the offer was off the table. Universal had heard that Douglas was also considering another project and, with no time to wait on a star to make up his mind between two films, they went elsewhere. Pierce Brosnan eventually starred in *Dante's Peak* – for considerably less than $20 million – while Tommy Lee Jones starred in *Volcano*, the rival project. *Dante's Peak* did get into cinemas first, with *Volcano* being delayed until the following year, but neither film was a huge box office hit.

The other film which Douglas was considering was a much more intriguing prospect. *The Game* was to be directed by David Fincher and its central character could have been written with Michael Douglas in mind. Nicholas van Orton is a tycoon whose life is dominated by the memory of his father's suicide. As he himself approaches the age at which his father killed himself, he is given a birthday gift which will change his life. He is enrolled in a game but he does not know when it will start, who else is involved, and has no idea of the rules. His life is turned upside down as he is socially discredited, financially ruined, almost killed, implicated in a murder and ultimately driven to the brink of madness and suicide. Throughout his ordeal he is never certain what is real and what is 'The Game', or where 'The Game' ends and his life begins again. *The Game* is a brilliantly constructed screenplay and after his success with *Seven*, David Fincher was regarded as one of the brightest and best talents in the business.

'I thought it was the best-structured script I had read in a long time,' said Douglas. 'I like the nervous edginess, the dark humour, the uncertainty in a time when big, predictable movies are doing well.'

There were potential advantages here for both men. The central role of Nicholas van Orton offered a lot to Douglas as an actor, on the other hand the film was so complex and potentially uncommercial that Fincher would require the presence of a major star like Douglas to smooth its path at the box office. The path would be even smoother, of course, if a major female star such as Jodie Foster were to co-star. At one point it seemed almost certain, it was even announced in the industry trade papers in March 1996, but within months the deal had degenerated into a welter of recrimination and lawsuits.

What is certain is that Foster was keen on playing what is effectively the supporting role in *The Game*, the person who enrols van Orton in the bizarre venture as a birthday gift. According to Douglas he was pitched the idea that Foster would be playing his younger sister and he had no problem with that. The difficulties began when he learned that Foster – who was only nineteen years his junior – wanted to play his daughter. Mathematically it was feasible, but Douglas had serious doubts about its dramatic potential. He pointed out that he felt this changed a lot of things and he was uncomfortable with the idea. Since PolyGram, who were producing the film, had given Douglas casting approval it was unlikely that he would go along with the idea.

Jodie Foster's side of events, as outlined by her brother Buddy in his book *Foster Child*, is a little different. She claimed she had agreed to work for four weeks in the summer of 1996 on *The Game* for a fee of $4.5 million plus five per cent of the box office, and as a consequence she had taken herself off the market. Foster claimed that PolyGram had no intention of ever using her in the film and had merely used her name to help raise finance. According to Buddy Foster, his sister was also horrified to learn that Douglas had script approval which meant that, in theory, he could change her lines to whatever he wanted. By June 1996 the trade papers were announcing that Foster had left *The Game*, although Buddy Foster puts it a little more plainly when he claims she was 'dumped' from the picture. However you describe it, Foster did not go quietly and she left in her wake a $54.5 million lawsuit in which she was suing PolyGram for breach of contract, fraud and defamation.

They were now left to look for a replacement for Jodie Foster and although Jeff Bridges was considered for a time, the role was finally played by Sean Penn who would be Nicholas van Orton's wayward younger brother, Conrad. For Michael Douglas, Nicholas van Orton was a character he knew well. Like Andrew Shepherd in *The American President*, van Orton is a man who has to deal with the isolation of power, as he spends his birthday alone in a big house with only the television for company. Douglas knew that feeling all too well, especially since his separation from Diandra so, in one sense, this was not too much of a challenge for him. He understood, however, when Fincher told him that if he came on board there would be no question of softening the character. Douglas agreed with Fincher that it was van Orton's very impersonal ruthlessness which made the character interesting.

Michael Douglas has made films which have been logistically difficult. *Romancing the Stone* and *The Jewel of the Nile* spring to mind, or more recently *The Ghost and the Darkness*, but few have been as difficult personally as *The Game*. The amount of distractions which were taking place in his personal life would have been enough to send most actors screaming for their trailer, but Douglas never missed a call despite overwhelming demands on his time.

There was, of course, his father's continuing recovery and his need to provide constant support. Then there was his own marriage to consider. After nearly two years of separation he and Diandra were finally going to divorce. Diandra had never got used to being the wife of a man whose face was known all round the world. She also could not abide the Hollywood lifestyle and, with Michael working and Cameron in boarding school, she was feeling increasingly isolated and unhappy. They had both tried and failed and it was time to call it a day. She realised now what she should have realised back at that White House inauguration. She and her husband were from different worlds. He was part of a group of wild and crazy guys, which included Warren Beatty and Jack Nicholson, who had the world spread out at their feet waiting for them to take advantage. She, on the other hand, came from a refined and cultured scholarly background.

'Now I realise how young and stupid I was,' she told *Vanity Fair* magazine. 'I appeared older because I had grown up in Europe and I had already coped with my father's drinking and his death. I was an only child who spent a lot of time with friends of my mother, who was an artist. I knew nothing about Hollywood but I did know that

I loved this man . . . My family didn't like the idea of my marriage. They wanted me to finish school.'

Diandra had tried to deal with life in Hollywood by making a life for herself. She had gone to college and tried to complete her degree, but when Cameron came along so early in the marriage those plans had to be abandoned. Being a new mother meant there was no way that Diandra could spend her nights at Hollywood parties. Michael Douglas began to resent this and, to prevent arguments, she simply stopped going to the parties. He did not stop going and, since he was there on his own, there were always women there to take Diandra's place. She did contemplate leaving him but Douglas insists there was never a question of him leaving her for another woman.

In the end it was her relationship with Cameron which saw her through the difficult periods and ultimately helped her end the marriage.

'We spent a lot of time alone when Michael was away doing pictures back-to-back,' Diandra continued. 'You can't have a healthy family life with children when you're away ten months of the year. But Michael was pursuing his vision of himself and I have never put myself in the position of saying "I don't want you to do this movie." Never.'

Ultimately Diandra and Cameron had spent so much time alone together they realised they had their own life. Michael Douglas had become an irrelevance in his own marriage. Eventually the intrusions, the invasions, and the innuendo associated with being married to Michael Douglas became more than she could take.

'It's very difficult,' she said. '. . . If you have a marriage to a movie star, you have to accept that your life is under the microscope. I don't have the power to change it. I'm sure I could dwell on certain things that have been painful and humiliating but I try not to do that.'

Diandra was going to move back to Spain where she kept their house, while he was moving to their apartment on Central Park West in New York; the house in Santa Barbara would be sold. The biggest crisis involved their son Cameron, whom Douglas had been determined to protect at all costs.

On 28 October 1996 the seventeen-year-old Cameron was driving along the street in Santa Barbara when he hit a car which was at a red light. That car then shunted into another car. This third car belonged to an off-duty Secret Service agent, who got out and tried to take the teenager's car keys from him. Cameron Douglas drove off with the agent hanging on to the car. According to the police the ensuing chase caused a three-car pileup before Cameron Douglas's car eventually hit a taxi which then collided with a fountain. The boy was arrested and charged with drunken driving, hit-and-run, as well as driving with a suspended licence. He was eventually released into his mother's custody. A pained Michael Douglas released a statement saying that he and Diandra would do what was appropriate.

'Anybody who is a parent,' said the statement, 'knows how difficult it is for Diandra and myself.'

Douglas had been called to Santa Barbara in the middle of the night to help deal with his son. He was back at work, on time, the following morning and most people working on *The Game* had no idea that anything untoward had happened until they saw the evening news or read the following day's papers.

'There is nothing like a family crisis,' said Douglas, 'especially a divorce, to force a person to re-evaluate his life. My divorce was my game. It certainly put my life into perspective.'

Throughout all of this David Fincher was astonished at the performance which Michael Douglas was contributing to his film. Fincher came to the conclusion that Douglas's best performances were fuelled by rage and what was going on in his personal life was providing an impetus and a well-spring for his professional life.

'It was absolutely uncanny,' says Fincher. 'Between shots Michael would be in his trailer on the phone talking to lawyers for his wife, son, and brother and talking to his father. You knew he was in pain but he was the consummate professional. He never brought any of his personal pain on to the set of *The Game*.'

There was more disappointing news for Michael Douglas. *The Ghost and the Darkness* opened in October just as he was completing filming on *The Game*. The film did not find much favour with either critics or audiences. It was involved in a three-way box office tie on its opening weekend with *The First Wives Club* and *The Long Kiss Goodnight*, although Douglas would later claim that their opening weekend of $9.215 million gave them first place. He was right, but in the end it didn't amount to much. Douglas was also furious at Val Kilmer who had not done a great deal to promote the film in the United States. It is pure conjecture as to whether it would have made much difference, but as far as Douglas was concerned this was part of the discussion they had had back in Africa. Promoting your film and supporting the release was part of your responsibilities as the star of the film. Douglas only had a supporting role but he was the executive producer and he ended up doing the bulk of the promotional work.

'Those things have a way of coming back to haunt you,' said Douglas ominously about Kilmer's lack of enthusiasm.

The film, which had cost $55 million to make, only took $34 million in the United States and $75 million worldwide. Constellation had missed out on its first two turns at bat, but there were still the big guns of *Face/Off* and *The Rain Maker* to come.

A PERFECT VILLAIN

Cameron Douglas became his father's main priority for the next twelve months. He went in to a clinic to be treated for substance abuse and he received all the support and affection that he required from both his parents. This was another difficult time for Michael Douglas, because his half-brother Eric had been arrested for driving under the influence of drink and drugs. Eric had previously been in jail for disrupting an internal flight from California to New Jersey. Although he felt for Eric and was concerned because this was a worry his father could do without, Michael Douglas's chief concern was for Cameron.

'I tried to be as supportive and loving as I could,' says Douglas. 'It's something I have learned from my father these past couple of years . . . When I was growing up I was always just Kirk Douglas's son. I had to fight for my own identity. Even though I had some success in the early Seventies with *The Streets of San Francisco*, I didn't come into my own until 1975 when I produced *One Flew*

Over the Cuckoo's Nest. Cameron is third generation. It's going to be even harder for him to carve out a niche for himself.'

Michael Douglas more or less returned to public life in the autumn of 1997 to coincide with the release of *The Game*. No matter what was going on in his personal life he would not avoid any of his responsibilities to the film.

'I'm just coming up for air after all the trials and tribulations in my personal life over the past three years,' he said. 'I'm really looking forward to a little bit of reflection. I'm trying to simplify, to allow myself time to think about what I want to do.'

As part of the pre-publicity for *The Game*, Michael Douglas made a small piece of Hollywood history. The film was scheduled to open at the famous Mann's Chinese Theater on Hollywood Boulevard on 12 September. Two days before that Douglas joined the elite in Hollywood whose hand or foot prints have been immortalised in cement in the courtyard in front of the famous cinema. His father's hand prints were already there and, with Michael joining the pantheon, he and Kirk were the first father and son to be commemorated in this landmark tourist attraction.

Once the publicity duties are completed the film's fate is in the lap of the gods and the skill of the marketing department. In this case the public embraced *The Game* on its opening weekend but, as is frequently the case with David Fincher's films, the enthusiasm of that first three-day period was not matched over subsequent weeks and the film faded quickly. However it was released almost simultaneously in Europe and the United States and foreign markets embraced the film as enthusiastically as they had most of Michael Douglas's films. When it finally finished its run *The Game* had taken more than $100 million internationally and returned a tidy profit. By this time Michael Douglas was taking a short break during which he would celebrate his 53rd birthday before throwing himself into another film role. Although they were still working out the terms of their divorce, Michael and Diandra Douglas remained on good terms and there was little acrimony between them. They talked regularly on the phone and he would often discuss his film projects with her. There was, however, an undisguised glee when he called to let her know about his latest film.

'I called her,' he laughed, 'and I said "Hey, guess what, I'm doing another movie" and she asked what it was about. "Murdering your wife," I said. "I don't think that's funny," she said and I said "No, I know you don't."'

In fact Douglas had signed on to star in *A Perfect Murder*, which was a new version of Alfred Hitchcock's *Dial M for Murder* which had been filmed in 1954. Producer Arnold Kopelson had been watching a laser disc of the 1954 movie with his wife and producing partner Anne when it occurred to them that it might be ripe for a remake. Unfortunately for the Kopelsons someone else felt the same way about Knott's play, for *Dial M for Murder* was one of a number of projects which independent producer Christopher Mankiewicz was developing for Warner Brothers. Mankiewicz had the property but Arnold Kopelson, who was coming off a string of hits including *The Fugitive*, had access to the talent. A partnership seemed the obvious solution.

The Fugitive proved something of a template for the new film which began with a working title of *Dial M for Murder*. A number of key crew positions were filled with people the Kopelsons knew from the Harrison Ford picture, but none more vital than director Andrew Davis. The Chicago-born Davis was a cinematographer turned director, who had earned a reputation as something of an action specialist when he moved behind the camera. In 1988 he had directed Steven Seagal's film debut *Above the Law* – also known as *Nico* – and had watched it become hugely profitable. Four years later both he and Seagal made it on to the A list with *Under Siege* which was an enormous international hit. The success of his next film *The Fugitive* confirmed Davis as a major studio name, but at the same time he was keen not to be pigeon-holed. His next film *Steal Big, Steal Little* was a comedy which flopped and even when he returned to the action genre with *Chain Reaction* he was unable to recapture his earlier box office success. *A Perfect Murder*, as the new film would be known, gave him the chance to break out of the action movie mould and concentrate on a more intimate drama.

Davis was working from a script by Patrick Smith Kelly, who had been brought in to update the original and make it more relevant for modern audiences. Unlike the Hitchcock, which was a deliberate and rather literal translation of Frederick Knott's hit play, the new version would use Knott's play merely as a jumping off point. The play was opened out completely and the locations switched from the stuffy snobbery of clubbable post-war London to the pre-millennial mayhem of modern Manhattan.

Steven Taylor is a wealthy industrialist who discovers that his beautiful trophy wife, Emily, is having an affair with a bohemian painter, David Shaw. She is slipping away from her job as an interpreter at the United Nations to spend passionate afternoons with her painter-lover in his abandoned loft studio. Taylor insinuates himself into Shaw's life on the pretext of buying some of his work. Then he drops a bombshell. He knows that Shaw is in fact an ex-con with a history of swindling wealthy women. If he tells the police then Shaw, a three-time loser, will go to jail for life. However if Shaw agrees to murder Emily then not only will he not go to the police but he will also pay Shaw a six figure sum. All is not as it should be with Steven Taylor's business empire and the murder of his wife would not only provide him with revenge for her infidelity, it would also provide him with access to her multi-million dollar trust fund to bail out his ailing business and avoid prosecution for financial irregularities. Taylor will arrange everything, all Shaw has to do is turn up and strangle his wife. At the last moment Shaw gets cold feet. He sub-contracts the job to one of his underworld contacts who bungles it. Emily survives, the would-be murderer is killed, and Taylor is faced with the realisation that Shaw is still alive and has information which could ruin him.

The part of Steven Taylor was ideal for Michael Douglas. It helped that Arnold Kopelson and Michael Douglas are friends and Douglas was immediately attracted to the part of a man who is both successful and charming as a man, but deadly and predatory as a husband. The challenge of finding something with which the audience could identify in a man who decides that the only suitable penalty for his wife's adultery is murder was something which appealed to Douglas as an actor. It echoed the ambivalence of the characters he had played in *Wall Street*, *Fatal Attraction*, *Basic Instinct*, *Disclosure*, and most recently in *The Game*. Although there is no one in *A Perfect Murder* who is completely innocent Douglas again found himself playing the ostensible villain of the piece.

'Villainry is wonderful for acting, villainry is so much fun, it's the most fun. I'm curious about why audiences love villains so much. I think it's because in the first place they can see what fun the actor is having. But I think also there is a part of us – we try so hard to be good and social and civil people – but there is a part of us which loves someone who just doesn't care what other people think about what they do. There is that animal instinct in us, so it's a lot of fun. Sometimes I am a little worried about becoming the Prince of Darkness. All of my movies are kind of contemporary movies and I keep wondering why I do these dark movies because I would love to play a hero. Then I realise that I don't know any contemporary heroes. In my father's period, or in World War II, we had good guys and bad guys, but since I've grown up I don't see any heroes. That's why I liked *The American President* but I haven't found too many of those parts, or maybe they don't come looking for me. They go looking for Tom Hanks.'

Like Gordon Gekko, Steven Taylor is another one of Tom Wolfe's Masters of the Universe, commanding everything that he surveyed. In many ways he is the man that Gordon Gekko could have gone on to become: wealthy, powerful, corrupting, manipulative, and still skirting on the edges of lawlessness. As played by Michael Douglas he prowls through the film, long hair swept back in a leonine mane, like a predator in the financial jungles of New York. It is a performance of both power and subtlety. His presence dominates the film even when he is off-screen, he turns up when he is least expected, he is incapable of being surprised. Yet, in a carefully nuanced portrayal by Douglas which once again invites the audience to feel some sympathy for an unfeeling monster, we see this man brought down by his own hubris.

The role of Steven Taylor's trophy bride went to Gwyneth Paltrow, while Viggo Mortensen played David Shaw. Mortensen, who is an artist in his own right, used his own paintings to double for those which were supposed to have been done by Shaw. But it was the casting of Paltrow which raised the most eyebrows. There was the obvious comment on the fact that Paltrow, who had been most frequently compared to Grace Kelly, was now taking one of the late star's most famous roles. This was a fact not lost on Paltrow herself. That aside the tabloids had a field day with one other aspect of her participation in the film. Paltrow is the daughter of actress Blythe Danner and television director Bruce Paltrow, both friends of Michael Douglas for thirty years. Douglas had known them almost since Gwyneth was born. He had bounced her on his knee as a child and here he was playing her husband in a film.

It was, on the surface at least, a situation which could have been fraught with tension but everyone concerned did their best to make light of it. When magazine stories appeared suggesting that Bruce Paltrow had phoned his old friend with a 'Hands off' message, both Paltrow and Douglas were quick to make it clear that it had only been a joke. In his press comments Michael Douglas resolutely refused to dignify the argument by taking the question seriously. He would invariably acknowledge the difficulty of someone thinking of their daughter conducting an on-screen romance with someone who had been a family friend for years, then make light of it by suggesting, for example, that he thought they made 'a lovely couple'.

The May-December relationship between Michael Douglas was heightened by the fact that it was simply one of many which were appearing on screen at the time. When the film was released in the summer of 1998 audiences had already seen Robert Redford and Kristin-Scott Thomas together in *The Horse Whisperer* and Harrison Ford and Anne Heche together in *Six Days, Seven Nights*, Jack Nicholson had wooed Helen Hunt in *As Good As It Gets*, and Warren Beatty had romanced Halle Berry in *Bulworth*. Sean Connery, meanwhile, was just about to start production of *Entrapment* in which he would enjoy a platonic relationship with Catherine Zeta-Jones, who was about to embark on a real-life May-December romance of her own.

Michael Douglas always believed that the casting of a younger woman in the role of Emily Bradford Taylor was absolutely vital to the story. Steven Taylor was a man who had ruthlessly acquired the best and most beautiful of everything. The acquisition of a wife who was younger, stunningly beautiful, and sexually potent was a logical addition to his lifestyle. He also believed that there were good practical reasons for so many older men being teamed with younger women in major studio films.

'You look at your main leading men in that historically central age group and you have Tom Cruise, Brad Pitt and Nicolas Cage. And then who? Tom Hanks is in his forties, Jim Carrey is a comedian. I don't ever remember a time in Hollywood history when there have been so few leading men. You have a whole bunch of young actors, but many of them are still seen as somewhat youthful or as not yet full-blown leading men, there is still a youthful quality about them. Then you have older actors such as myself and Harrison Ford and Jack Nicholson and Sean Connery, who are not quite ready to roll over just yet. If you give us the chance to play these parts then, absolutely, we are going to take them. If an actor is able to shave five or eight years off his screen persona and an actress is willing to put on five years then you get a fifteen to twenty year difference.'

Douglas personally felt that the criticism was a cheap shot levelled at himself and others of his generation. The fact that, as he pointed out, there have always been stories about older men and younger women seemed to be immaterial. The fact also that he was about to play a dissolute older man for director Curtis Hanson, or that he and Meryl Streep had announced they would play grandparents in Mimi Leder's *Still Life*, was never taken into account. In any event, the film business has always been more about business than about film, and there are sound commercial considerations for every one of those casting decisions, no matter how improbable the pairings might seem. Most of these considerations concern themselves with the ever-increasing cost of making a film, and who you can rely on to recoup that cost not only in the United States but in the increasingly important foreign markets.

'What's happened is that you have some youth comedies which have worked well in the States but do not translate into foreign markets. The foreign market has continued to grow, for example, my movies generally do twice the business outside the United States that they do in the United States. The foreign market has changed but it is still driven by the so-called stars, and they still want those oldies but goodies. These are people that they know they can count on in their territories, and they don't know anything about these young guys. They may think they are hot stuff, they have maybe two hit movies and they're in all the film magazines and fashion magazines and then they start dating each other. They get more press and they may think they are hot stuff but the rest of the world is saying "Who are you talking about?" That's a real dilemma.'

These arguments were still some months away when *A Perfect Murder* began filming in October of 1997. Logistically, it was a relaxed shoot for Douglas. The furthest afield from New York they ventured was to Long Island to shoot some scenes at Salutations, a turn of the century mansion built by the financier J.P. Morgan, which doubled as Emily's family home. The other locations were in and around New York city and, in keeping with Steven Taylor's lifestyle, many of them were close to Douglas's own West Side penthouse. He could, had he chosen to, have walked to work. Gwyneth Paltrow similarly found herself back in her old stamping ground, since some scenes were filmed across the road from her old school.

The use of J.P. Morgan's former home was symptomatic of a film in which the production values were nothing short of lavish. Almost every glimpse we see of Steven Taylor's life reeks of opulence, from his home, to his office, to his club. As a man reportedly worth anywhere between $150 million and $200 million himself, Michael Douglas felt quite at home in Steven Taylor's world. Many of the extras in the film's opulent charity gala sequence at the Metropolitan Museum were genuine members of New York's social elite, including several personal friends of Douglas and Arnold Kopelson.

The producer in Michael Douglas would have appreciated the lengths to which the Kopelsons were going in bringing the Taylors' social orbit to the screen. The final touch in creating Steven Taylor's world came in dressing Taylor himself. The costumes were designed by Ellen Mirojnick, Douglas's favourite designer, who did the costumes for *Wall Street, Fatal Attraction* and *The Game*. She knew exactly what was required for this role.

'Steven Taylor's clothing is all fine, fine fabric,' she explains. 'It's hand-tailored from top to bottom and, including his leather shoes, everything except for a tie or two was designed especially for Michael Douglas . . . Steven is made to look strong, powerful and elegant.'

Despite a shooting schedule that included some 70 different locations the filming of *A Perfect Murder* went ahead without any major problems. The film was due for release in around six months as adult counter-programming for the usual bubblegum summer fare. By the end of 1997, Andrew Davis was able to bid a fond farewell to his cast and crew, send them home for the holidays, and settle in to the post-production process.

THE MESSENGER

Michael Douglas had a number of things to consider at the beginning of 1998, not the least of which was the future of his production company. He had been partnered with his friend Steven Reuther in Douglas/Reuther Productions since 1994. As well as *The Ghost and The Darkness*, in which Douglas had starred, they had also been responsible for *Sabrina*, *Face/Off* and *The Rainmaker*. Of those films only *Face/Off* had been a huge hit in spite of an $80 million budget. *A Song for David*, of course, was still on the stocks, but it had not been made for reasons which had nothing to do with the film industry. The partnership had formally dissolved at the end of 1997 after production finance from their German partners Constellation Films had dried up several months earlier. Reuther had set up another company, Bel Air Entertainment, at Warner Brothers but Douglas wasn't rushing into anything just yet.

Douglas/Reuther had become rather more of a business than perhaps Douglas had intended when it was first set up. They had a distribution arrangement with Paramount Pictures, which meant that although Douglas wanted to be dealing with the creative side of things, he became involved in a lot more decision-making in the business sense than he would have cared to. While he admits to gaining a new-found respect for those involved in the decisions to give films the green light, he found the business side of the industry had leached away some of the enjoyment of the film-making side. He blames much of this on the structural changes in Hollywood where, throughout the Nineties, film studios became more and more corporate as they were swallowed up by major multinationals such as Sony and Newscorp. Douglas, who has been approached in the past to run major studios, felt that the emphasis on bottom line accounting, especially in the domestic market, meant that creative decisions were being sacrificed just for the sake of getting as many films into development as possible, in the hope that one of them would turn out to be a colossal hit.

'There's sort of a trickle-down development process where the responsibility for scripts keeps passing to lower executives,' he explains. 'By not having a single visionary with a point of view at the top, like in the old studio days, you get this homogenised collection of notes, so that a writer desperately tries to answer all of his or her chiefs, to the detriment of the original story.'

While he was pondering what to do as a producer, Michael Douglas also had a number of decisions to make about what he would do as an actor. There had been no shortage of scripts pouring in for him as an actor, regardless of those he was developing himself as a producer. He was approached to star in two very different military movies. In *U-571* he would play the commander of a World War II American submarine on a top secret mission, while in *The General's Daughter* he was to play a military policeman investigating a brutal rape and murder on an army base, which would uncover a far-reaching political scandal. In addition, despite their earlier reluctance, 20th Century Fox were now apparently interested in making a third film in the *Romancing the Stone* series. Just before he started shooting *A Perfect Murder* Fox announced that a third film was in development and a script was being prepared, Douglas was being actively courted by the studio, but he preferred not to commit himself until he had seen the script, which would still be several months away.

'For me now it's a question of the cultivation of my soul and developing new habits and interests,' he said. 'Now that my marriage is over and my son Cameron is an adult, I find this is a really exciting time for me. I don't know where it's going; I'm just part of the excitement. It's a fun time because I don't have anywhere near the personal responsibilities and obligations that I have had for the last 20 years. It makes me more responsible for myself than to others. Sometimes you can hide out behind others and being involved with others.'

With his film projects somewhat up in the air, Douglas found his attention turning to other spheres. A self-confessed news junkie Douglas is, unusually for a major star, passionately political. This is not in the sense of the single-issue eccentric causes to which a great many film stars attach themselves – Douglas is a genuine political animal. He has a strong sense of social justice and political awareness which he inherited from his father and which was shaped by his step-father. In the spring of 1998 he received a call which would give him the opportunity to put many of his sincerely-held beliefs into practice.

The United Nations appoints a number of Messengers of Peace, whom it describes as personalities with widespread media appeal who are devoted and committed to UN policies. The six existing Messengers of Peace include such luminaries as Luciano Pavarotti for his work with the charity War Child, and the basketball player Magic Johnson for his work with HIV. The approach from United Nations Secretary-General Kofi Annan could not have been better timed for Michael Douglas. Ever since his fiftieth birthday he had been considering what to do with his life. He seemed by choice to be easing his workload. There seemed to be fewer starring roles which he considered worthy of his attention, and his responsibilities as a producer were being slimmed down.

'I wondered how I wanted to spend the rest of my life,' he says of his thoughts on his half-century. 'If my father's genes mean anything I have a good forty years left. I marvel at my father's spiritual growth these past ten years since his plane crash and his stroke. His life did not end when his career ended and that is a great inspiration for me. This has taught me that there are innumerable ways of having a life rather than retiring. I've decided I'm going to do less producing and more acting. I'd also like to try my hand at directing. I enjoy acting more and more. They pay you so well and they pamper you so much. It really is the best of all possible worlds.'

Given that he was taking things a little less frantically now there was more time for him to become involved in issues dear to his heart. Despite the trials of the past few years he realised that life had been extraordinarily good to him and now there was the chance to perhaps give something back. The opportunity to make a difference was clearly too good to pass up and so Michael Douglas agreed to become the seventh United Nations Messenger for Peace.

Michael Douglas already had experience of the influence which celebrities could wield in the political arena. Political involvement is one of the things which he claims to have inherited from his father. Kirk Douglas was active in the United States Information Agency, a part of the American State Department which encouraged celebrities to go all over the world on goodwill missions speaking on important issues. This, coupled with his Hollywood celebrity, gave him access behind the Iron Curtain . It was Kirk Douglas, after all, who famously secured a meeting with Marshall Tito of Yugoslavia when the British Ambassador could not. Tito was a movie fan, Kirk was a movie star, and there was no way Her Britannic Majesty's representative could compete with that. So Michael Douglas was aware that sometimes it is easier to reach people in the entertainment section of the newspaper with things that they might just gloss over in the news pages.

Michael Douglas had already had some experience of this. He knew, for example, that *The China Syndrome* had played a key role in making people aware of the issue of nuclear safety. He had remained active as a campaigner against nuclear proliferation and would speak out against it many times. Douglas also believed passionately in the United Nations, which set him against many in his own country's government. The United States had been witholding its contributions to the UN for some time in protest at the way the organisation was run.

'The reason why I think the United Nations is so important,' Douglas explains, ' is that we are very close to the entire planet having the same form of government: constitutional, elective, parliamentary. We have a way to go – there are some pockets on the globe where this doesn't exist. But I think the United Nations is my hope for the millennium, that we can have an organisation that would in effect allow all governments to act as members of a world congress . . . I hate to see us (the United States) as deadbeats as far as the United Nations is concerned. It has taken me a while to define where I want to work and what I want to do, and that's the area that captures my imagination the most.'

The Messengers of Peace tend to focus on one specific issue. For Michael Douglas it was disarmament, and when his appointment was announced he said he hoped that his work with the United Nations would help in some small way to speed up the process of nuclear disarmament. There were other things that concerned him as well as simply nuclear weapons. Michael Douglas saw his UN mandate as the chance to take his campaign for small arms limitation, which had begun when John Lennon was shot only yards from his house, to a wider international arena. He was also aware that when he made that choice that he would be laying himself open to accusations of double standards. D-Fens, his character in *Falling Down*, had shot up a fast food restaurant in one sequence, and in his earlier film *Black Rain* he played a gun-toting cop who was inclined to shoot first and ask questions later. Douglas is aware of the apparent irony and the ease and frequency with which his industry is used as a scapegoat but defends his position vigorously.

'The movie business does not sell $10 billion worth of small arms around the world each year and I think it is really a cop-out to turn to the movie business as the reason. We don't support the sale of small arms in the world, we make movies which are fictional movies. Sometimes there is gratuitous violence, but quite honestly there are also a number of times when films speak very strongly about guns and weapons and violence . . .

'To always turn around to television and films as the culprit (is unfair), the entertainment business does not sell small arms. Basically the United States and France and the Soviet Union are the leading arms sellers in the world and half of those $10 billion worth of arms sales are being put to illegal use. It took $25 million worth of arms in Rwanda to create genocide and that is what we need to start addressing. Interestingly enough – and this is just one small statistic – we all think that World War II was the war to end all wars. Since World War II, the United Nations has charted approximately 170 conflicts. We know some of them from the Vietnam War, Northern Ireland, Chechnya. Since World War II 44 million people have died and 80 per cent of them were civilians. So, our armies may be getting smaller but civilians are arming themselves. This is atrocious and it is something which I think we should monitor.'

His role with the United Nations did not really take effect until the end of July 1998, when he was presented to the assembled media at the United Nations New York headquarters. Before then there was the release of *A Perfect Murder* to think about, a release which had suddenly become problematic. It is axiomatic these days that studios do not release major films without an intensive research programme. The film is screened for preview audiences, who are recruited blind without being told what they are going to see. They then watch the film and are invited to fill in response cards outlining what they liked and didn't like about the film. Occasionally some of the audience members are recruited into focus groups for more detailed analysis of their views. These screenings are the responsibility of the studio's marketing department and the findings are then passed back to the executives, and of course the film makers, for their comments and for remedial action if necessary. This can be an exhaustive process, especially in the case of comedies which can be test screened several times in several separate incarnations. Occasionally the studio will sanction more money to be spent to shoot extra scenes to clarify the situation, particularly in films which the studio expects to return that money handsomely. More frequently, however, the director will repair to the editing suite with his editor and a fistful of notes and try to re-cut the existing footage.

A Perfect Murder was not testing well. Or rather it was testing just fine until it came to the ending. Audiences disliked the ending in which Gwyneth Paltrow effectively shoots Michael Douglas in cold blood and David Suchet, as the sympathetic detective, is complicit in her alibi. Obviously they did not take to the notion of Gwyneth exacting revenge in as calculating manner as Michael Douglas had attempted. Something would have to be done and Andrew Davis went back to his original footage. The result is an ending in which the basic facts remain the same – Michael Douglas is still shot dead by Gwyneth Paltrow – but this time she is seen to be acting in self-defence under extreme provocation. The original ending is perhaps more intelligent, a little more provocative, and requires a little more work from the audience. The new ending, on the other hand, is more conventionally Hollywood. The difference only involves about a minute and a half of film but the audience preferred this one.

There was one other problem. *A Perfect Murder* was seen by Warner Brothers as an ideal counter-weight to the action-driven, teen-oriented menu of summer movies. This was the summer of *Godzilla* and *Armageddon* and Warner's own action franchise *Lethal Weapon 4*. The idea was that audiences tired of special effects and characters shooting each other without motive would embrace the Michael Douglas film as an oasis of mature entertainment in a desert of pyrotechnics. However the reality was that on its 7 June opening weekend, *A Perfect Murder* found itself going head to head with *The Truman Show* which, along with *Saving Private Ryan* later in the summer, was seen as not only the pick of the bunch of the summer releases, but also a serious Oscar contender. In short this was a film which was going to cut right across the audience for *A Perfect Murder*.

With reviews describing it as one of the greatest American films of the century and raves over Jim Carrey's first serious performance as a man whose every breath is transmitted live on television without his knowledge, *The Truman Show* not surprisingly cleaned up at the box office. It took just over $31.5 million on its opening weekend and would go on to pass the $100 million mark – although it would be surprisingly shut out at the following year's Oscars. But, significantly, *A Perfect Murder* also found an audience. It racked up just over $16.6 million on its opening weekend. More important, it also had what they call in the film business 'legs'. There was good word of mouth on the film and it played all through the summer. It finally left American cinemas on 13 September by which time it had grossed a very healthy $67,629,000.

In the week that *A Perfect Murder* finished its American run Michael Douglas had gone to France to launch the film in Europe. It would turn out to be one of the most significant weeks of his life.

ENTER CATHERINE

Deauville is a quiet seaside town in northern France. It is a popular tourist haunt, especially for Americans making pilgrimages to the nearby beaches where the Normandy landings took place. It is a quiet haven of French gentility but for ten days every September it is a mecca for major American stars. Deauville was immortalised in film in the Claude Lelouch romantic classic *A Man and a Woman* and the experience produced a surge in the tourist trade. Partly because of that Deauville became a home for the movies, especially American ones, and every September since 1974 it has played host to the Festival of American Film. The biggest stars in the world have been to Deauville to visit the Festival, which began as a celebration of all that was good about Hollywood film-making. Over the years the great names of the Golden Age have given way to their younger but no less stellar contemporaries, as the Festival has become the prime launching site for American films on their European late summer releases.

In 1998 *A Perfect Murder* was having its European launch in Deauville and Michael Douglas was also being honoured for his services to the film industry. He was being awarded the festival's Coup de Chapeau for his work both as a star and as a producer. The other honourees that year were Bob and Harvey Weinstein, the founders and driving force behind Miramax, the General Motors of the independent film sector. Michael Douglas was heading for Deauville energised and excited. He had already decided that the underwater adventures in *U-571* were not really for him, he passed on the project citing the age-old catch-all reason of 'scheduling difficulties'. He had also made up his mind that he would not be getting involved with *The General's Daughter* either. Not for the first time, other actors would benefit from the scraps from Michael Douglas's table. *U-571* was eventually rewritten for Matthew McConaughey and provided him with a box office hit and a genuine star-making role. *The General's Daughter* on the other hand eventually went to John Travolta, and he too had a big hit at a time when the box office returns of his films were not matching the critical praise for his performances. Douglas himself, however, had decided to team up with director Curtis Hanson for *Wonder Boys*, a romantic comedy which was to be Hanson's first film after his highly praised *L.A. Confidential*. The film would start shooting later that year.

As a producer, as well as someone who likes to keep himself up to date on what's going on in the world around him, Michael Douglas has to be aware of what's going on in the film industry as well. Sometimes he doesn't see movies when he should – by the time he got to Deauville that autumn, for example, he still hadn't caught up with *The Truman Show* which had opened on the same day as *A Perfect Murder* – but he usually catches up with them in the end. It was while he was doing some catching up, a few weeks before going to Deauville, that he found himself taken with a young actress he hadn't seen before. The film was *The Mask of Zorro* and the actress was Catherine Zeta-Jones. Douglas was bowled over by this young woman.

'I hadn't seen anybody since Julie Christie who was as beautiful, as strong a presence onscreen as Catherine,' he remembers. 'I went "Wow! Who is this girl?"'

Michael Douglas was not alone in being stunned by Catherine Zeta-Jones's memorable performance opposite Antonio Banderas and Anthony Hopkins in the stylish swashbuckler. Hollywood was already hailing her as a major new talent. And, like most overnight successes, it had only taken several years of hard graft to achieve it.

Catherine Zeta-Jones was 28 but she had been in the business for more than a decade since leaving her native Wales to seek her fame and fortune. She had always wanted to be a star, and when she was only 11 she took the lead in a local production of *Annie*. Her first big break came on the West End stage, when she appeared in the musical *42nd Street* when she was only 16. However it was at the age of 22 that she became a household name in Britain, when she starred in the television series *The Darling Buds of May*. This charmingly old-fashioned series about the Larkin family, led by the roguish patriarch Pop Larkin, took Britain by storm. Its sense of rustic decency and the notion that everything would turn out all right in the end was embraced by British audiences and it regularly topped the ratings charts. For Catherine, who played the beautiful daughter Marianne, it was the sort of exposure she had been looking for. There was scarcely a newspaper which did not feature her on an almost daily basis during the height of the show's short-lived but nonetheless phenomenal popularity.

It was fame of a kind, but not the sort that Catherine Zeta-Jones wanted. For her, as for so many others, being famous meant being in the movies. There were featured roles in a couple of British films but neither amounted to much. Although the Eric Idle comedy *Splitting Heirs* was shown in competition at Cannes it remained a flop. Similarly *Blue Juice*, a British surfing movie, also failed to find an audience despite Catherine and the added bonus of Ewan McGregor. Undaunted, she struck out for Hollywood, the one place in the world where you had to be if you wanted to be a movie star.

She had gone to Hollywood with her then boyfriend, Angus MacFadyen, who was playing the role of Richard Burton in a television mini-series. Soon Catherine began to attract the attention of casting directors and producers in her own right. Once again, however, the big break seemed to elude her.

She was cast as a villainous female aviator and pirate opposite Billy Zane in the big screen adaptation of the comic-strip *The Phantom*, but the film was a complete flop. By this stage she and MacFadyen had split up and she had put her career in the hands of film producer Jon Peters. It was Peters who started to introduce her to the right people, and by the time the pair of them split up Catherine Zeta-Jones's career was starting to look up. She had been cast as the female lead in another mini-series, *Titanic*. Just like the ship, the mini-series foundered but not everyone went down with the ship. *Titanic* turned out to have provided Catherine Zeta-Jones with a career lifeboat.

In a plot twist that would tax even the most gullible audience, those watching *Titanic* when it screened in the States included Steven Spielberg. He saw Catherine and felt she might have just the right qualities he was looking for in the spitfire female lead in *The Mask of Zorro*, which he was producing. He called the director Martin Campbell and, almost before she knew what had happened, Catherine Zeta-Jones found herself in period costume duelling with Antonio Banderas in the deserts of Sonora.

'I thought my agent was pulling my leg or something when he called and said Steven wanted to see me,' she says. 'But within a week I was down in Mexico being screen-tested.'

When *The Mask of Zorro* opened in the States in July 1998 it was an instant hit, a favourite with the public and critics alike. Everyone was raving about Catherine Zeta-Jones and that included Michael Douglas.

Douglas was committed to going to Deauville to receive his award and promote his picture but, to his surprise and delight, he found out that Catherine Zeta-Jones was also going to be there to promote *The Mask of Zorro*. Douglas sent his publicist and good friend Alan Burry on a mission. He had to ensure that Zeta-Jones was coming to Deauville, find out who she was going with, and see if he could arrange dinner. It wasn't long before Burry came back with the news. She would be going, she would be going alone, but as for dinner he'd have to wait and see.

One of the questions Douglas had been asked most frequently in recent interviews was whether or not he would remarry. His answer was always the same. He would have no hesitation, he insisted, on getting married again 'in a nanosecond' if the right woman came long. Douglas also volunteered that he would love to have more children, on the basis that he had learned from bitter experience and was bound to be a much better husband and father second time round.

That dinner with Catherine Zeta-Jones didn't happen, as it turned out, but the festival schedule was on Douglas's side. *A Perfect Murder* was due to be screened at Deauville on the Friday of the closing weekend, a gala at which he would be honoured. Her film, however, was scheduled for the following day, a Saturday. Douglas and Zeta-Jones met in the foyer of the Hotel Royal on the Saturday. He was relaxing, having finished all his publicity duties, while she was in the middle of hers and on her way to a dinner to celebrate the European launch of *The Mask of Zorro*. When she returned later that evening Douglas was in the bar waiting and they struck up an easy conversation. It was a 'date' of sorts, although both were chaperoned; she by her hairdresser and he by Alan Burry. Douglas and Zeta-Jones chatted into the night and it was plain that there was an instant and mutual attraction. He, according to Burry, asked her to have his children while she said she had heard a lot about him and found it refreshing to discover that it was all true. Whether that was meant as a compliment or not, Douglas was encouraged.

They went their separate ways the following day. Douglas went back to New York while Catherine Zeta-Jones headed to Mull, an island off the coast of Scotland to film some key scenes in

Entrapment with Sean Connery. Despite the relative remoteness of the island, she was met at the end of a day's filming by a huge bunch of roses. She was, according to Douglas, suitably impressed.

One of the things they had discovered they had in common during their tryst in Deauville was that they shared the same birthday, 25 September – albeit a quarter of a century apart. Douglas always marks the occasion with a very elite gathering in New York of similar high-fliers who share his birthday. Those who are invited – and they include television news presenter Barbara Walters, actor Christopher Reeve, and a number of film industry movers and shakers – refer to it as the 'Nine Twenty-Five' club. Naturally Catherine moved rapidly to the top of his guest list, but because of her commitment to *Entrapment* she was filming on the other side of the world in Kuala Lumpur and unable to make it. That was the way their relationship progressed in the early days with Douglas preparing to film *Wonder Boys* and Catherine filming *Entrapment*, there were very few windows in their respective schedules to get together. Nonetheless their phone bills were huge.

It was obvious, even at a distance, that their relationship was becoming closer and closer. Over the Christmas holidays, they finally had some time for each other and they got round to a set of important formal introductions.

'At Christmas time Catherine, who always spends her holidays in Wales, had brought her parents to Los Angeles because that's where she was working then,' Douglas remembers. 'Every time I took her out to dinner it was like taking the whole family . . . Then my mother had this little Christmas Eve party at her house and asked Catherine and her family to come.'

The party went without a hitch and a Merry Christmas was had by all.

At this stage the relationship between Michael Douglas and Catherine Zeta-Jones was more or less a family affair, known to only family members and a few trusted confidants. However it is hard to keep anything secret for long in an industry town like Los Angeles.

Hollywood is an industry town in exactly the same way that Detroit is an industry town, all that differs is the end product. In Detroit restaurants the gossip is of the motor business, in the chic restaurants of Beverly Hills and West LA the gossip is of the movie business. It was not long before Michael Douglas and Catherine Zeta-Jones were the subject of that gossip. It was becoming more and more difficult for them to keep their love secret, especially with Catherine in Los Angeles and Michael making frequent visits to the set of her new film *The Haunting*.

'Michael often whisked Catherine away into town for hours on end,' says cameraman Frank Lazar. 'And when he wasn't in town with her, he would often join her in her trailer. Everyone could hear them laughing and giggling and getting on like a house on fire. Whatever they were doing they were having a damn good time doing it. When I saw them together they were always flirting, saying things to one another with that little sexual edge to them. He was also always cheering her on and telling everyone what a great actress she was.'

Neither of them would comment in public about their relationship, insisting they were no more than good friends, but they became less and less discreet about being seen out together. Eventually in June 1999, almost six months after they had met, they found it impossible to deny that there was nothing more to their relationship than simple friendship. They had gone for a week-long holiday to Douglas's Spanish estate on Majorca for some sun, some swimming, some relaxation, and of course some golf. They were not as private as they thought they were and paid the penalty when a photographer with a long lens materialised. She was topless and stroking his back while he had one arm casually, but undeniably affectionately, draped across her shoulders. It was not the sort of situation you would expect to get into with someone who was merely a friend, no matter how good a friend.

Privately Douglas and Zeta-Jones must have known that the jig was up, but they still continued to tease the media in public. He was a surprise guest at the European premiere of *Entrapment* in Edinburgh while she delighted in appearing with a huge diamond ring on her engagement finger. While the press speculated furiously the couple took their time before revealing that the ring was merely on loan from a jeweller friend. Earlier in the day, at a press conference for the film, Catherine had teased the assembled journalists about her fondness for older men – her comments were ostensibly directed at her co-star Sean Connery who was also at the table, but she knew exactly what kind of spin the media would put on it.

Before the *Entrapment* premiere, which was effectively their formal coming out as a couple, there was one other family obligation to be taken care of. Michael Douglas had met Catherine Zeta-Jones's family, Catherine Zeta-Jones had met his mother, Diana Darrid, at that intimate Christmas Eve get-together. Now it was time for her to meet the Douglas clan. Just after they got back from Majorca, Michael Douglas arranged a private dinner party at a Los Angeles restaurant so that he could take his new girl home to meet his dad. Catherine confessed afterwards that she had been terrified at the prospect of meeting Kirk Douglas, as much because of his status as a Hollywood legend as because of his position as her boyfriend's father. She was equally nervous of meeting Michael's step-mother, Anne. As it turned out she need not have worried. She was charmed by them and she charmed them in return. Kirk Douglas was particularly taken by Catherine.

'She's a lovely girl and she plays a mean game of golf,' he said referring to another shared passion between his son and the new woman in his life.

After the *Entrapment* premiere neither of them could deny their relationship and they decided instead that the best way to approach things was to celebrate it.

'He's my boyfriend, why hide it?' Catherine said simply to one magazine. 'Everyone knows about it anyway. Have you seen what they are saying about us in the newspapers? Okay, we could try and lock ourselves away and pretend to everyone that it's not happening but, after a bit, that just creates more intrigue and ends up making your life ridiculous. So the answer to (the) question is yes, we're together and yes, we're very happy.'

With the pair having gone public it became open season on both of them as far as the media were concerned. They could not step outside without having their picture taken and almost every week there was speculation about when and where they would marry. Catherine had taken to wearing a ring on her engagement finger but insisted that it was merely one of many gifts from her new boyfriend, they were not getting married yet. He admitted that she had moved in to his New York apartment but, no, they were not getting married yet.

Despite this, in the first week in August, 1999 the *Sun* – the English tabloid which had published the Majorca photographs – announced in screaming headlines that the couple were to announce their engagement later that month. The obligatory anonymous source assured the paper that Catherine and Michael had 'found happiness at last'. Within 24 hours the story was roundly dismissed by spokesmen for both sides as being completely without foundation and totally groundless.

The media, however, would not be so easily deflected from what they had already decided was going to be the show business marriage of the decade. If they were not going to announce their engagement this month, then surely it would be the following month at the next annual meeting of the Nine Twenty-Five Club.

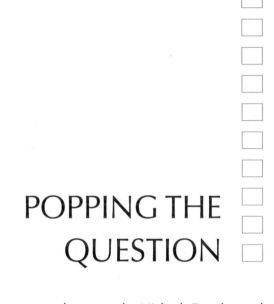

POPPING THE
QUESTION

Now that they were openly a couple Michael Douglas and Catherine Zeta-Jones were much more forthcoming about their relationship and their feelings for each other. He revealed that he admired her work ethic and was very impressed with the way she was handling her fame. To someone who was second generation Hollywood as he was, there was less emphasis on fame for its own sake and more emphasis on movies as an industry. Michael Douglas was pleased that she shared his pragmatic view of their ephemeral occupation.

The one thing which everyone brought up again and again was the age gap. Michael Douglas confessed that it was something that he too had been concerned about, but not for too long.

'Initially I was worried about the difference in our ages,' he said in a reflective interview with *US* magazine, ' but since the first three weeks it hasn't come up. Early on any doubts I had were because I realised I have had it all. But the great advantage of that is nothing would make me more excited, prouder than to watch Catherine explode – something a lot of guys couldn't handle unless they'd had their own success.'

Catherine Zeta-Jones had taken Hollywood by storm in the early roles of what might be termed the second phase of her career. Anthony Hopkins, who starred in *The Mask of Zorro*, had appeared with her before in a production of Dylan Thomas's *Under Milk Wood*. The Oscar-winner was full of praise for her talent and her work ethic. Similarly, Jon Amiel who had directed her in *Entrapment* was also a fan. He compared her to the great glamour names of the Golden Age of Hollywood such as Ava Gardner. In the course of her new career she had become used to answering questions about her relations with older men, but generally only in the sense of her co-stars. She had just finished working with Anthony Hopkins and then Sean Connery, both comfortably old enough to be her father. Now she found herself answering the same questions about a man who was sharing her love scenes for real and not just on screen. But whenever she was asked she was adamant that the quarter of a century gap between them was a matter of complete irrelevance.

'I'm not looking for a father figure in Michael,' she said. 'I already have the most fantastic father a girl could wish for at home in Wales and I'm certainly not trying to have him replaced or re-done or re-enacted in any way, shape or form . . . I don't spend a lot of time with people who are older, Michael doesn't seem like an older man to me, he's just Michael. The fact that he is older is just the way it worked out.'

They were both about to get another year older with their joint birthdays on 25 September and as the big day approached the media speculation intensified. Once again the media were thwarted. The next meeting of the Nine Twenty-Five club came and went and Douglas and Zeta-Jones remained resolutely unengaged.

Although the pair of them continued to act in flagrant disregard of the media's wishes by appearing to be blissfully happy in their unmarried state, there was still intense speculation about their future together. Zeta-Jones had moved into his Central Park West apartment and they were effectively living together as man and wife. Still there was no announcement. In an interview with *Harpers Bazaar* magazine Catherine appeared to pour cold water on the notion of a wedding when she said there had been 'no words of marriage' between them. This particular flame was fuelled by reports that Catherine would be spending Christmas of 1999 alone with her family in Wales. Was the relationship heading for the rocks? In fact it was stronger than ever. Zeta-Jones had only been travelling to Wales on her own to have some time with her family, Douglas joined her a few days later and they spent Christmas together in Wales.

'I love Mumbles,' says Douglas of the seaside town where Catherine's family live. 'It's a great area. They couldn't have been more hospitable. They're very gracious people. They have embraced me quite quickly and that makes me feel good.'

Immediately after spending Christmas in Wales, Michael Douglas and Catherine Zeta-Jones headed back to the United States. They would bring in the millennium at his holiday home in Aspen.

One development which had taken up some of Michael Douglas's time towards the end of 1999 was the launch of his own official website. This would enable him and his fans to keep in touch with each other, as well as raising money for Cease Fire and other good causes. The website had been up and running for a couple of months, but in the first few days of 2000 it got the showbusiness story which everyone had been looking for.

'I am very happy to announce,' said Douglas on the website, 'that I am engaged to Catherine Zeta-Jones. I proposed to Catherine on New Year's Eve at my house in Aspen. We plan to marry sometime this year, however, no date has been set.'

If Douglas and Zeta-Jones expected the announcement of their engagement to give them a break from media speculation they were wrong. All that happened was that the speculation switched from whether they would get married to where the ceremony would take place. Again, as they had throughout their relationship, neither one of the couple gave any clues about the location. But this soon paled into insignificance when it was announced that Catherine Zeta-Jones was pregnant. At the age of 55, Michael Douglas was to become a father again. He had often said he thought he would be a better father second time round and now he was being given the chance to prove it. Douglas was looking forward to fatherhood to the extent where he joked about becoming a house husband while Catherine took over the movie star role.

'As I get close to sixty I'll be happy to stay home with the kid and let Catherine go off and work as much as she wants,' he said. 'I'll be Mr Mom.'

Dylan Michael Douglas was born at 5.52 on the afternoon of Tuesday, 8 August at Cedars Sinai Medical Centre in Los Angeles. He came into the world just eight minutes before his new grand-parents touched down at the airport. Catherine's parents had come from Wales to support their daughter during the birth of her first child but their grandson arrived before they did. Dylan weighed in at 7 pounds 7 ounces and was 21 and a half inches long and he had the Douglas dimple, much to his grandfather Kirk's delight. Mother and baby were both fine, and after a day in hospital the two of them and Michael Douglas went back to Catherine Zeta-Jones' house in Santa Monica. The baby's birth, along with every other event of significance in his parents' lives, was announced on Michael Douglas's website.

The arrival of his second son was an emotional moment for Michael Douglas. He was present at the birth and cut the umbilical cord with tears in his eyes.

'I always wanted more children,' he told OK magazine, 'and it's actually an area I feel fairly confident about. It's not something that leaves me totally freaked out or anything. I enjoy children, I enjoy babies, I feel relatively comfortable handling them and I think it's inherent – something you never forget once you've had a child even though it's 21 years later. You remember that you can bounce them around pretty good, about burping and the physicalities about them. So I'd always hoped the opportunity would arise.'

With the birth of baby Dylan, Michael Douglas was now happier than he had been for a long time. He had reached a place in his life where he felt content. He was at ease with himself, with his father, with his new family, and with the world around him. The pain and the demons that had tormented the previous few years had been exorcised by a young woman from Wales and a seven-and-a-half pound baby. Douglas says he feels genuinely blessed to have met Catherine Zeta Jones.

'I was single,' he told *OK* magazine. 'I struggled in my past marriage for a long time, there was no question about that. I don't treat this lightly, the idea of a commitment or a responsibility, contrary to what some people try to write. So, any marriage that's going to end, it ends because it wasn't good, it wasn't rewarding.

'But that was all a while ago, so it is really a joy to fall in love. Love is something that's so rewarding – it just makes you feel great to have something to cherish, something to protect, something to nurture. All those clichès. And I think it's just been great that we have sort of taken the time. I mean, one of the extraordinary things for Catherine at this point, right at the height of her career when she's rocketing, is that this thing took off and she didn't think twice about it.'

Michael Douglas and Catherine Zeta-Jones were finally married on 18 November 2000. Despite all the rumours and guesses about various exotic locales, the ceremony took place in New York. The details were, of course, announced on his website.

Even by the opulent standards of Hollywood, the wedding of Catherine Zeta-Jones and Michael Douglas was a spectacular affair. Douglas had already insisted that his new bride could call the shots on the arrangements for the big day and seemed confident that there would be no unnecessary extravagance. It was was the biggest day of her life and she was to have her way.

The venue for the wedding had been the subject of much media speculation with early attention being focused on Skibo Castle in Scotland – where Madonna would marry some months later – as well as other possible venues in California near Douglas's home. Instead he quietly announced on his own website that the wedding would take place in the Plaza Hotel in New York in the magnificent Terrace Room.

When the festivities began at 6.30 in the evening it was obvious that, despite the presence of so many superstar names, this was still fundamentally a family wedding. There were 350 guests and more than 100 of them were family, members of the extended Douglas and Jones clans. Kirk Douglas and Diana Darrid were there, as was Michael's stepmother Anne Douglas of course, along with his three brothers. On the bride's side there were her parents, her brothers, her godson, her cousins and many old friends from her early days in Wales and her early career in England. The bride and her maids of honour were dressed by Lacroix who also dressed the bride's mother.

The important job of best man went to Michael's son Cameron but there was one other very important guest. Three month old Dylan – described by the Honourable Judith S. Kaye, chief judge of the state of New York, who officiated – as 'best boy'. Dylan was carried into the ceremony by his grandmother Anne Darrid and remained quiet and placid, though doubtless a little bemused, throughout the ceremony.

Catherine Zeta-Jones walked down the aisle, escorted by her father Dave, at one minute past eight. As she approached her groom to be she could not have helped but notice her soon to be father-in-law Kirk Douglas weeping unashamedly with the emotion of the moment. The ceremony was simple but dignified and at 8.15, completing the exchange of vows, Catherine Zeta-Jones said 'I do.' A few seconds later Judge Kaye presented 'Mr and Mrs Douglas' to the guests who responded with a standing ovation.

The dancing and partying went on into the small hours. The guests included Sir Anthony Hopkins, Oliver Stone, James Woods, Danny De Vito and his wife Rhea Perlman, Jack Nicholson, Meg Ryan, Russell Crowe, Quincy Jones, Goldie Hawn and Kurt Russell, Mick Hucknall, and – as a demonstration of the regard in which Michael Douglas is held outside the film industry – United Nations Secretary-General Kofi Annan. By any standards, given the amount of 'A' list talent in the room, this was the biggest showbusiness wedding in years.

The only cloud on the horizon came later when there was an unseemly squabble between two magazines over which had the exclusive rights to the wedding pictures. *OK!* magazine had done a deal for the rights but the rival *Hello* magazine managed to get hold of some photographs and tried to publish ahead of *OK!* The final outcome would eventually be decided by the courts. As they had done when they sold their baby pictures, no money was paid to either Michael Douglas or Catherine Zeta-Jones for the pictures, instead it went to a charitable trust in Dylan's name. The couple similarly asked for donations to the trust in lieu of wedding gifts. The theory is that when he is old enough Dylan can decide which charities will benefit from the money. Afterwards Michael Douglas defended the decision. He conceded that it did appear odd for the United States, but added that they had to consider the situation in Europe which, he insisted, was markedly different.

'Catherine is an international star,' he explained to *Movieline* magazine, 'and in England the paparazzi become like bounty hunters and go to extraordinary extremes to take a photograph they can sell. When you spend your whole life protecting your name and likeness, how do you deal with these people? I've been really open about it, saying "Look you want to take a photograph of me and sell it? We'll split the money and I'll give my half to charity." When we were going to have a baby, we knew a bounty hunt would happen. So when we were contacted by a magazine about their doing a layout, paying us for it, then syndicating it – a fairly common practice in Europe – we simply saw it as a way to build financial security for our new son and control what was going to be a madhouse.'

ACT TWO

There are no second acts in American lives, or so F. Scott Fitzgerald insisted. Michael Douglas has never been one for doing what is expected of him and he appears determined to do everything he can to prove Fitzgerald wrong. As an actor, as a producer, and as a man Michael Douglas is showing impressive signs of having discovered his second wind.

He had, first of all, decided to act his age. No one needed to tell him that he was reaching the stage in his life where the thought of any more of what he jokingly described as his 'pants-down' roles, was becoming a little embarrassing. It was Douglas who called it a day on that one. Similarly, he had proved he could play the shady tycoon to perfection, as he had in his other trilogy of *Wall Street*, *The Game* and *A Perfect Murder*. What he really needed to do was to stretch himself as an actor. His biggest critical success had come in *Falling Down* where he had the lead role but with what was essentially a character part. Playing D-Fens was like nothing we had ever seen from Michael Douglas – which is why it was such a success.

When director Curtis Hanson made a success of *L.A. Confidential* Hollywood sat up and took notice. This was partly because it was a superlative piece of film-making, but also because it came from such a surprising source. Hanson had been a successful director but he was essentially considered a journeyman, a safe pair of hands who could turn out films such as *The Hand that Rocks the Cradle* and *The River Wild*. No one expected the man who made these films to make such a rich, complex, morally ambiguous film as *L.A. Confidential*. As a result Hanson pretty much got a free hand to do what he wanted for his next project. He chose *Wonder Boys*, the screen version of the novel by Michael Chabon.

Wonder Boys is the story of Grady Tripp, a middle-aged college professor and failed writer who is deeply blocked on the follow up to his successful debut novel. It is seven years since that initial success, he has almost reached page 3000 of the manuscript, but there is no end in sight. Grady is a mess. He drinks too much, he smokes too much dope, he has been in too many marriages, and he is generally unable to cope with anything.

'What I loved about the material when I read it was the absence of political correctness,' says Hanson. 'I loved the way the characters and their eccentric behaviour was accepted. It was just saying "These are people that are doing weird and politically incorrect things but we like them because they are good souls and they're struggling to figure it out." There's a lot of behaviour in this movie that is unusual for a studio movie but that's what I like about it.'

When the script was sent to Michael Douglas he loved the idea of playing Grady Tripp, a man who spends a large part of the film unshaven, dishevelled, and wandering around in a ladies' pink candlewick dressing gown. Grady is a child of the Sixties in middle age, without having paid too much notice to the passage of time around him. Grady and Michael Douglas are about the same age and it would be unusual if Douglas did not think at least once that there but for the grace of God . . . He admitted that playing Grady reminded him a lot of his days at UCSB.

'Oh yeah,' he said. 'I was a bit of a hippie and liberal arts colleges are a unique phenomenon. You have this unique relationship with the professors that doesn't exist, say, in the chemistry department. They're half teacher and half friend. In liberal arts colleges, the teachers do not grow up.'

Douglas has always thrived on doing the unexpected. He once said that if the work doesn't stir the emotions then what was the point. There was no progress to be gained by playing it safe. For *Wonder Boys*, Douglas went further out on the limb than he had gone before by gaining around 25 pounds to play Grady Tripp. The trick apparently is to eat lots of cookies.

'It's nice not to have to worry about vanity or your image and I feel really blessed about that,' he says. 'Because there are actors in my general milieu who are probably more restricted.'

Douglas found himself completely unrestricted in the role and playing Grady Tripp was probably the most liberating experience of his career.

'Well you get told that people think of your characters as being kind of intense and aggressive,' he reasons, 'but then I keep thinking that I'm proud of the fact that there has been such a variety of roles. I certainly don't think there's been anyone like Grady in terms of the exterior persona. But I have done mostly dramatic roles and I don't think people necessarily think of me for comedies, so there's a particular satisfaction in getting some laughs and that is one of the reasons why I took this.'

If Grady Tripp was a first for Michael Douglas, so too was a cast like the one Hanson put together in *Wonder Boys*. Douglas has essentially worked in two-handers where he is teamed with one other big star whether it be Glenn Close, Sharon Stone, Charlie Sheen, Andy Garcia or Gwyneth Paltrow. In *Wonder Boys*, although he had the lead role, Douglas was part of an ensemble cast. Not only was it an ensemble, it was a high quality ensemble. There was Oscar-winner Frances McDormand, Robert Downey Jnr, Rip Torn, Richard Thomas, Philip Bosco and two of the brightest young actors of their generation in Tobey Maguire and Katie Holmes. If Douglas had tried to be a movie star he would have been slaughtered in company like this. He would have to be an actor if he was to make any kind of impression.

'Michael is such a star,' says Curtis Hanson, 'but what was great about him is that unlike some other stars who get defensive about their stardom and are just protecting it, Michael was bold and said "Let's confound expectations." That's what excited me about having him in this movie; the absence of vanity and his willingness to shed what one might think of as his star image. For us, as movie-goers, it's fun to see the star who surprises us.'

Michael Douglas's performance in *Wonder Boys* is a revelation. It is clever and nuanced and utterly self-deprecating. As Kathleen Turner pointed out in the films they did together, not once does he metaphorically wink at the audience to let them know that it's all just pretend. Douglas is brave enough to go out there as an overweight man in a ladies' dressing gown and make a complete fool of himself. He goes head to head with some superb talent in this film and emerges with his reputation enhanced. The critical reaction to his performance was overwhelmingly positive and, just like the last time he ditched his image in *Falling Down*, he got reviews an actor would kill for. In any other circumstance there would have been an Oscar nomination in it for sure but, thanks to a poor marketing campaign, the film never found its audience on its spring release. However, so bullish were the studio about Douglas's performance that they took the unprecedented step of re-releasing the film in the autumn of 2000 in the hope that he might yet catch the eye of the Academy voters. In the end, although he snagged a lot of attention in the year-end round of awards, the Oscar nomination, perhaps unfairly, eluded him.

Wonder Boys certainly reflects an encouraging change of pace and a change of direction for Michael Douglas. After several years of simply acting he was also getting back into producing again, but his previous experiences had taught him a lesson. His new company Further Films, which is based at Universal Studios, is not going to saddle him with the raft of business-related problems he ended up with at Constellation or Stonebridge. Further takes its name from the destination sign on the front of Hieronymous Bosch, the bus which former beatnik Neal Cassady drove across America in the Sixties. The bus, and the journey, were immortalised by Tom Wolfe in his book *The Electric Kool-Aid Acid Test*. In that sense the spirit of the San Francisco Sixties which informed Fantasy Films and *One Flew Over the Cuckoo's Nest* still informs Further Films.

That spirit also informs the type of films that the company will be making from now on. Douglas is no longer interested in a full slate of projects which faceless executives can leave to languish in development hell.

'We're going back to developing less material, but more material for myself to play,' he says. 'One of my disappointments when I was involved with so many pictures at once was that seldom did we have any pictures that were for me as an actor. We're concentrating on that more.'

Michael Douglas and his new bride both starred in *Traffic*. Directed by Steven Soderbergh and based on a British television mini-series, it was a powerful look at the war against drugs in America. Douglas played an American drugs tsar while Catherine Zeta-Jones played the wife of a drugs baron who eventually takes over his operation. Although they had no scenes together the film, which was a commercial success, it was a turning point for Catherine Zeta-Jones who was attracting attention as a serious actress. There was talk of an Oscar nomination for her performance but this turned out to be premature.

As he entered the second half-century of his life Michael Douglas found himself wandering down a rich and varied career path. After *Traffic* there was another cameo in *One Night at McCools* in which he appears to be doing an impression of his father as a younger man. The film was not a success but Douglas was having fun with his career, invigorated by his new family, and enjoying himself immensely.

'The hardest thing is for me to find the next picture that I want to do,' he says. 'I never know what my next picture is going to be. Most actors have got a slate. They have pictures lined up . . . I wish I was one of those people who could line up pictures, but I never really know what I want to do. And I'm pretty fortunate in that way because it allows me to follow my instincts. I love to act. And my job is to give the audience something that they want. And I don't know what's going to come next and sometimes it makes me a little nervous and antsy, but that's really just part of the fun.'

His desire to give the audience something they want would be severly tested with his next film. He had been shooting a thriller, *Don't Say a Word*, for director Gary Fleder in which he played a psychiatrist negotiating with kidnappers for the release of his daughter. She was being held by the gang as an incentive for Douglas to unlock the secrets contained in the mind of disturbed young woman Brittany Murphy. *Don't Say a Word* was due for release at the end of September 2001.

On September 11, 2001 America was dealt its worst peacetime blow with the terrorist atrocities at the World Trade Center. As the rescue crews clambered through Ground Zero film-makers made rapid decisions. Scenes of the Twin Towers were removed from films such as *Zoolander*, action films such as Arnold Schwarzenegger's *Collateral Damage* were removed from the distribution roster, and the film industry, like the country, was in a state of shock. As President George W Bush urged Americans to carry on life as normally as possible the film industry prepared itself to get back to business as usual. The first major release in the wake of September 11 was *Don't Say a Word*. Obviously, the audience found Douglas a reassuring presence because the film took a very healthy $17 million when it opened on 30 September on its way to a very respectable $55 million domestic gross.

Michael Douglas spent most of 2002 producing, in one way or another. He was able to wear both his hats on his long-awaited project with his father Kirk. The younger Douglas produced and starred in *It Runs in the Family*, which not only featured a role for Kirk but also for his mother Diana and his oldest son Cameron. Brother Joel also returned as an associate producer. He then went on to film *The In-Laws*. This is a remake of the Peter Falk–Alan Arkin comedy, with Albert Brooks as his comedy partner and due for a release in summer 2003. And then it was announced that Catherine Zeta-Jones was expecting a second child.

The pregnancy was announced not long before the last unresolved matter from their wedding would be decided. Their legal action against *Hello* magazine for the use of 'cheap and tacky' photographs of their wedding was finally coming to court. The Douglases maintained that by publishing the photographs the magazine had breached their right to privacy. The case, at the Old Bailey in London, was a sensation. Douglas and Zeta-Jones were held up to ridicule in some sections of the British media for their perceived vulgarity. Zeta-Jones' comment to the effect that a million pounds might seem like a lot of money to some people but not to them was particularly badly received.

For all its potentially laughable aspects the case had serious undertones and could have created a *de facto* privacy law in Britain had the judge found in favour of Michael Douglas and his wife.

As is the nature of the British legal system, the judgement was finally issued some months after the actual hearing. While the judge continued his deliberations, a by now heavily pregnant Catherine Zeta-Jones returned to Los Angeles to collect a Best Supporting Actress Oscar for *Chicago*, thus fulfilling the predictions of two years previously for *Traffic*.

In the end the court case effectively turned out to be a draw. The judge ruled that while the Douglases 'commercial confidence' had been broken there was no breach of privacy since at the time of their wedding there was no privacy law in Britain. In bizarre scenes after the verdict was announced, both sides claimed victory.

Within a few days of the court verdict being revealed it was also revealed that Catherine Zeta-Jones had given birth to a daughter. Carys Zeta Douglas was born on 20 April at Valley Hospital in Ridgewood near their home. The proud parents were able to preserve their privacy this time and their happy news did not break until two days after the baby was born.

Michael Douglas meanwhile was becoming more and more involved with Further Films. Their distribution deal with Universal had formally run out at the end of 2000 but he had been in no hurry to rush into anything else. However, at the beginning of 2003 he was able to announce that Further had signed a two-year, first-look deal with Warner Brothers for whom he was making *The Wedding Party*. One of their first ventures will be a comedy called *Monkeyface*, a heist movie in which Michael Douglas and his wife will appear together for the first time. The film, to be directed by British filmmaker Stephen Frears, is due to begin shooting in Florida in September 2003.

It Runs in the Family also opened in the month that Michael Douglas became a father again. In the film the elder Douglas is a retired lawyer who made his name as an aggressive litigator in private practice who is at odds with his son, played by Michael Douglas, who prefers to work as a public defender. Kirk's former wife Diana played his screen wife while Cameron Douglas plays Michael's son. The American media were delighted at the prospect of father and son doing the publicity rounds together. Kirk Douglas, now 86, insisted that he wouldn't work with just anyone so he had waited until Michael was a star before agreeing to do the film. Their interviews became a ritual of good-natured ribbing and bantering shot through with a fierce mutual pride in the other's achievements.

One exchange, however, in an interview for the Associated Press news agency in the United States, revealed just how much the film meant to them and how far they had come. It came at a moment when Michael Douglas was insisting to the reporter that this was not just a vanity production.

'It's just a bunch of actors playing a family, which doesn't have a lot of similarities to us . . . '

'Well, Michael, you know that's not quite true,' Kirk interrupted. 'The element that was autobiographical in the movie was when I say as the character to him, "You're a much better father than I was." And he answers with a smile, "Well, Dad, you didn't raise the bar too high." And he said it with so much conviction that I have a feeling he was telling me something!'

Michael Douglas was telling the world in the best way he knew, through the movies, that he had finally stepped out of the shadows.

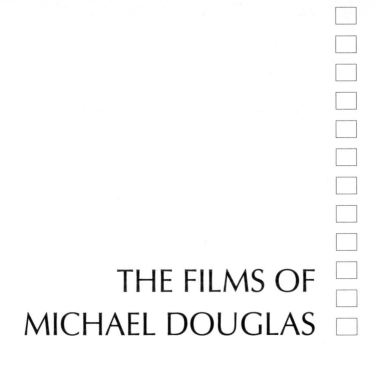

THE FILMS OF
MICHAEL DOUGLAS

Hail Hero (1969)
Producer: Harold D. Cohen
Director: David Miller
Cast: Arthur Kennedy, Michael Douglas, Teresa Wright, John Larch

Adam at 6AM (1970)
Producers: Robert W. Christiansen, Rick Rosenberg
Director: Robert Scheerer
Cast: Michael Douglas, Lee Purcell, Joe-Don Baker, Meg Foster

Summertree (1971)
Producer: Kirk Douglas
Director: Anthony Newley
Cast: Michael Douglas, Barbara Bel Geddes, Jack Warden, Brenda
Vaccaro

Napoleon and Samantha (1972)
Producer: Winston Hibler
Director: Bernard McEveety
Cast: Michael Douglas, Will Geer, Jodie Foster, Johnny Whitaker

Coma (1978)
Producer: Martin Erlichman
Director: Michael Crichton
Cast: Genevieve Bujold, Michael Douglas, Elizabeth Ashley, Rip
Torn

The China Syndrome (1979)
Producer: Michael Douglas
Director: James Bridges
Cast: Jack Lemmon, Jane Fonda, Michael Douglas, Scott Brady

Running (1979)
Producers: Robert Cooper and Ronald Cohen
Director: Steven Hilliard Stern
Cast: Michael Douglas, Susan Anspach, Lawrence Dane, Philip
Akin

It's My Turn (1980)
Producer; Martin Elfland
Director: Claudia Weill
Cast; Jill Clayburgh, Michael Douglas, Charles Grodin, Beverly
Garland

The Star Chamber (1983)
Producer: Frank Yablans
Director: Peter Hyams
Cast: Michael Douglas, Yaphet Kotto, Hal Holbrook, Sharon Gless

Romancing the Stone (1984)
Producer: Michael Douglas
Director: Robert Zemeckis
Cast: Michael Douglas, Kathleen Turner, Danny De Vito, Zack Norman

A Chorus Line (1985)
Producers: Cy Feuer and Ernest Martin
Director: Richard Attenborough
Cast: Michael Douglas, Alyson Reed, Terrence Mann, Janet Jones

The Jewel of the Nile (1985)
Producer: Michael Douglas
Director: Lewis Teague
Cast: Michael Douglas, Kathleen Turner, Danny De Vito

Fatal Attraction (1987)
Producers: Stanley Jaffe and Sherry Lansing
Director: Adrian Lyne
Cast: Michael Douglas, Glenn Close, Anne Archer

Wall Street (1987)
Producer: Edward R. Pressman
Director: Adrian Lyne
Cast: Michael Douglas, Charlie Sheen, Darryl Hannah, Terence Stamp

Black Rain (1989)
Producers: Stanley Jaffe and Sherry Lansing
Director: Ridley Scott
Cast: Michael Douglas, Andy Garcia, Ken Takakura, Yusaka Matsuda

The War of the Roses (1989)

Producers; James L. Brooks and Arnon Milchan
Director: Danny De Vito
Cast: Michael Douglas, Kathleen Turner, Danny De Vito, Sean Astin

Shining Through (1991)

Producers: Sandy Gallin, Howard Rosenmann, Carol Baum
Director: David Seltzer
Cast: Michael Douglas, Melanie Griffith. Liam Neeson, Joely Richardson

Basic Instinct (1991)

Producer: Alan Marshall
Director: Paul Verhoeven
Cast: Michael Douglas, Sharon Stone, George Dzundza, Jeanne Tripplehorn

Falling Down (1992)

Producers: Timothy Harris, Arnold Kopelson, Herschel Weingrod
Director: Joel Schumacher
Cast: Michael Douglas, Robert Duvall, Barbara Hershey, Tuesday Weld

Disclosure (1994)

Producers: Barry Levinson, Andrew Wald
Director: Barry Levinson
Cast: Michael Douglas, Demi Moore, Donald Sutherland

The American President (1995)

Producer: Rob Reiner
Director: Rob Reiner
Cast: Michael Douglas, Annette Bening, Martin Sheen, Michael J. Fox

The Ghost and the Darkness (1996)
Producers: Gale Ann Hurd, A Kitman Ho, Paul Radin
Director: Stephen Hopkins
Cast: Val Kilmer, Michael Douglas, Tom Wilkinson, Emily Mortimer

The Game (1997)
Producers: Cean Chaffin, Steve Golin
Director: David Fincher
Cast: Michael Douglas, Sean Penn, Deborah Kara Unger, James Rebhorn

A Perfect Murder (1998)
Producer: Arnold Kopelson, Anne Kopelson, Peter MacGregor Scott, Christopher Mankiewicz
Director: Andrew Davies
Cast: Michael Douglas, Gwyneth Paltrow, Viggo Mortensen, David Suchet

Wonder Boys (2000)
Producers; Curtis Hanson, Scott Rudin
Director: Curtis Hanson
Cast: Michael Douglas, Robert Downey Jnr, Tobey Maguire, Frances McDormand

Traffic (2000)
Producers: Laura Bickford, Marshall Herskowitz, Edward Zwick
Director: Steven Soderbergh
Cast: Catherine Zeta-Jones, Michael Douglas, Salma Hayek, Dennis Quaid

One Night at McCool's (2001)
Producers: Michael Douglas, Whitney Green, Allison Lyon Segan
Director: Harald Zwart
Cast: Liv Tyler, Matt Dillon, John Goodman, Paul Reiser, Michael Douglas

Don't Say a Word (2001)
Producers: Arnon Milchan, Arnold Kopelson, Anne Kopelson
Director: Gary Fleder
Cast: Michael Douglas, Brittany Murphy, Famke Janssen, Sean Bean, Oliver Platt.

The Wedding Party (2003)
Producers: Bill Gerber, Elie Samaha, Joel Simon
Director: Andrew Fleming
Cast: Michael Douglas, Albert Brooks, Candice Bergen, Ryan Reynolds

It Runs in the Family (2003)
Producers: Michael Douglas, Marcy Drogin, Joel Douglas
Director: Fred Schepisi
Cast: Michael Douglas, Kirk Douglas, Diana Douglas, Cameron Douglas

Michael Douglas has also been involved on the following films as producer:

One Flew Over the Cuckoo's Nest (1975)
Starman (1984)
Flatliners (1990)
Radio Flyer (1992)
Made in America (1993)
The Rainmaker (1997)
Face/Off (1997)

SOURCES AND ACKNOWLEDGEMENTS

The material on which this book is based comes from a number of sources.

Author's interviews

Michael Douglas (1995, 1996, 1998), Jon Amiel, Richard Attenborough, Annette Bening, Andrew Davies, Danny De Vito, Diana Hawkins, Stephen Hopkins, Val Kilmer, Barry Levinson, Rob Reiner, Ben Younger, Paul Verhoeven

Magazine articles

Seventeen (August 1969), *After Dark* (July 1971), *City* (October 1975), *Rolling Stone* (5 April 1979),*Esquire* (April 1984), *US* (30 December 1985), *GQ* (December 1985), *Rolling Stone* (16 January 1986), *Playboy* (February 1986), *American Premiere* (Summer

1986), *Rolling Stone* (5 November 1987), *Rolling Stone* (14 January 1988) *Premiere* (April 1992), *Calendar* (*Los Angeles Times*, 4 December 1994), *Vanity Fair* (January 1995), *Entertainment Weekly* (29 September 1995), *Los Angeles Magazine* (October 1997), *Cigar Aficionado* (June 1998), *Sunday Telegraph* (24 October 1999), *US* (25 September 2000).

Other material was drawn from various back issues of *Daily Variety* and The *Hollywood Reporter*

Books

The Ragman's Son by Kirk Douglas
Climbing the Mountain by Kirk Douglas
In the Wings by Diana Douglas Darrid
Michael Douglas by Alan Lawson
Foster Child: Jodie Foster by Buddy Foster and Leon Wagener
The Oscars by Anthony Holden
Citizen Jane by Christopher Andersen

I am also grateful to Siobhan Synnot and Anwar Brett for access to their interviews and to Leslie Pound for his help and advice.

My thanks to Lorna Russell at Robson Books and, as always, to my agent Jane Judd for her continued support.

INDEX